THE
NEW
PHONOGRAPHIC
PHRASE BOOK

PITMAN PUBLISHING

SIR ISAAC PITMAN AND SONS LTD.
Pitman House, Parker Street, Kingsway, London, WC2B 5PB
P.O. Box 46038, Banda Street, Nairobi, Kenya

SIR ISAAC PITMAN (AUST.) PTY. LTD.
Pitman House, 158 Bouverie Street, Carlton, Victoria 3053, Australia

PITMAN PUBLISHING CORPORATION
6 East 43rd Street, New York, N.Y. 10017, U.S.A.

SIR ISAAC PITMAN (CANADA) LTD.
495 Wellington Street West, Toronto 135, Canada

THE COPP CLARK PUBLISHING COMPANY
517 Wellington Street West, Toronto 135, Canada

ISBN: 0 273 42254 5

Text set in 10/11 pt. Monotype Times New Roman, printed by letterpress, and bound in Great Britain at The Pitman Press, Bath
G4—(S.203:24)

PUBLISHER'S PREFACE

THE discovery of the possibility of employing phraseography in the practice of Pitman Shorthand was not made till the system had been in extensive use for some years. Its first introduction into the textbooks is to be found in the "Manual" published by the Inventor of Phonography in 1845. In this work it is stated that "to promote expedition in writing, the advanced phonographer may join two or more words together, and thus sometimes express a phrase without removing the pen." Examples are then given of over fifty simple phrases, most of which have been used in the system ever since, while a few—which did not prove in every way satisfactory—never came into general use.

In one of his contributions to the history of Phonography, the late Thomas Allen Reed has described the feelings of pleasure he experienced on seeing the first phraseogram, in a letter either from the Inventor of Phonography or from his brother Joseph Pitman. It was the now well-known phrase ︶︵⁀, but it came upon Mr. Reed as a revelation, and the possibilities which this simple little outline opened out at once presented themselves to Mr. Reed's mind. But, for a considerable time after the introduction of "Phraseography" in the "Manual," the method was used sparingly and with great caution by phonographers, and, in works issued in phonographic characters, phraseography is conspicuous by its absence for several years subsequent to 1845.

Ten years later, in 1855, Mr. Reed, who had devoted considerable attention to the phraseographical powers of Phonography since they were first introduced to his notice, compiled "The Phonographic Phrase Book, a General Explanation of the Principle of Phraseography; or, the writing of entire phrases without lifting the pen, as applied to Pitman Phonetic Shorthand: with several thousand illustrations." A note expressive of approval of Mr. Reed's labours from the pen of Isaac Pitman was included in the work. Subsequently the Inventor of Phonography himself issued the "Phrase

Book," in an improved and enlarged form, and from time to time new editions have made their appearance.

In response to the continued and increasing demand for the book, Miss Emily D. Smith, B.Sc.Econ., has at our request prepared this completely revised and much enlarged edition. Miss Smith, who is the only holder of the National Union of Teachers' Certificate for 250 words a minute and who has seven other First Place awards in Pitman Shorthand, is thoroughly aware of the requirements of the shorthand writer at all stages of speed development. This new edition is, therefore, designed to give shorthand writers, in the elementary as well as in the advanced field, careful guidance in the formation of phrases based on the principles of Pitman Shorthand. Ample practice in the application of the principles is provided in the form of *Facility Drills* and reading and dictation exercises.

A major difference between this NEW PHONOGRAPHIC PHRASE BOOK and the older one is that the latter offered a general survey of the principles of phrasing whereas the present volume contains a definite step-by-step course of detailed instruction in the subject. It is assumed throughout that the reader has already gained a knowledge of the principles of the system, as this allows for the "interlocking" of the different principles of phrasing to be explained in a way that is not possible in a beginner's textbook.

Those who are still learning the theory of Pitman Shorthand are strongly advised to use the *Phrase Drill Notebook*.

SIR ISAAC PITMAN & SONS LTD.

CONTENTS

FOREWORD

THE Pitman system of Shorthand, because of its consonantal structure, lends itself to extensive phrasing, and offers to the interested writer possibilities both rich and varied. Expert shorthand writing does not, of course, depend upon the unregulated use of miscellaneous short-cuts. It is the skilled application of the *principles* of phrasing that marks the trained writer, principles of phrasing that are embodied in the Pitman system and have grown out of the experience of Pitman writers over a period of more than a century. The unhesitating and unerring use of these principles gives to shorthand notes an added beauty and a greater conciseness, with consequent higher speed and increased reliability.

When Pitman Shorthand was first invented in 1837 each outline was written separately, and the shorthand writers of those far-off days experienced a thrill of wonder and delight when for the first time they saw outlines joined together to make a "phrase." They had not imagined that such speed and beauty of outline was possible, but we today cannot imagine shorthand writing without phraseography, so accustomed are we to "phrasing" from our earliest lessons. All shorthand writers use phrasing to a greater or less degree, and it is the purpose of this book to ensure that shorthand writers apply the principles of phrasing to the greatest extent compatible with facile writing and assured legibility.

The advantages of phrasing are at once apparent when we compare the following ways of writing the sentence: *I shall be glad if you will consider the matter.* If each outline is written separately the

shorthand rendering is: ⟨shorthand outlines⟩ If

phrasing is used the shorthand may become: ⟨shorthand outlines⟩ or, if

the writer is more advanced: ⟨shorthand outlines⟩

In the first example we have ten separate outlines with nine lifts of the pen and several changes of position in relation to the line of writing. In the second case we have only three outlines, with two lifts of the pen and good lineality. In the third case we have only one outline. The saving of time in the second and third examples is immense, not only because the phrases are quickly written but also because the hand has travelled so short a distance. The time taken for the hand to travel from outline to outline and from one line to the next is as important a factor in rapid shorthand writing as is the time taken to write the actual outlines. At the rate of 240 words a minute four words have to be represented in every second—that is, each word can be allocated only a quarter of a second of time. Clearly, every fraction of a second saved is precious to the writer.

An awareness of the value of the "saved second" is, however, apt to lead some writers astray at times. Seeing others write more quickly than they themselves can, they jump to the conclusion that the ability to write at high speeds must depend upon some secret knowledge of an extensive range of short-cuts unknown to them. If they can learn enough phrases, they tell themselves, and if they can master enough short-cuts, they too will automatically be able to write at two hundred words a minute and over. They are then disillusioned and surprised to see from the notes of myself and other fast writers that it is possible to achieve high speeds while writing what may be termed "textbook" shorthand. Where, they ask themselves, are all those mysterious short-cuts that they imagined were the reason for the high speed?

My advice to young writers who wish to acquire shorthand speed and to pass the examinations of the public examining bodies is to keep at first to the principles of phrasing as set out here and in *Pitman's Shorthand Instructor*. Gradually, as experience grows, those principles can be more and more fully exploited and built upon. Only when that stage has been reached and passed should more daring experiments be indulged in—and only then when the writer is very experienced and the material being reported lends itself to the use of special phrases. Some hints on the formation of such advanced phrases will be found in Appendix Two, p. 111 and in List Three of Section 15, p. 82.

This book develops more fully the principles of phrasing taught in *Pitman's Shorthand Instructor*. The writer is not asked to learn the phrases shown by heart but to learn the principles herein set out and to understand the application of those principles. Ample material is included for both reading and writing practice.

Phrases may be divided into three main types—

1. Those phrases in which outlines are simply joined together without any change of form, the only change, if any, being one of position. Examples of such phrases are—

I am glad	I shall have	do you	may we
with which	that is not	we will	last year

2. Those phrases in which one or more of the outlines making up the phrase is written either differently or incompletely. In such

phraseograms outlines are also quite frequently omitted altogether. Examples are—

      able to   better than   at all   in our

      of the world   of us   as we may   if it were

3. Those phrases in which one or more of the outlines comprising the phrase is omitted but there is no change in the remaining outlines. Examples are—

      for a time   more or less   larger and larger

All three classes of phrase should be used to the fullest extent. An endeavour has been made throughout these pages to show that a principle should not be accepted simply for the few examples that considerations of space permit to be included in textbooks. The phrases given with each principle in the textbooks should be regarded as an indication of how the principle can be used: the examples are not intended to be exhaustive but to act as a guide to the further formation of like phrases. All students seem to remember, for instance, that the final N Hook may be used to represent the word *than* in phrases, and they faithfully use it in such cases as *better than, smaller than, rather than*; but the hook can safely be used for a very much larger body of phrases than the few stock ones to which it is usually applied: it should be used instead of the full outline on every possible suitable occasion. Again, the use of the large initial circle for *as we* is confined by many students to the few examples that it is possible to give in a small textbook, whereas the large Circle Sway can, in fact, be widely applied.

These are just two examples out of many, and it cannot be too strongly stressed that the accepted and clearly stated principles of phrasing offer almost unlimited scope for the formation of phrases of an orthodox and reliable type. An orthodox phrase may be defined as one supported by basic principles of the Pitman system but allowing some licence in the application of those principles. An unorthodox phrase is one which is quite arbitrary and is not based

on any recognized principle, e.g.   for *all round the world* and

for *whether or not*. Such unorthodox phrases are sometimes found by reporters to be very useful, but the average high-speed writer should be very wary of straying far from orthodoxy.

One important point that should not be overlooked is that phrasing remains a personal matter for the writer, and the intensity with which phrasing is used necessarily varies from writer to writer. It is very unlikely that the shorthand notes of any two writers would show identical phrasing because the freedom of choice is great, and the writer is influenced by the immediate circumstances. Nor can it

be said to be "wrong" to write ⟍⟍ instead of ⟍⟍ for *better than* or

to write ⟍⟍ instead of ⟍⟍ for *as we think*, but it can be said that it is foolish to do so because it is time-wasting. Every lift of the pen takes a fraction of a second, and conversely every time a lift of the pen is saved a fraction of a second is saved. As has been pointed out, in the shorthand writer's scale of time fractions of a second are extremely important.

This book is not primarily a "list of useful phrases" although a list has been included for reference purposes on pp. 115–156; it is a guide to the *principles* of phrasing, so that the student who studies it can use an ever-widening range of phrases, a range capable of almost indefinite extension.

The NEW PHONOGRAPHIC PHRASE BOOK is intended for use after the student has completed a first study of the textbook. A knowledge of the principles of Pitman Shorthand is assumed throughout. For example, the use of the small and large circles in phrasing is shown in its application to other principles, from the simplest to the most advanced. Again, the use of the initial and final hooks is shown in connexion with all principles of the system, regardless of whether such principles are taught in the textbooks before or after the hooks are dealt with. Each section, therefore, gives an over-all picture of the principle with which it is dealing and shows its relationship to other principles, thus achieving a much more comprehensive survey than is possible in a strictly graded book. It is in this respect similar to *A Student's Review of Pitman's Shorthand*.

Each section of the PHRASE BOOK should be studied with care, working in the following four stages—

1. The instructional pages of a section should be carefully read and thoroughly mastered.

2. The *Facility Drills* should then be practised. One line of the *Drills* should be copied into a notebook on the top line of the page, and then copied and re-copied on the following lines until the page is quite full. It is only by such repetition practice that the use of phrases can become automatic. Each line of each *Drill* should be dealt with in this way.

3. The third stage is to read the *Shorthand Exercises* over and over again until they can be read at very high speed. These *Exercises* can also be used for facility practice, and should be written from dictation where practicable.

4. The dictation material should then be written, preferably from dictation. Because this dictation material consists largely of phrases quite high speeds should be reached by the enthusiastic writer.

A *Key* to the *Drills* and *Exercises* will be found at the end of this book.

EMILY D. SMITH

PART ONE

Phraseograms in Which There Is No Change in the Form of the Component Outlines

SECTION ONE

The Joining of Outlines

As explained in the *Foreword*, phraseograms may be formed by simple joining, by changing the form of one or more of the outlines, or by omission of part or the whole of an outline. This section deals with the first type of phrase, those in which two or more outlines are joined without change of form, although there is often a change of position. Some rules that must be observed in the use of such phrases are—

1. The phrase must have good lineality. It should not ascend too far above nor descend too far below the line of writing.

2. The phrase should be simple and easy to write. Elaborate joinings that cannot be written easily are a handicap rather than an advantage to the writer.

3. Each outline should be clearly distinguishable: the parts should not blend into one unrecognizable sign.

4. The joining should result naturally from the English speech-pattern. Words that naturally flow together in speech may be represented as a phrase in shorthand, but words that are clearly separated by a pause in speech should not as a rule be represented by joined outlines in shorthand.

These four points may usefully be elaborated.

1. Lineality

(*a*) The first outline of a phraseogram retains its correct position in relation to the line of writing. The position of the remainder of

1

the outlines follows naturally. For instance, in the simple phrase
I am glad that you are, the outlines for the words *I am glad that* are written above the line in their proper position, but the outlines for *you* and *are* do not rest on the line in their normal position but are lifted above the line in order to become part of the whole phraseogram. On the other hand, in the phrase *I think that you are* the outlines for *that, you,* and *are* are written below the line out of their normal position.

The three phrases *do you, if you, that you* further illustrate this point, the outline for *you* appearing on the line, below it, and above it, according to the position of the outline to which it is attached.

The simple rule is, therefore, that the first outline of the group takes its proper position in relation to the line of writing, but the position of following outlines is governed by the preceding outline or outlines.

(b) A Grammalogue or Short Form that is normally written above the line may be slightly raised or lowered to permit a following outline to fall into its proper position, as—

with much		of those
with which		of this
with each		of these

It must be noted, however, that the first outline is in all cases still written *above* the line and is clearly in the first position. In no circumstances should such an outline, when it is at the beginning of a phrase, be allowed to approach too near to the line of writing. Such pairs as the following must always be clearly distinguished—

of each		as these
to each		is this

(c) Phraseograms should not be so rambling that they are allowed to interfere with the writing on other lines, either by dropping too far below the line or by climbing too high above it. Here, for instance, is a legible but thoroughly bad phraseogram—

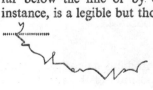

I shall be glad if your receipt can be sent to me by return mail.

It is a bad phrase for several reasons, but first and foremost because it has destroyed the possibility of successfully writing on the next two or three lines of the notebook. It is bad also because far too many outlines are joined together, with the result that, instead of giving increased facility of writing, the phrase is a very real handicap to facility and requires slow and careful writing. A more practical rendering would be—

There is no interference in this case with other lines of writing, and each part of the sentence can be rapidly written and easily read.

A second example of a thoroughly bad phraseogram is—

A little later Leslie left.

This phrase climbs too high and interferes with shorthand already written. In this case the outlines would be much better written separately, as—

A second rule for students is, therefore, that a phraseogram should not descend too far below the line of writing nor ascend too far above it. A reasonable general statement is that a phrase should not drop more than two strokes below the line or climb much more than two above it. For instance .... *to have your* is a satis-

factory form but .... *to have your order* descends too far

below the line and is better written .... ; .... *to refer* is

acceptable but .... *to refer later* ascends into the previous line

of writing and is better written ....

2. Simplicity

Phrases should not be complicated and should not be used for long and involved sentences. An over-zealous phrase-maker might take down the beginning of a company report as follows—

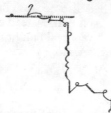

> The Chairman, in the course of his address, said that he thought that they had reasonable cause for satisfaction.

Not only does this phrase break the rules for lineality: it also fails in simplicity and common sense. It cannot be written without careful concentration, and certainly would not be used by an experienced high-speed writer, who would prefer to represent the sentence in the following way—

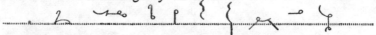

A third rule is, then, that outlines should be joined only when a definite advantage results from the joining. There should be no joining merely for the sake of joining.

3. Legibility

Outlines should not be joined together unless such joining distinctly shows. A shorthand writer, taking advantage of the fact that *he* may be represented by ....ι.... when joined to a preceding outline,

might write: ....|...ϰ What does this mean? Only the shorthand writer who wrote it is likely to know that the phrase was intended to mean: *Oh, he died, did he?* and he will probably forget. The phrase is easy to write, and no complaint can be made about its lineality, but it offends seriously in the matter of legibility, and common sense demands that such "straight line" phraseograms should not be used.

Another example of the same type of phrase is: .... for *I can cook cake*—an example to be avoided.

Again, outlines such as .... *might* and .... *not* must not be joined, as the resultant phrase .... is not sufficiently legible.

A very common fault among inexperienced shorthand writers is to join the outlines for such words as *that I, to see,* etc. Such joinings are not clear and lead to confusion in transcription.

A fourth rule for phrasing is, therefore: outlines should not be joined if the strokes blend into one another and cannot be clearly distinguished. Joinings in phraseograms should be very clear.

4. Speech Pattern

A phraseogram should follow naturally from the pattern of the English language. It is well known that the addition or the omission of a comma can alter the sense of a sentence. The following two sentences differ only in the commas: (i) *Frank said the girl was a fool to go.* (ii) *Frank, said the girl, was a fool to go.* In one case the girl has been called a fool, and in the other Frank is stated to be the fool.

In shorthand the use or non-use of phrasing can correspond to the change of position of a comma in longhand. In the shorthand for: *"It is said, Alice, . . ."* the writer would use the phrase for

it is said and write: ⎍ But in the shorthand for: *"It is,"*

said Alice . . ." the writer would not use the above phrase but would

write: ⎍ The separation of *said* from *it is* has in the second case acted in the same way as the comma in longhand. When the notes are transcribed the reader will know at once that Alice is the speaker.

A further illustration of the art of phrasing according to the speech-pattern may be found in the sentence: *It was, the speaker said, the wiser course.* In this case the good shorthand writer would

not use the Tick The in either instance but would write: ⎍

⎍ If the tick were used, as: ⎍

the pattern of the sentence would be changed. Difficulty would probably be experienced in transcription because the reader would naturally at first say: *It was the speaker . . .* and would then hesitate.

A fifth rule for phrasing is, therefore, that the phrases should reflect the meaning of the longhand. The experienced writer, following the sense of the passage being dictated or writing a letter to a friend, will automatically adjust the phrasing to comply with meaning.

Emphasis. An outline that is normally joined to another may sometimes be written separately to convey the emphasis given to a word by a speaker. If a speaker says: **"That** *was the reason . . ."*

the shorthand writer should write ⎍ rather than

_____ *In the first case emphasis is implied without under-lining. If a speaker says: "*I want to know* if *he said this*" the short-hand should be: _____ but if he says: "*I want to know if he said* this." the shorthand would be _____ _____ If the word *I* were emphasized, then the outline

for *I* would not be joined to that for *want*. In such subtle ways inflexions of speech can be indicated in shorthand notes and the work of transcription greatly facilitated.

Examples of "distinguishing" phrases are given in Section Seventeen, p. 97.

The *Facility Drills* on the following page provide examples of straightforward joinings. They are representative of the thousands of phrases that are possible as a result of simple joining, and should be practised vigorously, the principles being applied in actual note-taking. It is seldom necessary to vocalize a phraseogram.

FACILITY DRILL 1

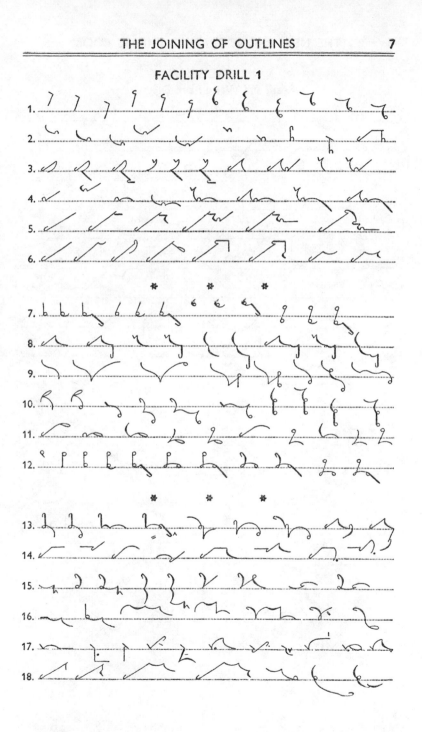

EXERCISE 1A
Read, and Write from Dictation

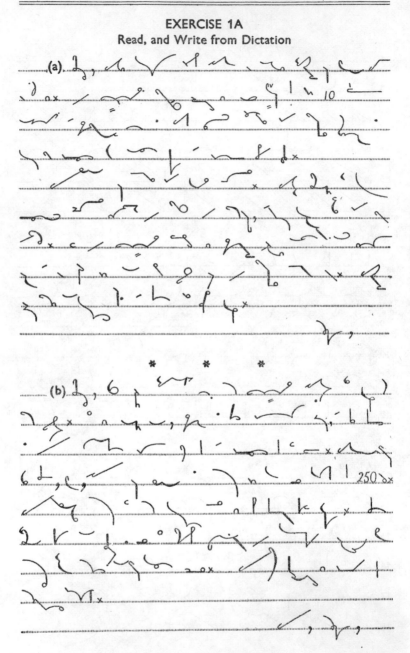

EXERCISE 1B
Write from Dictation Several Times

(Phrasing is suggested by hyphenation)

If-you wish to-make yourself an expert writer of[10]-shorthand it-is-necessary for-you to-master the fascinating[20] art of-good phrasing. This-does-not mean that-there[30]-is one correct way only of-representing groups of-words:[40] there-may-be two or even more equally good-ways[50] of-grouping the shorthand-outlines for a series of-words.[60] There-may, of-course, also-be some incorrect ways of[70]-grouping them. In illustration of-this we-may take-such[80] a sentence as: *I think that they have not yet*[90] *been.* The sentence could-be represented as-one long phrase,[100] but it-would-not-be advisable to-write it in[110]-that-way. The resultant phrase would-not give good lineality,[120] and a writer would-gain nothing in-speed or in[130] legibility by-its use. The words would-be better represented[140] in shorthand by grouping into two phrases such-as: *I*[150]-*think-that-they have-not-yet-been* or *I-think*[160]-*that they-have-not-yet-been.* Either of-these groupings[170] is satisfactory but a trained writer would choose, probably, the[180] second grouping as-it-has better lineality and does-not[190] separate *they* from *have* to-which it-is-naturally attached.[200]

You-can-see then that-there-are-several-ways in[210]-which a quite simple sentence can-be-written in shorthand.[220] The way in-which a speaker groups his words may[230]-have a considerable influence on a writer's use of-phrases.[240] The speaker may hesitate after a word: the pen is[250] lifted and poised ready for what-has-to-be-written[260] next. In practical writing there-is-little or no-point[270] in going-back and-completing a phrase once the pen[280] has-been so lifted. Phrases are, of-course, intended to[290]-prevent unnecessary lifts, and-if-such a lift has-been[300] already-made the best thing to-do is-to-move[310] forwards, not backwards. Your phrasing then will-be influenced by[320]-many-considerations, and-will possibly not-be exactly like-that[330] of-your neighbour, but all-your shorthand-notes should show[340] a good knowledge and use of-phrasing. (347)

PART TWO

Phraseograms in Which There Is Some Change in the Form of One or More of the Component Outlines

---

THIS second class of phraseogram covers a wide field and shows how the principles of Pitman Shorthand can be extended to apply not only to simple consonants and syllables but to whole words. This is an extremely fruitful source of time-saving devices, and every shorthand writer seeking to write rapidly should master these sections. The principles should be applied as extensively as possible, keeping in mind at all times the common-sense requirements of facility, legibility, and lineality, as set out in Section One.

As mentioned in the *Foreword*, the Principle of Omission is often combined with this type of abbreviation to achieve advanced forms.

SECTION TWO

Tick The; Diphthongs; He

1. Tick The

The is the most common word in the English language, and in Pitman Shorthand it has been given the shortest possible sign—a dot on the line. A dot, however, cannot be joined to another outline, and it is often advantageous to join the sign for *the* to a preceding outline. For purposes of phrasing, therefore, the word *the* is represented by a little tick which is almost as quickly written as the dot and which saves the fraction of time that would be lost by lifting the pen to write the dot. It is faster to write ⌐ than ⌐ for *take the.*

Furthermore, another outline can be added after the tick, thus saving another lift of the pen, e.g. ⎣⎤ *take the matter*, the phrase being much more quickly written than the separate outlines.

The little tick for *the* should be used in all cases permitted by the following rules—

(*a*) Tick The is always sloped in the direction of *chay* ╱ Note the difference between ⟋ *know the* and ⟋ *now*, and between ⟋ *is the* and ⟋ *is to*.

(*b*) Tick The is always attached to a preceding sign and is *never* written at the beginning of an outline, as: ⟍ *book the* but ⟍ *the book*; ⎿ *set the* but ⎿ *the set*; ⟍ *drop the* but ⟍ *the drop*.

(*c*) Tick The may be written either upwards or downwards according to which direction gives the clearer joining—

Downwards:	⟋ give the	⟋ of the	⎿ for the
	⟋ are the	⟍ face the	⟋ and the
Upwards:	⎿ which the	⟍ gave the	⟍ gain the
	⟍ win the	⟍ or the	⟍ miss the

After ⟍ *p* and ⟍ *b* the tick is written downwards: ⟍ *up the*, ⟍ *be the*, ⟍ *rob the*, ⎿ *dip the*. If, however, there is a final circle or hook attached to the ⟍ *p* or ⟍ *b* Rule (*c*) above applies, e.g. ⟍ *pave the*, ⟍ *above the*, ⟍ *pass the*, ⟍ *open the*.

(*d*) Tick The is used medially in a phraseogram, as ⟋ *to take the matter*, ⟍ *in the art*, ⎿ *at the time*.

(Note: ⟍ *by the by*, but ⟍ *by-and-by*.)

(*e*) Tick The is not used if the preceding outline does not lend itself to its easy addition. Tick The is not used, for instance, after a Stee or Ster Loop, Ns or Nses Circle, as: ⟍ *passed the*, ⟍ *master the*, ⟍ *rinse the*, ⎿ *dances the*.

(*f*) When Tick The is added to the signs for ⌣ⵏ... *but* and ⵏ... *on*, the phrase is made to slope a little, as: ⵏⵉ... *but the*, ⵏ... *on the*.

(*g*) It is not advisable to add Tick The to a half-length straight stroke standing alone and having no initial or final attachment: ⵏ... *pat the*, but ⵏ... *repeat the*, ⵏ... *paint the*.

(*See* Section Sixteen, p. 87, for notes on the omission of the sign for *the* in phraseograms.)

2. Diphthongs

The diphthong-signs ⵏ... IE and ⵏ... UE also represent the words *I/eye* and *you* respectively, and they are extensively used in phrasing—

ⵏ... I have	ⵏ... you are
ⵏ... I think	ⵏ... do you
ⵏ... I had	ⵏ... you may

In these cases the diphthong-signs are unchanged, but in many phraseograms a slight change is made in the signs, as explained below.

(*a*) **The Diphthong IE.** Where the second half of the sign would blend with a following form, only the first part is written, thus:

ⵏ... *I will*, ⵏ... *I may*, ⵏ... *I refer*, ⵏ... *I trust*, ⵏ... *I pray*, ⵏ... *I play*.

The sign ⵏ... is also abbreviated for reasons of facility in a few frequently occurring phrases: ⵏ... *I can*, ⵏ... *I go*, ⵏ... *I gave*, ⵏ... *I went*, ⵏ... *I crossed*.

The full sign is, however, used when there is no advantage to be gained from such abbreviation: ⵏ... *I feel*, ⵏ... *I see*, ⵏ... *I join*, ⵏ... *I took*.

(*b*) **The Diphthong UE.** The sign ⵏ... *you* is turned on its side if a more convenient phraseogram results—

ⵏ... to take you	ⵏ... let you
ⵏ... to agree with you	ⵏ... what you
ⵏ... to give you	ⵏ... in you
ⵏ... are you	ⵏ... would you

In such cases it is slightly faster or more facile to tilt the diphthong-sign, but in the majority of cases the ordinary form is quite convenient, e.g. ...↙... *which you*, ⌒ *for you*, ↳ *if you can*, ⟍ *saw you*.

The Diphthong UE is never tilted at the beginning of a phrase.

3. He

The form ...⟋... *he* is used in phraseograms when *he* is the first word of the phrase, as: ⟋ *he is (has)*, ...⟋... *he can*.

The sign ...ı... *he* is used when it can be attached to a *preceding* stroke, as: ...ʃ... *when he is (has)*, ..ꞁ... *if he can*.

The sign ...ı... *he* resembles Tick The in that it is not used when standing alone or at the beginning of a phraseogram. The following pairs of outlines illustrate the use of the forms ...⟋... and ...ı... in phrases

...⟋... he may	*but*	ꞁ if he may	
...⟋... he can	*but*	.ʃ. when he can	
...⟋... he will	*but*	.ϒ. that he will	
...⟋... he was	*but*	...ı... as he was	

FACILITY DRILL 2

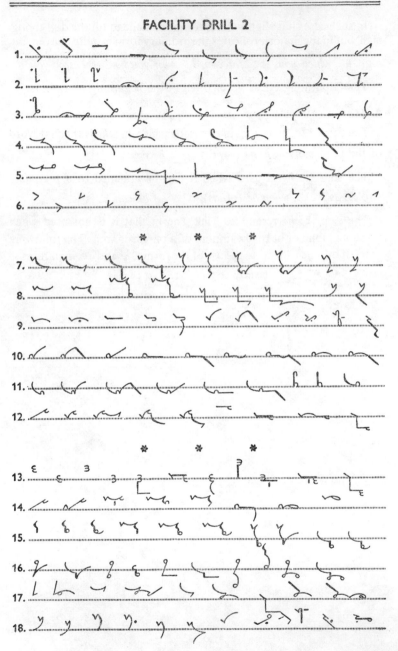

EXERCISE 2A
Read, and Write from Dictation

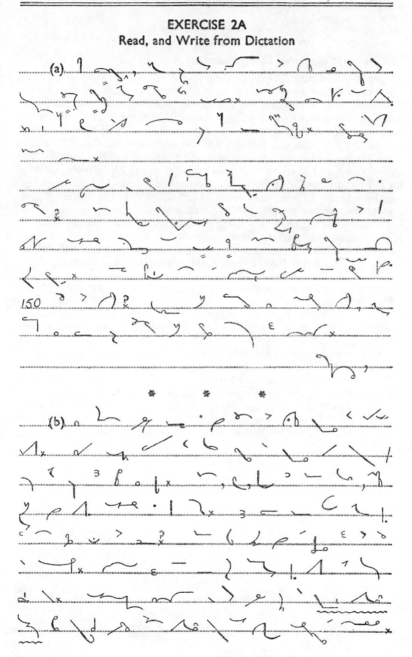

EXERCISE 2B
Write from Dictation Several Times
(Phrasing is suggested by hyphenation)

(a) It-is advisable for-you to develop-the art of[10]-phrasing as-much-as you-can in-the-course-of[20]-your writing. When-you-consider-that when-you write-the[30] shorthand for 120 words in-one-minute[40] you-are representing two-words in-each second you-will[50] realize-the necessity for-the adoption of-time saving devices.[60] For-you as writers of-shorthand time is divided not[70] into-the minutes and-the hours and-the days of[80]-every-day life; it-is divided into seconds and-fractions[90] of-the second. To-lift-the pen and to-make[100]-contact with-the paper again is-the work-of a[110] moment but-the moments add up in-the-course-of[120]-the dictation, and-the saving of a moment means an[130] addition to-the speed. If-you-write two separate signs[140] for-the-words *with-you* you-are wasting time; if[150]-you join-the two signs you-are gaining time. You[160]-should, then, do what-you-can to-phrase when-you[170] take shorthand-notes, always remembering that-the phrases used should[180]-not-be long and difficult but should-be those-that[190] add to-speed and to-the-ease of-reading back. (200)

(b) I-ask-you now to-turn to-the report and[10] to-the statement of-the-Directors. In-the two documents[20] you-will-find all-the information that-you-require regarding[30]-the affairs of-the-organization. You-will-no-doubt have[40] already studied-the report and-the figures given in-the[50]-accounts, and-I-am-sure that-you-will-agree-with[60] me that-they show that-the-trading for-the-year[70] has-been very-satisfactory. I-am-pleased to-be-able[80] today to-tell-you that I-have-heard from-the[90] Chairman. He-is-making a rapid recovery from-the illness[100] that afflicted him when-he-was travelling abroad recently. It[110]-is-not-yet certain when-he-will-be resuming his[120] duties but I-know-that-he-is hopeful of-returning[130] in-the near-future. I-am-sure-you-will join[140] with me in-sending-the united wishes of-the-meeting[150] for-his speedy restoration to-good health. (157)

SECTION THREE

Circle S

IN addition to representing the words *is*, *his*, *as*, and *has* the Circle S is used in phrasing for the word *us*. In more advanced phrases it may replace the Stroke S for *say*.

The circle is also combined with the N Hook for the quick representation of *once*, and with the Shun Hook for *association*. It is used with the Halving and Doubling Principles to provide a wealth of first-class phrases.

Further, the circle replaces the Stee Loop in a wide range of useful phrases, and coalesces with R Hook in yet one more group.

All these uses of Circle S in phrasing are explained in the following notes.

1. The General Use of The Circle S

(*a*) The small circle provides an excellent link in many phraseograms—

    it is not   yours truly

    this time   it seems

    please inform   because it is

    dear sirs   for several years

(*b*) To achieve greater scope, the normal direction of the circle may be reversed—

    please take *but*   please make,   please accept;

    it is time *but*   it is really,   it is important

In such cases the direction of the circle is that required for the phrase as a whole.

An exception is made in the case of such phrases as   *this matter*,   *these men*, where it is an advantage to retain in the phrase the direction of the circle that would be employed were the outlines written separately.

2. Is, His, As, Has

The circle representing these words should be joined to a preceding or following outline whenever possible—

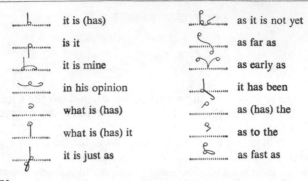

	it is (has)		as it is not yet
	is it		as far as
	it is mine		as early as
	in his opinion		it has been
	what is (has)		as (has) the
	what is (has) it		as to the
	it is just as		as fast as

3. Us

The Stroke S must be used for the word *us* when the outline stands alone, but the Circle S should usually be used in phraseograms. It will be found a very useful aid to the rapid representation of many common expressions—

	tell us		with us
	from us		before us
	please inform us		asking us
	let us see		help us
	to give us		against us

(See also Section Eight, p. 41.)

4. Say

In advanced shorthand writing the circle may be used for the word *say*—

	we can say that	to say a few words
	asked to say that	I would like to say a few words

5. Once, N-Us

Combined with the N Hook to straight strokes the circle provides a quick representation for *once* and may also be used for *us* following N—

	at once	upon us
		depend upon us

(*See also* Section Eight, p. 41.)

6. Association

The Shun Hook and Circle S are used together to afford an easy termination for *association* in such phrases as—

medical association   welfare association

political association   Commonwealth association

7. As-R Hook

The circle blends with the R Hook to straight strokes to form many useful phrases beginning with *as*—

as per   as produced

as promised   as contrasted

as compared (with)   as compared with last year

8. The Circle S—Halving Principle

The circle may be added to a stroke that has been halved to represent *it*—

if it is (has)   in which it is (has)

if it is (has) not   in which it has been

from its   I do not think it is necessary

9. The Circle S—Doubling Principle

The circle may also be added to a stroke that has been doubled to represent *there*—

I know there is (has)   if there is (has)

I know there has been   if there is (has) not

(*Note also* such advanced phrases as: to render us,

hinder us.)

10. The Use of The Circle S Instead of The Stee Loop

A large and useful group of phrases is formed by employing the Circle S in place of the Stee Loop—

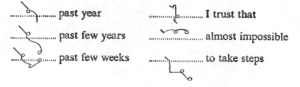

past year   I trust that

past few years   almost impossible

past few weeks   to take steps

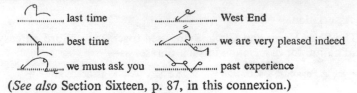

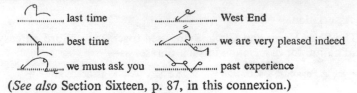 last time   West End

 best time   we are very pleased indeed

 we must ask you   past experience

(*See also* Section Sixteen, p. 87, in this connexion.)

11. The Circle S—Circles Sway and Sez

An outline normally consisting of simple Circle S sometimes loses its identity by blending with another S or a W, the large circle being used, as: ⟨image⟩ *as is,* ⟨image⟩ *this city,* ⟨image⟩ *as we can,* ⟨image⟩ *as soon as possible.*

This is fully explained in Section Four.

Very occasionally the final S of one word and the initial S of a following word are represented by a single Circle S, as: ⟨image⟩ *chairman's speech.*

FACILITY DRILL 3

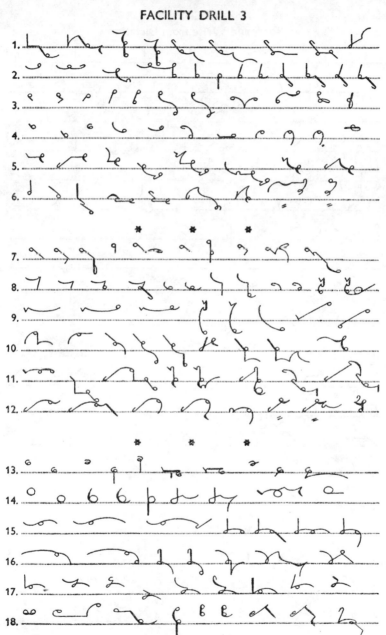

EXERCISE 3A
Read, and Write from Dictation

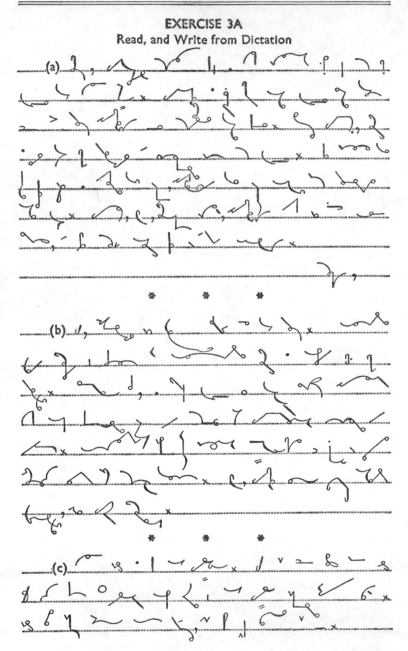

EXERCISE 3B
Write from Dictation Several Times
(Phrasing is suggested by hyphenation)

(*a*) Dear-Sirs, We-have-just-received your price-list. As[10]-far-as we-can-see your-prices are very-satisfactory[20] as-compared-with-those of-your-competitors, and-we-suggest[30] that your Mr.-Lester should call-upon-us the next[40]-time that-he-is in-this-town. We-trust-that[50]-he-will bring-with him actual samples of-your products.[60] We-are-proposing to-take immediate-steps to-extend our[70] factory, and it-is-most-important that delivery dates shall[80]-be firm. We-trust-that-you-will keep-this in[90] mind when quoting prices and dates for delivery. You-may[100] depend-upon-us to pay promptly so-that it-is[110] in-your interests as-much-as in-our-interests that[120] nothing shall occur to hinder-us in-the completion of[130]-the work. We-trust, therefore, that-you-will render-us[140] all possible assistance. Yours-truly,   (145)

(*b*) I-would-like-to-say-a-few-words to all[10]-those shorthand-students who-are-present this-evening. I-am[20]-very-pleased-indeed to see so-many-of-you and[30]-I-trust-that-you-are going to-be most-successful[40] in-the shorthand-speed tests next-week. The entries are[50] large as-compared-with-last-year and as-compared-with[60]-the year before but, as-promised, we-shall take-steps[70] to-mark-the papers as-soon-as-possible and-I[80]-do-not-think-there-is any-doubt that-the-results[90] will-be ready by-the last-day of-this term.[100] It-is-important that-you bring-with-you a notebook[110]-containing first-rate paper for your notes and-that-you[120] ensure that your fountain-pen is in first-rate-condition.[130] During-the-next-few-days you-should take-steps to[140]-practise your shorthand both with your teacher and-from-the[150] radio, and-I-must-say that-you-would-be well[160]-advised to-practise facility drills as-much-as you-can.[170] There-is-no-time to-waste if-you-are to[180]-do well in-the-examinations next-week, and-I-feel[190] certain-that-you-are going to-do as-well-as[200]-can-be expected from-you. The Rapid-Association has had[210] an excellent reputation for-the past-few-years, and-I[220]-am-certain-that-you-are worthy representatives of-the-Association.   (230)

SECTION FOUR

Circles Sway and Sez

THE large circle offers useful scope for phrases. Its uses include the representation of the following combinations—

Initially: *as-w, as-we,* and (irregularly) *as-s*
Finally: *s-is/has, is-his, s-s/z,* etc.
Medially: The final *s/z* of one word and initial *s* of the next
Alone: *is-as, is-his, as-is, as-has,* etc.

These various uses of the large circle are explained below.

1. The Initial Use of The Large Circle

(*a*) **As We.** The most important use of the large circle at the beginning of a phrase is for the representation of the words *as we*, and these words should be represented by the circle whenever facility and legibility permit. Suggestions for its use are given here, but its full use covers a much wider range of phrases than can be listed—

as we can	as we feel
as we can be	as we explained
as we know that	as we may have
as we may	as we jumped
as we are	as we ran
as we have	as we do

In certain cases, such as ⟨outline⟩ *as we went*, the large circle cannot be used.

The use of the large circle for *as we* may be combined with the halving principle and with the doubling principle—

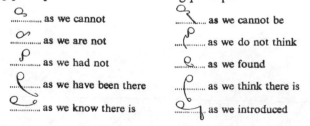

as we cannot	as we cannot be
as we are not	as we do not think
as we had not	as we found
as we have been there	as we think there is
as we know there is	as we introduced

The large initial circle is also combined with the R Hook to straight strokes to form further phrases—

as we trust   as we promised
as we trusted   as we brought

(b) **As-W.** This use of the large initial circle is confined to a small but very important group of common phrases—

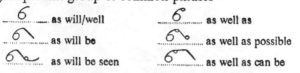

as will/well   as well as
as will be   as well as possible
as will be seen   as well as can be

(c) **As-S.** The irregular application of the Circle Sez initially to a small group of phrases is justified by the frequency of the combination As-S and by the clarity of the resulting outlines—

as soon as   as satisfactorily
as soon as possible   as certain as
as soon as we can   as has been
as satisfactory as   as said

2. The Final and Medial Use of The Large Circle

(a) **S-Is/Has**

this is/has   it is his
this has been   this is done

(b) **Is/Has/His-S**

it is certain   for his sake
it is/has certainly   it is satisfactory
it has certainly been   it is said
it is seen   it is suggested

(c) **S-S**

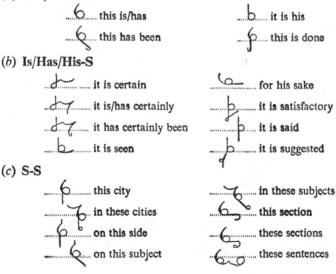

this city   in these subjects
in these cities   this section
on this side   these sections
on this subject   these sentences

3. The Large Circle Standing Alone

.............O............ as is, as has, as his, has his

.......O....... is as, is his, his is

The examples given above will suffice to show that there is much to be gained from a generous use of the large circle in phrasing.

FACILITY DRILL 4

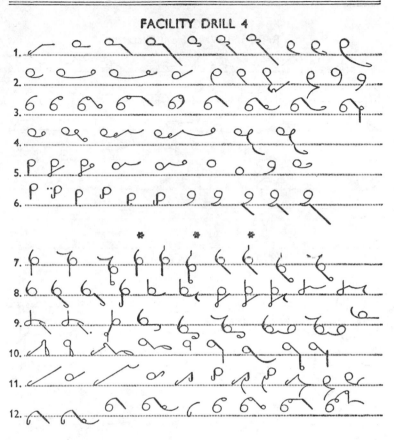

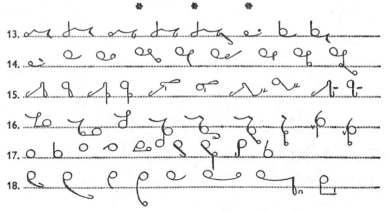

EXERCISE 4A
Read, and Write from Dictation

EXERCISE 4B
Write from Dictation Several Times
(*Phrasing is suggested by hyphenation*)

(*a*) As-we-can-see from here, they-have already started[10] to-build on-this-side-of-the new road. As[20]-soon-as-we-know-there-is a house available we[30]-shall try to buy it as-we-wish to-live[40] in-this area. The agent states-that all-the houses[50] on-this-side-of-the road have already-been bought[60] but-that this-is-not-the case on-the-other[70]-side. We-have asked-him to-reserve a house for[80]-us in-this-section of-the road as-we-do[90]-not-wish to-be a long-way from-the shops[100] and-the station as-we-have-no car. The houses[110] are-not expensive, and it-is-certain-that-we-can[120] sell our present house for a fair sum. We-are[130] writing to-Mr.-Smith on-this-subject as-we-promised[140] to-tell-him as-soon-as-possible should our house[150] become available.   (152)

(*b*) The figures now put before-you are as-satisfactory-as[10]-the figures for-last-year. This-has-been achieved in[20]-spite-of rising-costs and it-is-certain-that-such[30] fine results could-not-have-been obtained unless each member[40]-of our staff had worked as-well-as-possible. The[50] report contains little information about-the new plant as-we[60]-shall-not-be in a proper position to estimate-the[70] results of-this-section until it-has-been in operation[80] for-some-months. It-is-certain, however, that-this-section[90] of-our factory is-as busy as-we-thought it[100]-would-be, and-this-is a source of-satisfaction to[110]-us. Whilst on-this-subject I-must tell-you that[120] if-the new plant is-satisfactory we-shall build a[130] similar one as-soon-as-possible as-we-think-that[140]-the present is-as good a time for development as[150]-we-are likely to-have for-a-long-time.

As[160]-will-be-seen from-the report, it-is-suggested that[170]-the dividend shall-be one per-cent higher-than last[180]-year. This-is proposed as-we-have-done well during[190]-the past-year and as-we-expect to-do as[200]-well or even better during-the current-year.   (208)

SECTION FIVE

The Stee Loop

THIS small loop forms a useful link in many phrases, and in addition use is made of it to represent the words *first* and *next*.

1. The General Use of The Stee Loop

The medial use of the loop allows distinctive phrases to be formed—

2. The Stee Loop and The Circle S

Circle S follows the small loop to represent *as* or *us*—

.... as fast as   .... against us

3. First

The small loop may be used initially, medially, or finally for the representation of this word. When *first* occurs at the beginning or in the middle of a phrase, the sign *.l....* is generally retained, but when occurring at the end of a phrase the word is represented by a Stee Loop attached to the stroke in the ordinary way.

Initially: .... first time   .... first place

.... first thing   .... first prize

.... first class   .... first instance

.... first quality   .... first-hand information

Medially: .... at first cost   .... for the first time

.... at first hand   .... in the first instance

Finally: .... at first   .... very first

(*See also* Section Sixteen, p. 87.)

4. Next

Combined with the N Hook the loop is used to represent *next*—

.... Sunday next   .... Monday next

(*See also* Section Eight, p. 41, and Section Sixteen, p. 87.)

FACILITY DRILL 5

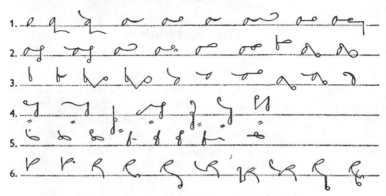

EXERCISE 5A
Read, and Write from Dictation

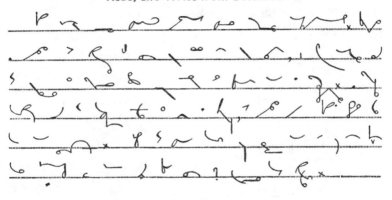

EXERCISE 5B
Write from Dictation Several Times

(Phrasing is suggested by hyphenation)

Dear-Sirs, I-am interested just-now in buying some[10] first-class office furniture, and-I-shall-be-pleased if[20]-you-will in-the-first-instance let-me-have-your[30] price-list. I-wish to-have-this list by Friday[40]-next, and-I-shall-be interested to know whether-the[50] furniture is available just-now. I-am working as-fast[60]-as I-can to-set up a new branch in[70]-this-town. It-is essential that-the furniture shall-be[80] of first-quality only as first-appearances are all-important[90] in-such-cases. During-the-last-few-days I-have[100] visited several showrooms but have-not-found any furniture just[110]as- high-class as I-require. Yours-faithfully,   (118)

SECTION SIX

The R Hook

THE R Hook to both straight strokes and curves lends itself well to the creation of facile and legible phraseograms. Perhaps the most common of its uses is in the representation of the words *are, our,* and *order,* but the use of the R Hook is extended to cover several other words not normally represented by the hooked form, among which may be mentioned: *appear, per, park, part, assure, far, forth.*

The hook is also used in the intersections for *Colonel, Professor, Superintendent,* and *Corporation.*

Details of the application of the hook to the above words is given below, but the R Hook has a wide range of utility, and advanced writers may safely adapt its use to their special requirements.

1. The R Hook to Straight Strokes

(*a*) **Appear**

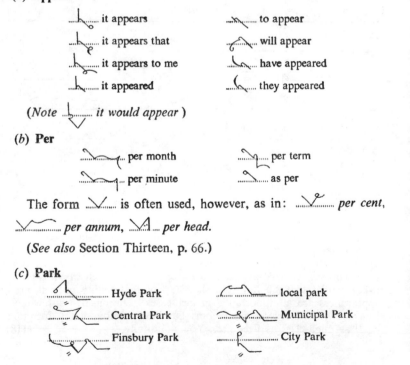

it appears   to appear

it appears that   will appear

it appears to me   have appeared

it appeared   they appeared

(*Note*   *it would appear*)

(*b*) **Per**

per month   per term

per minute   as per

The form ⟍⟍ is often used, however, as in: *per cent,*   *per annum,*   *per head.*

(*See also* Section Thirteen, p. 66.)

(*c*) **Park**

Hyde Park   local park

Central Park   Municipal Park

Finsbury Park   City Park

(*d*) **Part.** The R Hook combines with the Halving Principle to represent *part* in a large number of extremely useful phrases—

.... in all parts   .... your parts

.... in all parts of   .... for my part
the country

.... various parts   .... some parts

.... various parts of   .... to take part
the world

.... your part   .... for the most part

(*Note* .... *part of*, when the phrase stands by itself.)

(*See also* Section Nine, p. 47.)

2. The R Hook to Curves

(*a*) **Are.** The hook is used for the representation of *are* following *they*: .... *they are*, ... *they are not.*

In other cases Ray is used: .... *we are*, ... *you are*, etc.

(*b*) **Our.** The hook is used for the representation of *our* following *in*—

.... in our   .... in our interests

.... in our country   .... it is in our interests

In other cases Ray is used: .... *to our*, ... *of our*, etc.

(*c*) **Order.** The hook is combined with the Doubling or the Halving Principle for the representation of *order* following *in*—

.... in order   .... in order to

.... in order that   .... in order to be sure

In other cases the double-length R is used: .... *your order.*

(*See also* Section Twelve, p. 61.)

(*d*) **Assure**

.... I can assure you   .... if you can assure us

.... we are assured   .... to assure the

(e) **Far**

...🖊️...... how far   ...🖊️...... by far the most

...🖊️...... so far   ...🖊️...... by far the most important

...🖊️...... very far   ...🖊️...... is it far

(f) **Forth**

...🖊️...... set forth   ...🖊️...... put forth

3. Intersections

The R Hook is used in the representation of the words *Colonel*, *Professor*, *Superintendent*, and *Corporation*.

(a) **Colonel**

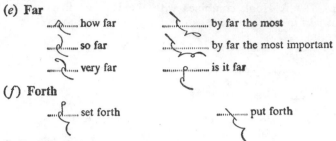

...🖊️...... Colonel Johnson   ...🖊️...... Lieut. Col. Baker

...🖊️...... Colonel Churchill   ...🖊️...... Lieut. Col. Brown

(b) **Professor**

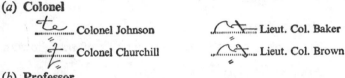

...🖊️...... Professor Robbins   ...🖊️...... Professor of Music

...🖊️...... Professor Smith   ...🖊️...... Professor of Chemistry

(c) **Superintendent**

...🖊️...... Superintendent Cousins   ...🖊️...... Superintendent of
                                              the Line

...🖊️...... Superintendent Wilson   ...🖊️...... College Superintendent

(d) **Corporation**

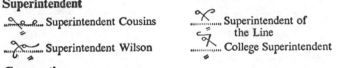

...🖊️...... Electricity Corporation   ...🖊️...... Rubber Corporation

...🖊️...... Broadcasting Corporation   ...🖊️...... Corporation of
                                              Industries

(*See also* Section Fifteen, p. 77.)

4. The R Hook and Circle S

Occasionally the R Hook at the beginning of one outline is blended with the final Circle S of a preceding outline in order to form a useful phrase—

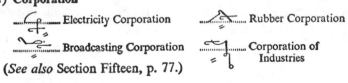

...🖊️...... purchase agreement   ...🖊️...... it is agreed

(*See also* Section Sixteen, p. 87, for examples of the omission of the R Hook in phrases.)

FACILITY DRILL 6

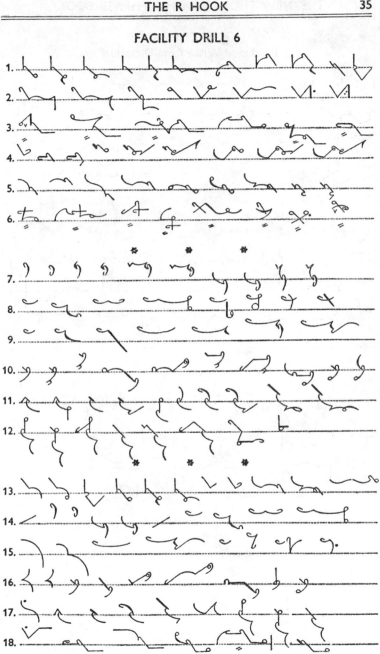

EXERCISE 6A
Read, and Write from Dictation

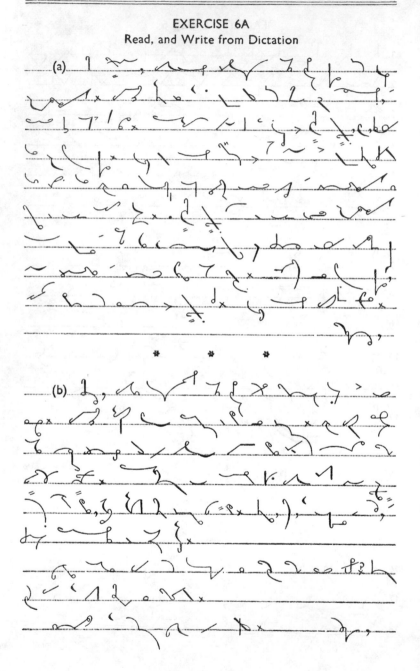

EXERCISE 6B
Write from Dictation Several Times
(Phrasing is suggested by hyphenation)

(*a*) It-is in-our-interests to-attend-the lectures that[10] are to-be held in-various-parts of-the City[20] during-the-next-few-weeks. It-appears-that-the speakers[30] include Professor-Jones, who-is Professor-of-Chemistry at-the[40] Central-Park University, and-Professor-Smithson who-is Professor-of[50]-History at-the Green-Park College. In-order-to-be[60]-sure of-finding a place at-such popular lectures we[70]-are advised to-purchase tickets for-the whole course very[80]-far in-advance. Programmes are available which set-forth in[90] detail the subjects of-the lectures together-with dates and[100]-places, and-members of-this-Corporation would-do well to[110] book early in-order-that-there shall-be no disappointment[120] later. We-can-assure-you that-the-Committee tried to[130] obtain a special fee for our members but it-appears[140]-that they-have-not-been successful in-this as-the[150] demand for tickets is so great.   (156)

(*b*) During-the course of-my holiday I-visited various-parts[10]-of-the-country in-order-that I might learn more[20] about-the wild life and-the wild flowers to-be[30]-found in different-parts-of-the-country. I-did-not[40]-have to-go very-far to-find out that great[50] differences exist between different-parts-of-the-country. I-suppose[60]-that if I-were fortunate enough to-be-able-to[70] visit various-parts-of-the-world I should-find that[80] even greater differences exist than I-had imagined. In-some[90]-parts-of-the-world, for-instance, trees shed-the leaves[100] in-the hot season. Flowers can-be-found in various[110]-parts that bloom profusely during long dry periods but do[120]-not bloom if-it rains. In-our-part-of-the[130]-world our trees have-their heaviest foliage during-the hottest[140] season and-without water flowers fade away. In-our-country[150] cats like to-sit in-the-sun in-order-to[160] warm themselves but very-far away in-the hot places[170] cats like to-sleep in-the shade all-day in[180]-order-to keep cool and to-come out only in[190]-the evening when-the-sun has set.   (197)

SECTION SEVEN

The L Hook

THE use made of the initial L Hook covers a more limited field in phraseography than that made of the R Hook but the few phrases in which it is employed are very useful. The words which it affects are *all*, *only*, and *fellow*.

The L Hook is also used in the intersection for the word *application*.

1. The L Hook to Straight Strokes

The L Hook is attached to the beginning of the outlines for *at* and *by* to add the word *all*, as—

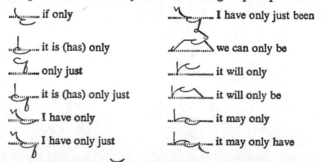

at all   by all

at all costs   by all means

at all events   by all accounts

at all times   by all reports

In such phrases as ⌣ *in all*, ⌣ *for all* there is no advantage in using the hook.

2. The L Hook to Curves

(*a*) **Only.** The large initial hook to curves is used with the stroke N for the representation of *only* in a valuable group of phrases:

if only   I have only just been

it is (has) only   we can only be

only just   it will only

it is (has) only just   it will only be

I have only   it may only

I have only just   it may only have

(*Note:* in the phrase ⌣ *only been*, where the form stands alone, the full outline for *only* is more satisfactory.)

(*b*) **Fellow.** The form ......⌒...... may be used for *fellow* in frequently used expressions, as—

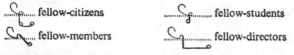

......⌒...... fellow-citizens   ......⌒...... fellow-students

......⌒...... fellow-members   ......⌒...... fellow-directors

3. Intersection

The hooked form ......⌒..... is used for the word *application* when it can conveniently be intersected, as: ......⌒...... *to make application.*

(*See also* Section Fifteen, p. 77.)

FACILITY DRILL 7

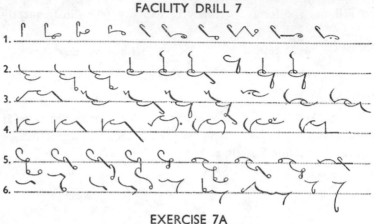

EXERCISE 7A
Read, and Write from Dictation

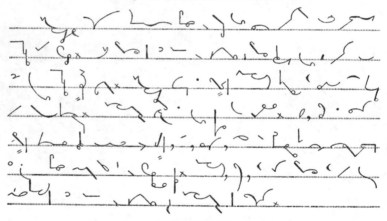

EXERCISE 7B
Write from Dictation Several Times

(Phrasing is suggested by hyphenation)

Dear-Sir, We-thank-you for-your-letter, and-we[10]-can-only-say that-we-are-sorry-that-there-has[20]-been some delay regarding-the signing of-your-contract for[30]-the supply of-building-materials. It-has-only-just-been[40] officially decided to-proceed with-the-erection of new buildings[50] at-all our branch premises. We-can-assure-you that[60]-it-will-only-be a matter of-days now before[70]-the-contracts are formally-completed. By-all-means, however, come[80] in and see us if-you think-it-will facilitate[90] matters. We-can-only-hope-that once work actually begins[100] everything will move smoothly at-all-times. Yours-faithfully,   (109)

The N Hook

THE N Hook to both straight strokes and curves lends itself well to
the formation of very facile phraseograms, and speed writers should
lose no opportunity of availing themselves of its use. Among the
words that may be represented by the use of this hook are *been*,
than, on, own, not, once, next. The hook is also used in the intersections for *beginning* and *convenience*.

Details of the uses of the hook are given below, and advanced
writers may safely adapt its use to their particular requirements.

1. The General Uses of The N Hook
(*a*) **Been**

I have been	recently been
I had been	only been
already been	certainly been

The Doubling Principle may be applied to such phrases to add the
word *there—*

I have been there	recently been there
I had been there	only been there
already been there	certainly been there

The N Hook is not applied to such phrases as: *has not been*,
it has been, etc.

(*b*) **Than.** The use of the N Hook to represent the word *than*
provides the shorthand writer with an extremely wide range of
phrases, of which the following are examples. The hook should be
applied in all suitable cases—

better than	bigger than
greater than	larger than
fewer than	smaller than
more than	quicker than
rather than	longer than

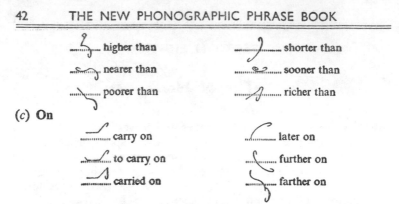

.... higher than   .... shorter than

.... nearer than   .... sooner than

.... poorer than   .... richer than

(c) On

.... carry on   .... later on

.... to carry on   .... further on

.... carried on   .... farther on

(d) **Own.** The N Hook may generally be used for *own* but after
.... *my* the vocalized stroke is used, as: .... *my own,* ....
in my own case. The stroke is also used after .... *his* and .... *in
their,* as: .... *his own,* .... *in their own.*

Examples of the hooked form for *own* are—

.... your own   .... for your own

.... her own   .... in her own

.... our own   .... on our own

.... their own   .... for their own

(e) **Not.** The N Hook combines with the Halving Principle to
represent the word *not*—again offering the shorthand writer a wide
range of useful phrases—

.... I am not   .... certainly not

.... you are not   .... it is (has) certainly not

.... you will not   .... this will not

.... I do (had) not   .... this will not be

.... I did not   .... is it not

.... we do not know   .... were not

(*See also* Section Eleven, p. 54.)

(f) **Once.** Circle S blends with the N Hook to represent *once* in the
phrase .... *at once.*

(*See also* Section Three, p. 17.)

(g) **Next.** The Stee Loop blends with the N Hook to represent *next*, as in: ⎯⎯ *Monday next,* ⎯⎯ *Wednesday next.*

(*See also* Section Five, p. 30.)

2. Intersections: Beginning, Convenient/ce

The intersection ⎯⎯ is employed for *beginning* while ⎯⎯ is used for *convenient/ce*:

⎯⎯ at the beginning   ⎯⎯ if it is convenient

⎯⎯ from the beginning   ⎯⎯ is it convenient

⎯⎯ from beginning to end   ⎯⎯ at your convenience

3. Miscellaneous Phrases

The N Hook occurs in a few miscellaneous phrases, such as ⎯⎯ *against us,* ⎯⎯ *upon us.*

(*See also* Section Three, p. 17.)

FACILITY DRILL 8

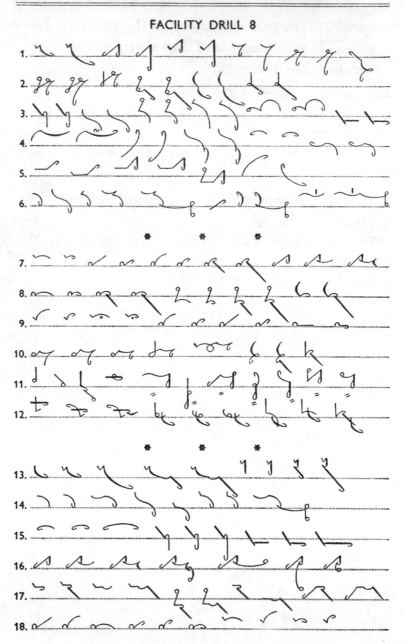

EXERCISE 8A
Read, and Write from Dictation

(a)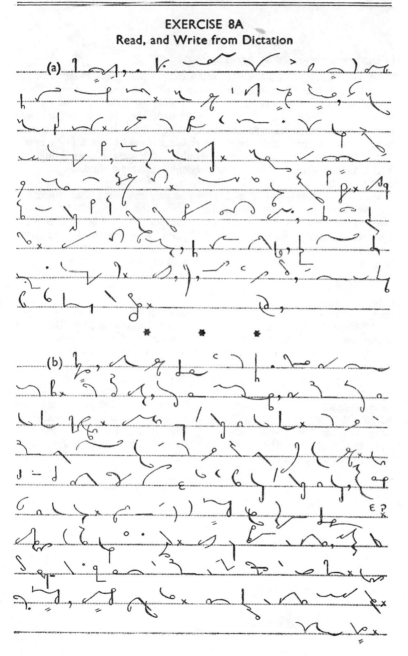

EXERCISE 8B
Write from Dictation Several Times

(Phrasing is suggested by hyphenation)

(a) Dear-Lucy, You-are-not unaware of-the fact that[10]-we-have recently-been house-hunting, for I-have-told[20]-you so-many-times about our experiences. It-seems that[30]-we-shall almost-certainly-not-be moving house in-the[40] very near-future as-we-have decided that to-build[50] our-own house is better-than to buy an existing[60] one. In-this-way we-can-have a house bigger[70]-than would-be possible if-we bought a fairly new[80] suburban house and-smaller-than would-be-the case if[90]-we bought a Victorian mansion. So-far we-have-been[100] unable-to-find anything of a suitable size.

We-are[110]-certainly-not able-to give-you any real details at[120]-present, and-we-do-not-know even where-the site[130]-of-the house will-be but-we-are-sure that[140]-it-will-not-be very-far from-you as-we[150]-both love your-part-of-the country better-than other[160]-parts. As-soon-as our plans have advanced farther-than[170] they-have so-far we-shall let-you-know what[180]-has-been decided. In-the-meantime we-send our kindest[190]-regards to-you all. Maisie.   (195)

(b) As my summer holiday will-be shorter-than usual this[10]-July I-shall go no farther-than-the South Coast.[20] This-will-not-be a hardship for-me as I[30]-like-the fresh sea-breezes of-Brighton, and-I-shall[40]-be-there for about ten days. The reason for-my[50] holiday lasting for no-more-than ten days is-that[60] I-have-been asked to-carry-on-the work-of[70] assistant accountant at-the office while-the assistant himself is[80] taking leave for rather longer-than usual on-account-of[90] poor health. He-has-recently-been very ill, and he[100]-may-not-be-able-to carry-on at-all if[110]-he-is-not given long leave of absence now. He[120]-will almost-certainly-not return before October. It-is-indeed[130] in-my-own-interests to comply with-this-suggestion as[140] otherwise I-cannot get-the training I-need and, more[150]-than that, I-shall-be-able-to take a holiday[160] at Christmas for rather longer-than-the usual four days.   (170)

SECTION NINE

The F/V Hook

THE words *have, of,* and *off* may be represented in phraseograms by the F/V Hook. The hook is also used to provide convenient forms for expressions containing the words *afternoon, evening, event,* and *effect.*

1. Have

While the form ....ᒾ.... *have* is generally retained in phraseograms (as ....ᒾ.... *I have,* ....ᒾ.... *we have,* ....ᒾ.... *can have,* etc.) the F/V Hook is used to form a small group of frequently occurring phrases—

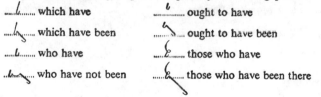

....ᒾ.... which have   ....ᒾ.... ought to have

....ᒾ.... which have been   ....ᒾ.... ought to have been

....ᒾ.... who have   ....ᒾ.... those who have

....ᒾ.... who have not been   ....ᒾ.... those who have been there

2. Of

The F/V Hook may be added to a great number of outlines to add the word *of.* It is an extremely useful and legible type of phrase, and the hook should be used on all suitable occasions.

....ᒾ.... out of   ....ᒾ.... exchange of

....ᒾ.... set of   ....ᒾ.... report of

....ᒾ.... rate of   ....ᒾ.... part of

....ᒾ.... total of   ....ᒾ.... present state of

....ᒾ.... plenty o'   ....ᒾ.... instead of

....ᒾ.... range of   ....ᒾ.... in spite of the

....ᒾ.... group of   ....ᒾ.... in support of

....ᒾ.... copy of   ....ᒾ.... in support of the

....ᒾ.... state of things   ....ᒾ.... rate of interest

....ᒾ.... state of affairs   ....ᒾ.... sort of

(*See also* Section Eleven, p. 54, for examples of the use of the F/V Hook following a half-length stroke.)

The Doubling Principle may be combined with the use of the F/V Hook—

...... out of there (their)   ...... which have their

3. Off

...... set off   ...... to make off

...... paid off   ...... better off

...... paid off their   ...... to take off

4. Afternoon

After, when occurring in phrases as part of the word *afternoon*, is represented by the F/V Hook as shown in the following examples—

...... Monday afternoon   ...... Sunday afternoon

...... Wednesday afternoon   ...... yesterday afternoon

(*Note* ...... *this afternoon*, ... *tomorrow afternoon*)

5. Evening

Even, when occurring in phrases as part of the word *evening*, is represented by the F/V Hook—

...... Tuesday evening   ...... Saturday evening

...... Thursday evening   ...... yesterday evening

(*Note* ...... *this evening*, ... *tomorrow evening*)

6. Event

The hook is used in a few phrases containing the word *event*, as:

...... *at all events*, ... *such events*, ... *which events*.

(*Note* ...... *in the event* (*of*))

7. Effect

Into effect is written: ...... The full form for *effect* is generally used, however, as: ...... *in effect*, ... *to effect*.

FACILITY DRILL 9

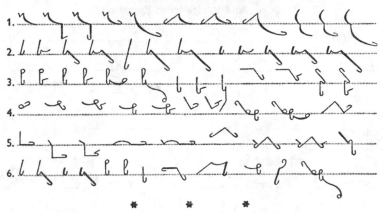

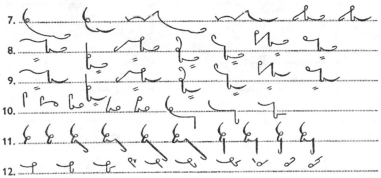

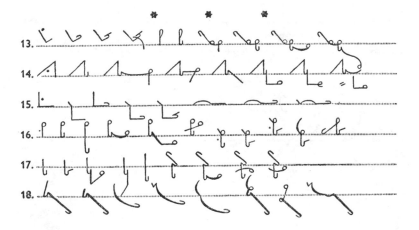

EXERCISE 9A
Read, and Write from Dictation

(a)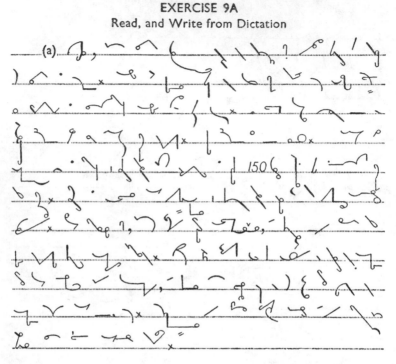

* * *

(b)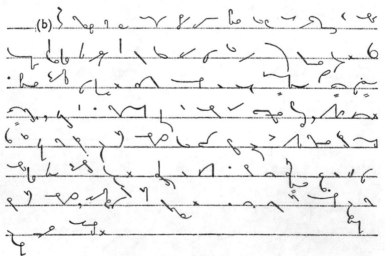

EXERCISE 9B
Write from Dictation Several Times

(Phrasing is suggested by hyphenation)

(a) Dear-Miss Weston, I-am-enclosing a set-of proofs[10] of-the report-of-the Chairman's-speech at-the meeting[20] held on-Friday-evening last. Kindly return-the set-of[30] proofs corrected ready for-the printer.

I-am-enclosing also[40] for-your approval a draft programme for-the Conference in[50] August. As you-will-see, the items include a Dinner[60] and Dance on-Friday-evening, the 17th; an Official Reception[70] and Lecture on-Saturday-morning, the 18th; four o'clock tea[80] on-Saturday-afternoon, by kind invitation of-the-President, with[90] social events on-Saturday-evening. On-Sunday-evening at 8.[100]30 I-am-proposing that-there shall-be informal Discussion[110] Groups. There-will-be two lectures on-Monday-morning, Discussion[120] Groups on-Monday-afternoon, and a Concert on-Monday-evening.[130] There-will-be a further two lectures on Tuesday-morning,[140] and on Tuesday-afternoon the President will give a general[150] Summing-up of-the Conference. On Tuesday-evening I-suggest[160] a Farewell Banquet.

I-shall-be-glad to-have-your[170] views on-this-suggested Programme and to know if-you[180] think-that-it-is-the sort-of thing required. I[190]-feel that-it-will give those Members who-have-not[200] attended a Conference before plenty-of opportunity to-meet other[210]-Members and plenty-of scope for-the exchange-of ideas.[220]

Kindly return-the draft copy-of-the Programme at-your[230]-convenience. Yours-sincerely,   (233)

(b) Dear-Sirs, Thank-you for-the copy-of-the illustrated[10] catalogue and-for-the set-of leaflets. You appear to[20]-be making-the sort-of materials in-which-we-are[30]-interested, and-we-shall-be-glad if-you-will send[40]-us a set-of-the samples offered on page 21[50] of-the-catalogue.

We-think-that your range-of[60] colours is rather limited and-we-shall-be-glad if,[70] when sending-the set-of samples, you-will state whether[80] colours can-be blended. If, after receipt-of your further[90] letter, we-are-interested in-your product we-suggest that[100] our representative should call at-your premises on-Thursday-afternoon[110] of next-week for a personal inspection-of-the range[120]-of your products. Yours-faithfully,   (125)

SECTION TEN

The Shun Hook

USE is made of the Shun Hook for the brief representation in phrases of the words *ocean, information.* and *association.*

1. Ocean

.... Atlantic Ocean   .... Pacific Ocean

(*Note* .... *Indian Ocean*)

2. Information

.... for your information   .... further information

(*Note* .... *for his information,* .... *any information,* etc.)

3. Association

.... Medical Association   .... Technical Association

.... your association   .... Traders Association

4. The Direction of The Shun Hook

The direction taken by the Shun Hook occurring in the course of a phraseogram is governed by the requirements of the outline as a whole, and may differ from the direction taken in an outline standing alone, as—

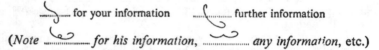

.... occasion   .... on such occasions   *but*   .... on this occasion

.... section   .... in these sections   *but*   .... in some sections

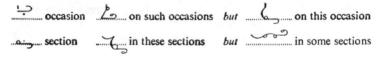

Facility of writing is of first importance in this connexion.

FACILITY DRILL 10

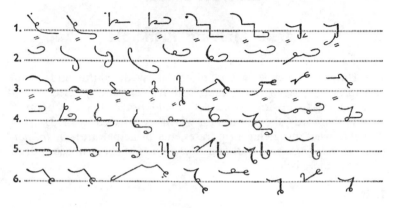

EXERCISE 10A
Write from Dictation Several Times

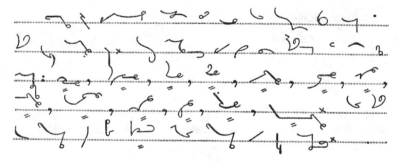

EXERCISE 10B
Read, and Write from Dictation

(Phrasing is suggested by hyphenation)

Dear-Miss-Thomas, We-thank-you for-your-information of[10]-yesterday and-have-pleasure in-enclosing pamphlets dealing-with-the[20] Pacific-Ocean. We-think-that-the pamphlets will-be of[30]-great-interest to-the new members of-your-Association. We[40]-are-enclosing also further-information about our booklets regarding-the[50] South Atlantic-Ocean.

We-draw your special-attention to-those[60]-sections that deal-with-the seasons of-the-year. In[70]-these-sections you-will-find recent Reports of-the Weather[80]-Association regarding-conditions to-be expected in-the oceans of[90]-the-world at different seasons of-the-year. Yours-truly, (100)

SECTION ELEVEN

The Halving Principle

THE Halving Principle is one of the most delightful and useful principles of Pitman Shorthand, and it is naturally used extensively in the formation of attractive and practical phraseograms. Among the words, the outlines for which are affected by the Halving Principle when occurring in phrases, the principal are: *it, to, not, word, would, time, part, out,* and *state.* Each of these words is dealt with separately below.

1. It

A preceding stroke may be halved to add the word *it.* A following outline may be joined to the half-length stroke—

.... if it

.... if it is

.... if it is not

.... in which it is

.... to make it clear

.... depend upon it

.... from it

.... I think it is

.... I think it is necessary

.... until it is

This list is not exhaustive, and the experienced writer will find many opportunities for the further application of the Halving Principle to the representation of *it.*

(*Note* .... *for it,* .... *if it*)

2. To

In the outlines .... *able* and .... *unable* the stroke B is halved to add *to.* A following outline may be joined to the half-length stroke—

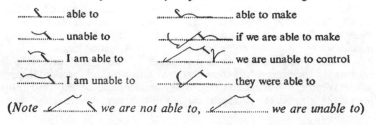

.... able to

.... unable to

.... I am able to

.... I am unable to

.... able to make

.... if we are able to make

.... we are unable to control

.... they were able to

(*Note* .... *we are not able to,* .... *we are unable to*)

3. Not

A stroke may be hooked for N and halved to add *not*, either finally or in the middle of a phrase. This principle offers wide scope to the phraser, and the following outlines are representative—

	I am not		I do not think it is necessary
	I will not		they are not
	you will not		certainly not
	you are not		it is (has) certainly not
	you were not		almost certainly not
	I do not		is it not
	I do not know		this will not
	I did not know		they will not be

Certain groups of outlines should be noted—

	I had not		I do not
	I did not		
	we do not		we did not
	are not		we are not
	you are not		they are not
	it is not		is it not
	they will not		this will not

(*Note* ___ *have not*)

Note also the following—

	shan't		we're
	won't		he'll
	can't		she'll
	haven't		they'll
	isn't		I'm
	wasn't		I'll
	you're		weren't

(*See also* Section Eight, p. 41.)

4. Word

Word may be represented by half-length Way .... in phrases if a more facile form is thereby achieved—

.... those words   .... in other words

.... in these words   .... few words

.... in his own words   .... to say a few words

.... common words   .... in many words

In such phrases as .... *in the words,* .... *words a minute,* etc., no advantage is obtained from a change of form.

5. Would

This word may also be represented by half-length Way .... in phrases if a more facile form results—

.... I would   .... this would

.... we would be   .... these would be

.... they would not be   .... these would not be

In such phrases as .... *he would not,* .... *it would not,* etc., no advantage is obtained from a change of form.

6. Time

Many interesting phrases are obtained by applying the Halving Principle to the stroke preceding the word *time,* as the following examples show. These examples are not exhaustive and the principle should be applied whenever practicable—

.... some time   .... from time to time

.... at some time   .... at all times

.... at the same time   .... modern times

.... for some time   .... valuable time

.... for some time past   .... lunch time

.... at one time   .... more time

In such phrases as .... *no time,* .... *at any time,* the Halving Principle cannot be employed.

7. Part

To represent this word briefly in phrases the Halving Principle is coupled with the initial R Hook, as shown in the following illustrative cases. The student should not limit himself to the examples given but should apply the principle whenever possible—

.... in all parts (of)

.... in all parts of the world

.... various parts of the country

.... part and parcel

.... for my part

.... for your part

.... greater part (of)

.... larger part (of)

(*See also* Section Six, p. 32.)

8. Out

The following phrases are useful time-savers—

.... set out

.... carried out

.... brought out

.... to set out

9. State

An extremely valuable set of phrases can be formed on the following lines—

.... to state

.... this statement

.... another statement

.... recent statement

.... this state

.... several statements

10. General Note

The F/V Hook may be added to halved strokes to represent the word *of* in many frequently occurring phrases using half-length strokes—

.... sort of

.... in spite of

.... instead of

.... part of

.... present state of

.... present state of affairs

The F/V Hook for *of* is not, however, used when *part* is represented by .... A distinction is thus obtained between *part of* and *number of*, as: .... *great part of* but .... *great number of*.

(*See also* Section Nine, p. 47.)

FACILITY DRILL 11

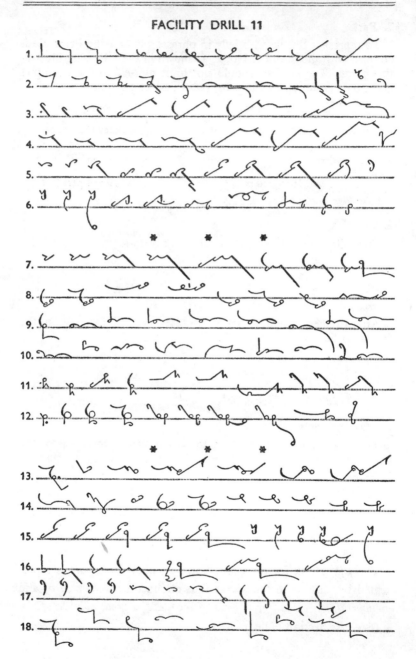

EXERCISE 11A
Read, and Write from Dictation

(a)

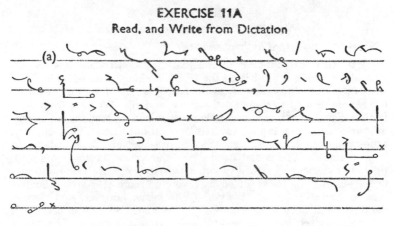

* * *

(b)

* * *

(c)

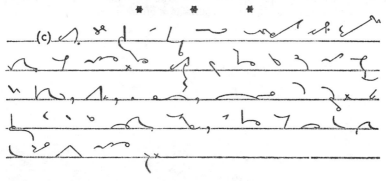

EXERCISE 11B
Write from Dictation Several Times
(Phrasing is suggested by hyphenation)

(*a*) I-wish to-make-it-clear to-you that-the[10] undertaking has-not-yet-been-able-to make a profit[20] on-the year's working. I-do-not-think-you-will[30]-be-surprised to-hear this, as-the past-year has[40]-been one in-which-it-has-been difficult to show[50] satisfactory working. We-have from-time-to-time carried-out[60] large orders but-we-are-not-yet really well-known[70] in-spite-of-considerable press advertising in various-parts-of[80]-the-country. I-am-confident, however, that-the-present-state[90]-of-affairs will-not-be long-continued. The actual details[100] of-our year's trading are set-out fully in-statements[110] already circulated to-you, and-I-do-not-think-there[120]-is-anything to-be gained by taking-up more of[130]-your valuable-time in further-comment. I-would-like-to[140]-say, however, that-during-the three-months since-the accounts[150] were prepared we-have carried-out extensive market research, and[160] it-is-certainly-not through any fault of-ours that[170]-the-accounts now presented are-not better-than they-are.   (180)

(*b*) I-have-been asked to-say-a-few-words about[10]-the present-state-of-the Club's finances. This-will-not[20] take-up much of-your valuable-time as I-intend[30] to-keep to-my undertaking and to say only a[40] *few* words. As you-will-have-seen from-the figures[50] set-out in-the Annual Report of-your Club, the[60] organization has for-some-time had a large-amount of[70]-cash in-hand and your-Committee believe-that in-the[80]-present satisfactory-state-of-the Club's finances they-are able[90]-to-recommend an extension of-the-premises to include a[100] hall in-which-it-is suggested that-such functions as[110] dances, cinema shows, lectures, should-take-place. This-sort-of[120] accommodation would greatly enhance the prestige of-the Club, and[130]-I-trust-you-will-not-consider-the-Committee wrong in[140] putting this proposal to-you. The Committee members regret that[150]-they-are-not able-to put a finished plan before[160]-you but-they did-not-wish to incur expense in[170]-this-connexion until they-had your-consent to-the general[180] scheme. I-would-therefore appreciate it if-you-would indicate[190] to-me this-afternoon your views on-the-matter.   (199)

SECTION TWELVE

The Doubling Principle

THE Doubling Principle is used extensively in phrasing to represent the words *their/there, other, dear*. The outlines for *therefore* and *order* undergo a change of form in certain double-length phraseograms.

The extra time taken to write a double-length stroke is so extremely small that the doubling of strokes to represent an additional word must be considered a most valuable time-saving device, and shorthand writers should avail themselves of its use whenever an opportunity presents itself.

1. Their/There

A stroke may be doubled in length to add either of these words, care being taken to maintain proportion and to show clearly that the stroke is doubled. A Circle S may be added.

Finally hooked strokes may be doubled for the addition of these words.

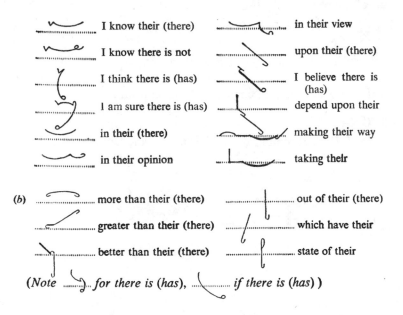

I know their (there)   in their view

I know there is not   upon their (there)

I think there is (has)   I believe there is (has)

I am sure there is (has)   depend upon their

in their (there)   making their way

in their opinion   taking their

(b)   more than their (there)   out of their (there)

greater than their (there)   which have their

better than their (there)   state of their

(*Note*   *for there is* (*has*),   *if there is* (*has*))

2. Other

A preceding stroke may be doubled to add the word *other*—

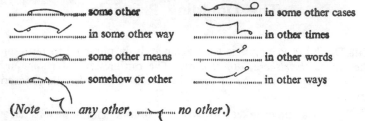

.... some other   .... in some other cases

.... in some other way   .... in other times

.... some other means   .... in other words

.... somehow or other   .... in other ways

(*Note* .... *any other,* .... *no other.*)

3. Dear

Doubling for the word *dear* principally occurs after the outline for the word *my*, but it is useful in a few other cases—

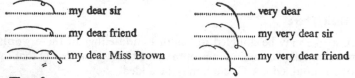

.... my dear sir   .... very dear

.... my dear friend   .... my very dear sir

.... my dear Miss Brown   .... my very dear friend

4. Therefore

The form for *therefore* is occasionally changed in order to avoid a lift of the pen—

.... I shall therefore   .... I was therefore

In such phrases as .... *I have therefore,* .... *I think therefore,*

there is no advantage in changing the form from ....

5. Order

The R Hook is combined with the Halving and Doubling Principles to form some very useful phrases containing *order*—

.... in order to   .... in order

.... in order to avoid   .... in order that

(*See also* Section Six, p. 32.)

FACILITY DRILL 12

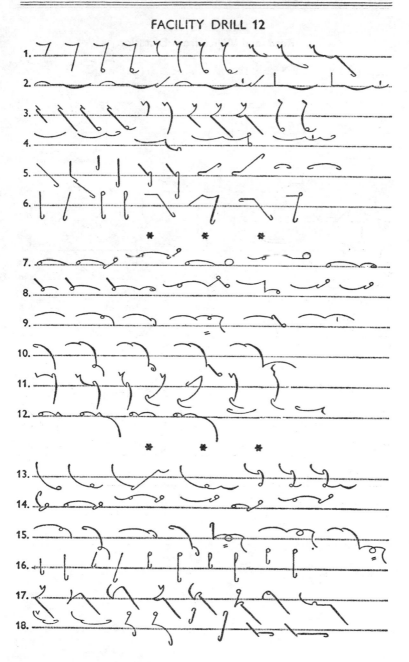

EXERCISE 12A
Read, and Write from Dictation

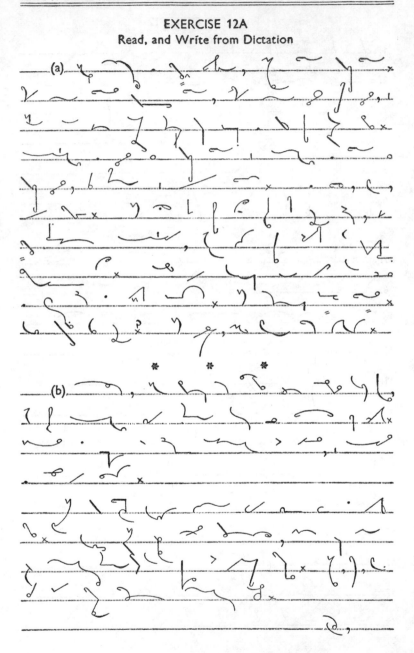

EXERCISE 12B
Write from Dictation Several Times
(Phrasing is suggested by hyphenation)

(*a*) The lecturer said: My-dear-friends, I-am-sure-there[10]-is no-one here to-night who-is-not happy to[20]-find himself among friends. In-other-words, I-hope-there[30]-is no-one who feels lonely. If-there-is, I[40]-trust he-will, as-soon-as-the formal meeting is[50] over, make himself known for-he-will-find that-there[60]-are very-dear-friends here.

You-may-have noticed that[70]-the audience is larger-than usual. This-is because-the[80] near-by Southern Branch has sent a group-of-their[90] Members to represent them at-this meeting, and-they-have[100] asked-me to arrange that a group-of Members from[110] this Branch shall make-their-way to-the next meeting[120] of-the-Southern Branch. I-shall-therefore be-glad if[130] at-the termination of-the-meeting Members who-would like[140] to-attend a meeting of-that-Branch will let-me[150]-know. If-you-can-be-there in large-numbers you[160]-will-be very welcome.   (164)

(*b*) Ladies-and-Gentlemen, I-think-there-is little that I[10]-can add to what-the Chairman has said, although-there[20]-is much that might interest-you if-there-were time[30] for-me to-speak to-you about-my personal visits[40] to-Ceylon. I-have-been-there many-times, and-I[50]-expect most of-those present have-been-there also. I[60]-have quite recently-been-there, however; in-fact, I-returned[70] only yesterday, and-I-think-therefore that-my information is[80] probably as up to-the-minute as-is possible even[90] in-this jet age. I-was-there indeed to-represent[100]-the interests of a rival-company of-which I-am[110] a Director, and-the picture I-saw of-the range[120]-of-their interests suggests to-me that somehow-or-other[130] your-company, of-which I-am a shareholder, should by[140]-some-other-means and-in-some-other-ways extend its[150]-interests in Ceylon.   (153)

SECTION THIRTEEN

Consonants R, L, W, H

WHERE alternative signs have been provided for the representation of a consonant the form used in single outlines is sometimes varied in a phrase in order to obtain a good phraseogram. In a few cases the signs for W or H are entirely omitted.

1. Consonant R

Words in which the form of R varies in phraseograms are: *were, world, war, wire, sir, per, appear, door(s)*. Examples are—

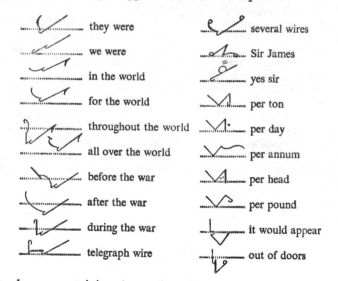

they were	several wires
we were	Sir James
in the world	yes sir
for the world	per ton
throughout the world	per day
all over the world	per annum
before the war	per head
after the war	per pound
during the war	it would appear
telegraph wire	out of doors

In phrases containing the outlines for *world* or *war* the Tick The is included or omitted as convenient.

(*See also* Section Six, p. 32.)

2. Consonant L

The direction taken by stroke L may be varied in a phraseogram to enable the outline as a whole to conform to the rules for the use of upward and downward L.

(a) **Downward L and Circle S**

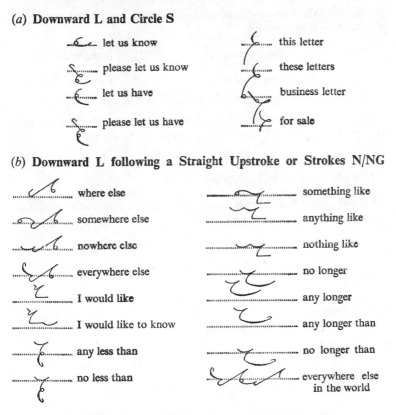

let us know

please let us know

let us have

please let us have

this letter

these letters

business letter

for sale

(b) **Downward L following a Straight Upstroke or Strokes N/NG**

where else

somewhere else

nowhere else

everywhere else

I would like

I would like to know

any less than

no less than

something like

anything like

nothing like

no longer

any longer

any longer than

no longer than

everywhere else in the world

3. Consonant W

(a) **Omission of W.** An initial representation of *w* is often omitted entirely in phrases containing *week, will, well, were*:

this week

next week

last week

you will

I will not

that he will

so well

very well

you were

you were not

The phrases _____ *we will*, _____ *that was* should be noted.

(*See also* Section Sixteen, p. 87.)

(*b*) **Stroke W.** The stroke is used instead of the initial semicircle if a better joining results:

telegraph wire   in the world

during the war   they were

In these phrases the forms for both W and R are changed.

(*c*) **Week.** This word is often represented by a simple K, as shown above. In other cases, however, a stroke *way* is used:

few weeks   past few weeks

(*See also* Section Sixteen, p. 87.)

(*d*) **As-W.** Initial W blends with a preceding S in a useful group of phrases, the *sway* circle being used:

as well as   as will be seen

as we can   as well as possible

(*See also* Section Four, p. 24.)

4. Consonant H

The aspirate is omitted in some phraseograms, particularly in the outlines for *house, hope, happen.*

in the house   I hope that you will

to the house   what has happened

I hope that   what is happening

we hope there is   in the House of Commons

The dot *h* is added in .... *to him,* .... *for himself,* etc. to distinguish the phrases from .... *to me,* .... *for myself,* etc.

Tick H is used in phrases, as: .... *for whom,* .... *in here.*

FACILITY DRILL 13

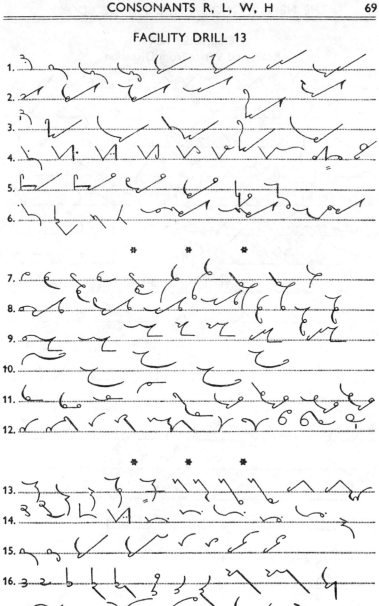

EXERCISE 13A
Read, and Write from Dictation

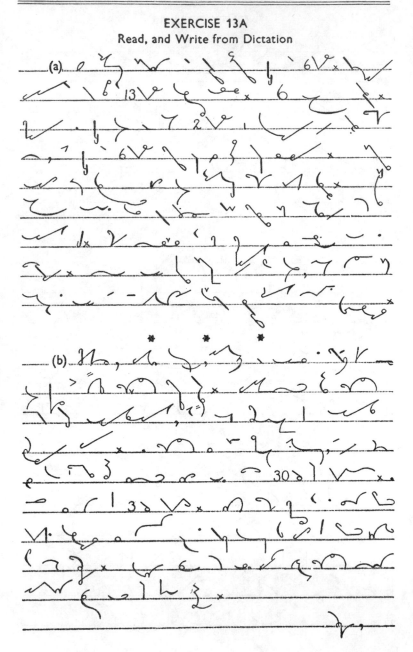

EXERCISE 13B
Write from Dictation Several Times
(Phrasing is indicated by hyphenation)

(a) Dear-Madam, As-requested, we-enclose copy-of-the College[10] Prospectus, and-we-hope-that-you-will decide to-send[20] your daughter to-us for tuition. You-will-see-that[30] for a Course covering Shorthand, Typewriting, English, and Book-keeping the[40] cost is £70 per-annum. This-is subject to[50] a five per-cent deduction if-the whole sum is[60] paid before instruction-commences. There-are three terms per year,[70] and you-may-prefer to pay £25 per[80]-term.

The hours of instruction are five per-day, the[90] hours being from nine until four with a lunch-time[100] break from twelve until two o'clock. There-are fourteen weeks[110] per-term. Students who-remain at-the-College for two[120]-years can always-be very-well-placed at good salaries[130] at-the-end of-their Course.

We-hope-you-will[140] decide to entrust your daughter to-our care, and-we[150]-assure-you that she-will obtain tuition superior to-that[160]-which she could obtain anywhere-else-in-the-world. Yours[170]-truly, (171)

(b) We-are-not very-well able-to predict our trading[10] figures in-advance because-this-House deals in a commodity[20] that serves a wide range-of purposes. Some-people order[30] in-such small quantities that-we-have to-quote prices[40] at so-much per-pound while others demand such great[50] quantities that-we-quote prices at so-much per-ton.[60] Some buyers request a delivery per-month while others buy[70] so-much per-annum. Our total output is-now something[80]-like 76,000 tons per-annum and it-is[90]-no-longer possible for-us to-expand our undertaking unless[100]-we-can-have larger premises. Nothing-else is available for[110]-us in-this area, and-we-may-therefore decide to[120]-go somewhere-else if suitable property can-be-found during[130]-the-next-few-weeks. (134)

SECTION FOURTEEN

Prefixes and Suffixes

THE application to phrasing of the rules for the representation of prefixes and suffixes is shown below. It will be seen that where a suffix also represents a complete word that word may often be represented in a phrase by the sign employed for the suffix.

1. The Prefix Con-, Com-.

When these prefixes occur at the beginning of a word they are represented in phrases by writing the part of the outline following the *con-*, etc., close to the preceding outline and omitting the dot.

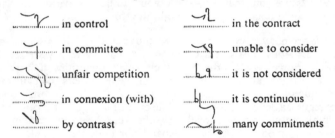

<table>
<tr><td>in control</td><td>in the contract</td></tr>
<tr><td>in committee</td><td>unable to consider</td></tr>
<tr><td>unfair competition</td><td>it is not considered</td></tr>
<tr><td>in connexion (with)</td><td>it is continuous</td></tr>
<tr><td>by contrast</td><td>many commitments</td></tr>
</table>

This method of indicating *con-*, etc., by proximity is not used following a single dash sign written downward, as: _____ *on committees*, _____ *of committees*; nor is it used following a dot, as: _____ *the committee*.

The phrase _____ *Income Tax* shows a useful extension of this principle.

In phrases for some frequently occurring expressions the syllable *con-*, etc., is omitted altogether, when the outline lends itself to such omission—

_____ it has been considered   _____ in conclusion

_____ it is considered   _____ come to the conclusion

(*See also* Section Sixteen, p. 87.)

2. Suffixes

The following examples show that the use of single strokes to represent suffixes can be extended to the representation of words in phrases. Such phrases are, however, more suitable for the high speed writer than for the beginner.

(a) Ability

.... your ability   .... our ability

.... best of your ability   .... best of our ability

(b) Reality

.... in reality   .... there is no reality

.... no reality   .... to face reality

(c) Logical

.... it would be logical   .... it is not logical

.... you are not logical   .... if we are logical

(d) Mentality

.... of low mentality   .... of this mentality

.... your mentality   .... poor mentality

(e) Ship/ment

.... several ships   .... new ship

.... this ship   .... some shipments

.... for shipment   .... these ships

(f) Fullness

.... in the fullness of time

(g) Yard

.... several yards   .... dozen yards

The half-length Yay for *yard* should be used only when the sign .... *yard* does not join easily.

FACILITY DRILL 14

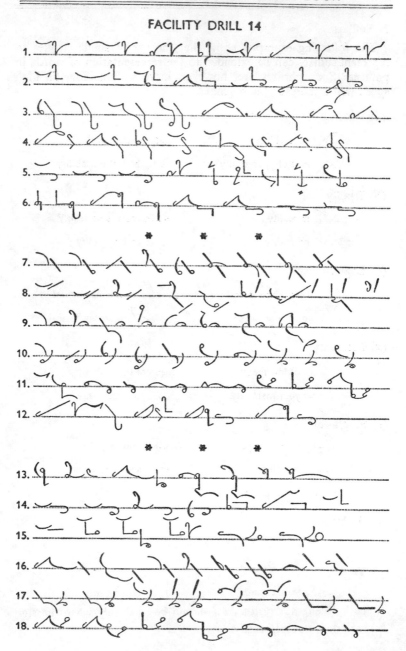

EXERCISE 14A
Read, and Write from Dictation

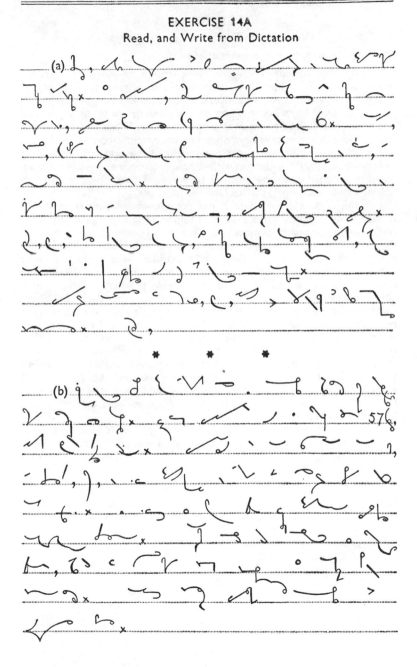

EXERCISE 14B
Write from Dictation Several Times

(Phrasing is suggested by hyphenation)

We-hope-that-you-are-controlling your-writing of-shorthand[10] to-the best-of-your-ability. In-reality, it-is[20]-simple to-achieve perfect-control. In-this-connexion we-may[30]-mention that-there-should-be no-considerable pressure of-the[40] fingers on-the pen or of-the nib on-the[50] paper. At-first you-must-control your pen movements-consciously,[60] but with experience you-will-find that-you have developed[70] an unconscious-control of-the pen when writing. While learning[80] you-must-make a constant endeavour to-keep-the-contact[90] of-the pen with-the paper as light as possible,[100] and-one-of-your chief-concerns must-be to ensure[110] that no-signs of-your-writing can-be-seen on[120]-the back-of-the page.

This fine-control comes with[130] practice and-in-this-connexion it-can-be-said that[140] facility drills may-be-considered-the finest of all-means[150] of-developing-complete pen-control. When-you-commence work on[160]-the drills in-this-book you-should first-consider all[170]-the details in-connexion-with your-writing. You-should-consider[180]-the quality of-your pen and-confirm that-it-is[190]-clean. You-should-confirm also that-the nib is fine[200] but flexible and-completely suitable for shorthand work. When-you[210]-have-confirmed that your pen is good and-that-the[220] ink flows smoothly from-its nib, you-can-consider-the[230] grip that-you take on-the pen. Your fingers should[240] make light-contact only. Do-not-consider it necessary to[250]-grip-the pen as-if-you expected someone to steal[260] it from-you. Allow your-little finger to-make light[270]-contact with-the paper. It-should-not-be tucked away[280]-completely inside-the palm of-your hand but should glide[290] across-the page, making light-contact with-the paper. The[300] point of-the nib should touch-the paper very-lightly,[310] and-no-considerable pressure should-be put on-the nib[320] for-the formation of-thick strokes.

In-conclusion it-may[330]-be-said that perfect-control of-the pen, first-consciously[340] and later unconsciously, is an essential factor in high-speed[350]-writing.   (351)

SECTION FIFTEEN

Intersections

INTERSECTIONS provide many of the most legible and time-saving of all phrases. The Principle of Intersection is to write a stroke representing a whole word through another outline—or, if it is not practical actually to intersect the stroke, it may be written very close to the preceding outline, e.g. .... *political party* but .... *Labour Party;* .... *this company* but .... *new company.*

If an intersected stroke is to be read first it is written first and the rest of the phraseogram is written afterwards; if the intersection is to be read last the stroke is struck through the completed outline, e.g. .... *railway ticket* but .... *Metropolitan Railway;* .... *Society of Commerce* but .... *Commerce Society.*

Intersections provide a very fruitful source of "personal" phrasing, that is, the invention of phrases specially adapted to the work being done by a particular shorthand writer, and examples of such "personal" phrases are given in List Three of this section.

An intersection may be raised or lowered to allow the remainder of the phraseogram to be written in its proper position, e.g. .... *party leader,* .... *party reform,* .... *party ranks.*

It will be found that the Principle of Intersection is often combined with the Principle of Omission (*see* Section Sixteen, p. 87.), e.g. .... *Department of Commerce,* .... *draw your attention to the fact.*

List One

The following is a list of the intersections that may be regarded as "textbook" and that should be used by all shorthand writers in their practical work.

.... P for *PARTY*:

.... party loyalty, ... political party

.... PR for *PROFESSOR*:

.... Professor Jones, ... Professor Smith

.... SPR for *SUPERINTENDENT*:

.... Superintendent of the Line, ... Police Super-intendent

.... B for *BANK*.

.... Provincial Bank, ... Westminster Bank, ... Bank Bills, ... Bank of London

„ -*BANKMENT*:

.... sea embankment, ... Thames Embankment

„ *BILL*:

.... Education Bill, ... Bill of Lading

.... T for *ATTENTION*:

.... your attention, ... best attention, ... some attention

.... D for *DEPARTMENT*:

.... department stores, ... in our department, ... in several departments

.... CH for *CHARGE*:

.... higher charges, ... freight charges, ... there is no charge

„ *CHANCERY*:

.... Chancery Appeal, ... Chancery Judge

.... J for *JOURNAL*:

.... Office Journal, ... Commercial Journal

.... K for *COMPANY*:

.... oil companies, ... Smith & Company

„ *COUNCIL*:

.... County Council, ... District Council

„ *CAPITAL*:

.... issued capital, ... new capital

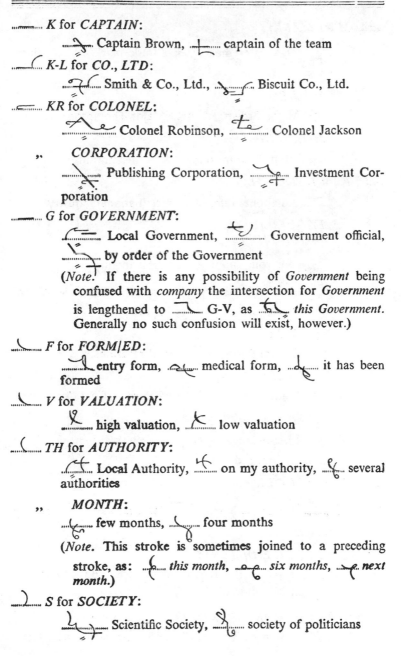

.... *K* for *CAPTAIN*:

.... Captain Brown, ... captain of the team

...... *K-L* for *CO., LTD*:

.... Smith & Co., Ltd., ... Biscuit Co., Ltd.

...... *KR* for *COLONEL*:

.... Colonel Robinson, ... Colonel Jackson

,,   *CORPORATION*:

.... Publishing Corporation, ... Investment Corporation

.... *G* for *GOVERNMENT*:

.... Local Government, ... Government official,

.... by order of the Government

(*Note.* If there is any possibility of *Government* being
confused with *company* the intersection for *Government*
is lengthened to .... G-V, as .... *this Government.*
Generally no such confusion will exist, however.)

.... *F* for *FORM/ED*:

.... entry form, ... medical form, ... it has been
formed

.... *V* for *VALUATION*:

.... high valuation, ... low valuation

.... *TH* for *AUTHORITY*:

.... Local Authority, ... on my authority, ... several
authorities

,,   *MONTH*:

.... few months, ... four months

(*Note.* This stroke is sometimes joined to a preceding
stroke, as: .... *this month,* .... *six months,* .... *next
month.*)

.... *S* for *SOCIETY*:

.... Scientific Society, ... society of politicians

M for *MARK*:

⎯⎯ high-water mark, ⎯⎯ trade-mark, ⎯⎯ finger marks

„   *MAJOR*:

⎯⎯ Major Brown, ⎯⎯ Major Thompson

„   *MORNING*:

⎯⎯ tomorrow morning, ⎯⎯ this morning

N for *NATIONAL*:

⎯⎯ national interests; ⎯⎯ national industry

„   *ENQUIRE/D/Y*:
„   *INQUIRE/D/Y*:

⎯⎯ for your enquiry, ⎯⎯ this inquiry

⎯⎯ letter of enquiry, ⎯⎯ several inquiries, ⎯⎯ will you enquire, ⎯⎯ we have inquired

⎯⎯ for *LIBERAL*:

⎯⎯ Liberal Party, ⎯⎯ liberal measures

„   *LIMITED*:

⎯⎯ limited company, ⎯⎯ Brown & Co. Ltd.

AR for *ARRANGE/D/MENT*:

⎯⎯ these arrangements, ⎯⎯ new arrangement, ⎯⎯ it has been arranged

RAY for *RAILWAY*:

⎯⎯ British Railways, ⎯⎯ local railways, ⎯⎯ railway station

„   *REQUIRE/D/MENT*:

⎯⎯ to meet the requirements, ⎯⎯ do you require, ⎯⎯ if he required

S-RAY for *CONSERVATIVE*:

⎯⎯ Conservative Party, ⎯⎯ conservative measures

List Two

Further examples of useful intersections suitable for the more advanced writer are given in this division.

.... *P* for *POLICY*:

.... new policies, ... policy of the Board

.... *B* for *BISHOP*:

.... Bishop of Croydon, ... local bishop

.... *F* for *FORTH*:

.... to call forth, ... to give forth

(*Note* .... set forth, ... put forth.)

(*See* Section Six, p. 34.)

.... *S* for *SCIENTIFIC*:

.... scientific research, ... scientific work

.... *PL* for *APPLICATION*:

.... to make application, ... form of application

.... *PN* for *PUNISHMENT*:

.... some punishment, ... severe punishment

.... *BS* for *BUSINESS*:

.... new business, ... our business, ... recent business

(*Note.* .... BS is sometimes joined, as in: .... *business man*, ... *business letters*.)

.... *GN* for *BEGINNING*:

.... at the beginning, ... from the beginning, ...

from the beginning to the end, ... from beginning to end

.... *VN* for *CONVENIENT/CE*:

.... is it convenient, ... at your convenience

.... SH-S for *ASSURANCE*:

.... life assurance, ... ordinary assurance

.... SM for *SIMILAR*:

.... similar letters, ... similar results

.... N-S for *INSURANCE*:

.... new insurance, ... fire insurance

.... N-SHUN for *COMMUNICATION*:

.... any communication, ... further communication

List Three

The experienced shorthand writer will naturally invent intersections of his own, and these will vary according to the type of work undertaken. If we examine for a moment List Two we find three intersections that would naturally be used by a writer in an insurance office, namely, the intersections for *policy, assurance,* and *insurance.*

The writer interested in theological work would use the sign for *bishop,* while the court reporter would no doubt find the intersections for *application* and *punishment* extremely useful.

As new phrases come into popularity the shorthand writer will need new intersections to deal with them. A few years ago the word *atomic* was seldom or never written by the average shorthand writer but now it is a common word, and the shorthand writer employed in science or industry probably finds it useful to intersect the stroke T for *atomic, as:* .... *atomic energy,* .... *atomic power,* .... *atomic power plant.*

Uranium is another word now in common use, and the intersection .... will be found sufficient for those who have to write the word often, as: .... *uranium ore,* .... *enough uranium.*

The phrase .... *hydrogen bomb* is another example of the adaptation of the Principle of Intersection to particular uses.

Other examples of the special use of strokes for special purposes are: .... *Royal Commission,* .... *Royal Family,* .... *resistance coil,* .... *current density,* .... *alternating current,* .... *low general average.*

The important point for the shorthand writer to remember is that the intersection, once decided upon, should be used at every opportunity. Careful thought should be given in advance to any possibility of clash. The shorthand writer in the scientific world should not, for instance, decide to use an intersected stroke T for both *atomic* and *titanium*. If both words occurred frequently it would be necessary to allocate ⌐ *t* to *atomic* and ⌐ *t-n* to *titanium*. The stroke Ray could usefully be intersected for *radar* provided it were not also used for *radio*. In the selection of signs common sense must be applied.

The fields of human activity and interest are so vast that it is not possible here to take them one by one and suggest intersections, but the serious student of phrasing should understand the Principle of Intersection and apply it in his own work to those expressions that occur most frequently.

The following list gives a few miscellaneous but well-known phrases using the intersecting device that all advanced shorthand writers could usefully memorize.

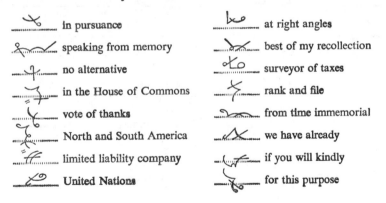

in pursuance	at right angles
speaking from memory	best of my recollection
no alternative	surveyor of taxes
in the House of Commons	rank and file
vote of thanks	from time immemorial
North and South America	we have already
limited liability company	if you will kindly
United Nations	for this purpose

FACILITY DRILL 15

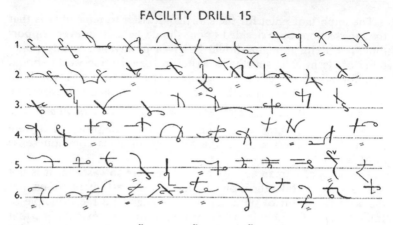

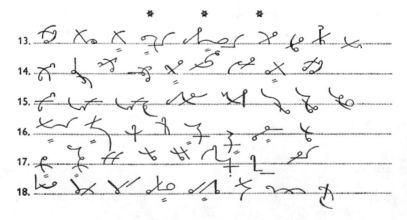

EXERCISE 15A
Read, and Write from Dictation

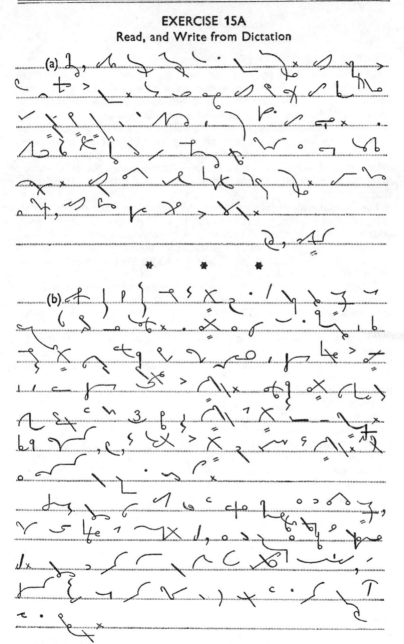

EXERCISE 15B
Write from Dictation Several Times
(Phrasing is suggested by hyphenation)

(*a*) It-is-interesting to-learn that-the big department-stores[10] are abandoning-their-policy of-keen-competition for a new[20]-policy of at-least partial co-operation. Their first step is[30]-to-be-the publication at-the-end of-this-month[40] of-the first number-of a monthly-journal. This-journal[50] will-be-sent free-of-charge to all business-men[60] and-trading-companies who-make-application for-it on-the[70] entry-form to-be-found in-all issues of-the[80] national-newspapers this-week. The cost of-producing-the-journal[90] will-be shared by six leading department-houses but it[100]-is-hoped that after a few-months revenue from advertising[110] will cover all printing-charges.

The journal will-contain information[120] regarding trade-marks, profit-margins, staff salaries, numbers of-employed[130] persons, transport costs, and many similar-features. A Professor-of[140]-Economics, Major-Robinson, is-to-be-the first editor. Major[150]-Robinson's books have-already called-attention to-his new theories,[160] and-we-may-expect to-find a liberal-policy in[170]-the-journal.

We-are hopeful that-this exchange-of information,[180] from-the business-man and-trading-companies to-the journal[190] and-from-the-journal to-commerce generally, will-be in[200]-the national-interests.   (203)

(*b*) I-would-like to-call-the-attention of-the local[10]-authority to-the bad state-of-the roads in-my[20] area. Neither carriage-way nor pavements have-been repaired for[30]-several-months, and-the recent extremely cold-weather, which-was[40] followed by heavy rains, has caused-the surface to-break[50]-up. Is-it-the responsibility of-the local Urban-Council[60] to-repair-the roads in-this district or does-the[70] responsibility rest with-the Highway-Authorities? A conservative-estimate suggests[80] that a sum of £5,000 would-be adequate[90] to-repair-the roads now but if-they-are left[100] to disintegrate for-several-more-months they-will-require greater[110]-attention and-the conservative-estimate might be increased to £20,000.[120]

I-must-also call-the-attention of-the[130] local-authority to-the dangerous state-of-the high-embankment[140] along-the railway-line just-before-the South-Bridge. Further[150] heavy rain might cause a fatal accident at-this spot.   (160)

PART THREE

SECTION SIXTEEN

The Principle of Omission

THERE can be no faster way of representing a word in shorthand than not to write it at all! That sounds paradoxical, but the fact is that the Principle of Omission is used in the formation of a great variety of extremely facile, legible, and reliable phraseograms. Letters, syllables, and whole words are omitted, and yet the resulting phraseogram is faster to read as well as being faster to write than is a string of single outlines.

Examples of omission have been included in preceding sections when occurring in conjunction with another principle. In this section attention is focused on the omissions. The consonants that are omitted are for the most part those that are very lightly sounded or are repeated, as in *bes*(*t*) *time*, *mos*(*t*) *important*, *prime* (*m*)*inister*. The syllables and words that are omitted are generally those that could be easily supplied were they left out in longhand writing. In the sentence "*I am structed to say . . .*" it is a simple matter to divine that the syllable *in-* has been omitted before *structed*. It would not require a genius to supply the missing word in the sentence "*I wish to see you in connexion this matter.*" *With* would be automatically added by the reader.

Here, then, for the shorthand writer's delight is superb scope for the invention of legible and time-saving phraseograms. Before setting out examples of this type of phrase, however, it is desirable to warn shorthand writers against the use of phrases that represent a great many words in one very short outline. Often several words are omitted from such phrases, and the omission could be filled in in more than one way. Such phrases are reasonably satisfactory for advanced verbatim work but are full of pitfalls for the examination candidate who must be exact at all times if he wishes to secure high marks. Error can arise in the following way. A Parliamentary reporter will frequently be faced with the expression "*I wish to call the attention of this House to the fact*" and he is not likely to waste time and energy by writing the expression in full. He will probably invent his own phrase which may be ⌇⌇⌇ In fact, that would be an excellent little phrase for such a reporter to use. BUT the phrase is not one that can be recommended to examination candidates. Candidates in speed examinations are usually writing at a speed approaching their highest rate. A student who had mastered the above phrase might be taking down an examination passage in which occurred the words: "*I wish to call the attention of the House to the fact.*" The chances are quite high that the student will use the old phraseogram and will either not notice or will forget that the words were not exactly the same. He will thus lose a mark for transcribing *this* instead of *the*.

Again, the Parliamentary reporter would probably find the phrase ⌇⌇⌇ *Rt. Hon. Gentleman has said* very satisfactory but in an examination passage the words could well be *Rt. Hon. Gentleman said.* If the phrase were used and the difference unnoticed a mark would again be lost.

It must be emphasized and understood that what is good for the reporter is not necessarily good for the shorthand examination candidate. It must also be remembered that reporters are for the most part men of very considerable mental ability and agility, with a vast background of experience. They develop a feeling for what is right, based on practice. Plainly a student, however able, who attends speed classes two or three evenings a week cannot compare in experience with the professional verbatim reporter who is spending his working life taking notes. The reporter may rely upon judgment and instinct; the classroom candidate must rely upon as complete an accuracy of notes as is humanly possible.

Therefore, before inventing phrases that cover more than four words or so, the shorthand writer is advised to study possible outlines searchingly to make sure that the outlines contain no traps. Extreme alertness can save a writer from falling into a trap but it is better for him not to set the trap that he might fall into. Provided shorthand writers remember this warning they will find that there is immense scope for the invention of phrases based on the principle of omission. The following lists are general in character, and are applicable to a wide field of work. The lists are by no means exhaustive, and should be regarded as an indication of the bases of such phrases. Upon the bases countless further phrases can be built to meet the special requirements of the individual writer.

1. Omission of a Consonant

(a) Lightly Sounded Consonants

T: .... most important .... take steps

.... almost impossible .... West End of London

.... almost certain .... there is still

.... last time .... shorthand students

.... in your last letter .... past few months

.... past year .... first rate

D: .... very pleased indeed .... enclosed receipt

(b) Repeated Consonants

K: .... take exception .... take cover

L: .... animal life .... political life

.... family life .... hardly likely

M: .... some measure .... Prime Minister

R: .... better results .... satisfactory results

.... poor results .... satisfactory record

SH: .... British ships .... machine shops

(c) Miscellaneous Examples

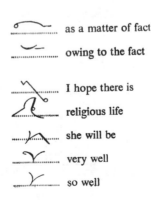

F: .... in fact .... as a matter of fact

.... owing to the fact

ITH: .... worth while

H: .... I hope you will .... I hope there is

L. .... long life .... religious life

W: .... this week .... she will be

.... next week .... very well

.... it will be .... so well

2. Omission of a Hook
(a) Initial R Hook

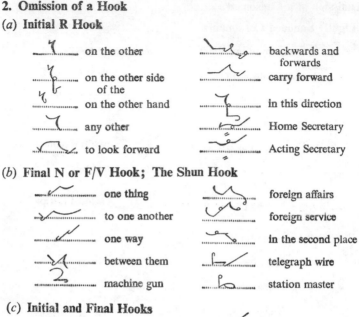

on the other

backwards and forwards

on the other side of the

carry forward

on the other hand

in this direction

any other

Home Secretary

to look forward

Acting Secretary

(b) Final N or F/V Hook; The Shun Hook

one thing

foreign affairs

to one another

foreign service

one way

in the second place

between them

telegraph wire

machine gun

station master

(c) Initial and Final Hooks

General Secretary

Foreign Secretary

3. Omission of a Syllable

The following lists, which give examples of words that are incompletely represented in phraseograms, should be studied and practised, and additions made to meet the writer's personal requirements—

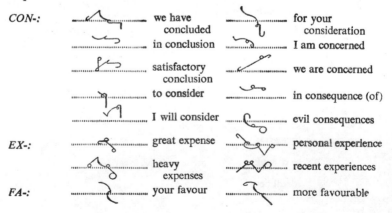

CON-:

we have concluded

for your consideration

in conclusion

I am concerned

satisfactory conclusion

we are concerned

to consider

in consequence (of)

I will consider

evil consequences

EX-:

great expense

personal experience

heavy expenses

recent experiences

FA-:

your favour

more favourable

-HAND:		shorthand writer	shorthand writing
HERE-:		enclose herewith	to send herewith
-IBLE:		if possible	as soon as possible
		if it is possible	as well as possible
IN-:		your instructions	if you will instruct
		I am instructed	musical instrument
-INGDOM:		Kingdom of Greece	United Kingdom
-ISH:		British Museum	British Empire
-LY:		extremely sorry	distinctly understood
		extremely regret	
MA-:		in this manner	only manner
-MENT:		Act of Parliament	Member of Parliament
NA-:		stage manager	general manager
-NICAL:		technical education	Technical College
		technical terms	technical institution
OB-:		we have no objection	there is no objection
PRE-:		high pressure	steam pressure
		low pressure	excessive pressure
RE-:		in reply	we shall be glad to receive
		in reply to your letter	in regard (to)
		your reply	as regards
		we have received	having regard to the
-STY:		Her Majesty	His Majesty
		Her Majesty the Queen	His Majesty the King
-TED:		I am requested to inform you	you are requested to call

4. Omission of Words

(a) Short Forms

A/AN: for a time   for a minute

                 for a long time   at a loss

                 in a way   as a rule

AND: ladies and   now and then
                 gentlemen

                 Mr. and Mrs.   first and foremost

                 here and there   larger and larger

                 over and above   again and again

AND plus a   deeper and   better and better
syllable: deeper

                 blacker and   thicker and
                 blacker   thicker

                 longer and   rougher and
                 longer   rougher

COME (to   I have come to   we have come to
the):   the conclu-   the conclusion
                 sion

HAVE: must have   would have been
                 been

                 there must   seems to have
                 have been   been

                 there have   it must have been
                 been

IN: bear in mind   keep in mind

OF: difference of   freedom of trade
                 opinion

                 expression of   loss of life
                 opinion

                 point of view   loss of time

                 packet of   City of London
                 matches

OF THE: fact of the   freedom of the
                 matter   press

                 facts of the   freedom of the
                 case   people

                 out of the   sign of the times
                 question

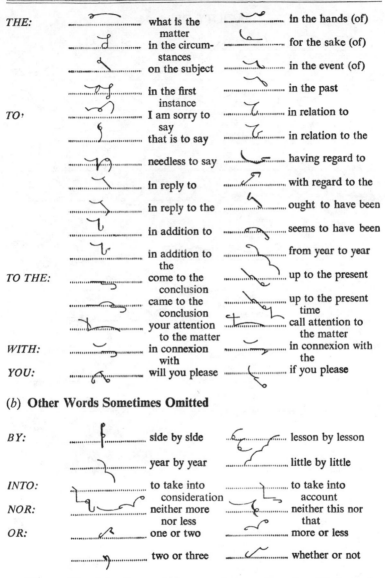

THE:
..... what is the matter
..... in the circumstances
..... on the subject
..... in the first instance

TO:
..... I am sorry to say
..... that is to say
..... needless to say
..... in reply to
..... in reply to the
..... in addition to
..... in addition to the

TO THE:
..... come to the conclusion
..... came to the conclusion
..... your attention to the matter

WITH:
..... in connexion with

YOU:
..... will you please

..... in the hands (of)
..... for the sake (of)
..... in the event (of)
..... in the past
..... in relation to
..... in relation to the
..... having regard to
..... with regard to the
..... ought to have been
..... seems to have been
..... from year to year
..... up to the present
..... up to the present time
..... call attention to the matter
..... in connexion with the
..... if you please

(b) Other Words Sometimes Omitted

BY:
..... side by side
..... year by year

INTO:
..... to take into consideration

NOR:
..... neither more nor less

OR:
..... one or two
..... two or three

..... lesson by lesson
..... little by little
..... to take into account
..... neither this nor that
..... more or less
..... whether or not

(*Note.* The joined vowel-sign *aw* is sometimes omitted, as in: ..... I am also, ... it is also.)

As has been stated, these lists are not exhaustive but are intended to guide the student in the application of an important principle.

FACILITY DRILL 16

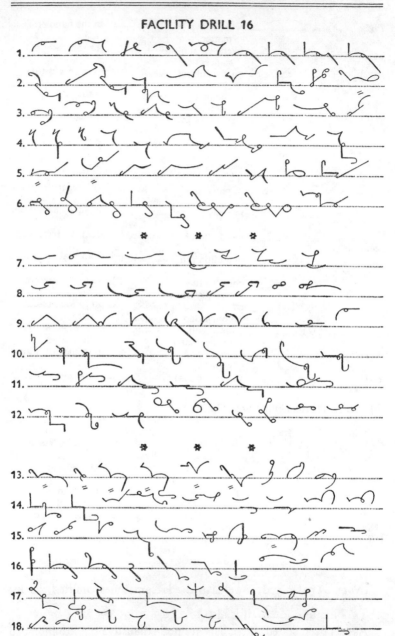

EXERCISE 16A
Read, and Write from Dictation

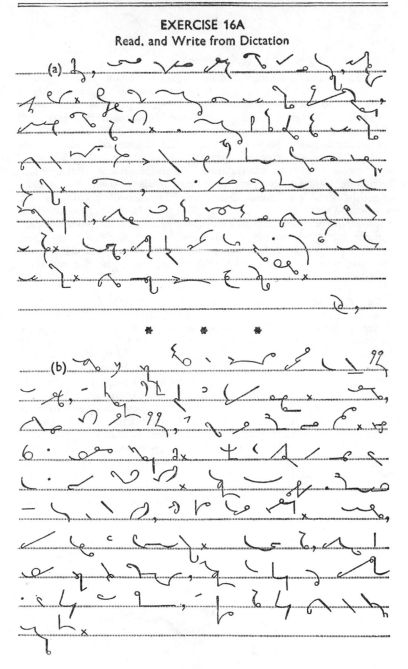

EXERCISE 16B
Write from Dictation Several Times
(Phrasing is suggested by hyphenation)

(*a*) Ladies-and-Gentlemen, I-have again-and-again drawn your[10]-attention-to-the-fact that our rates-and-taxes become[20] higher-and-higher while less-and-less is-received in[30] return for-their payment. Side-by-side with-this is[40]-the fact that-the quality of-the-Municipal-services becomes[50] lower-and-lower. We-have-come-to-the-conclusion that[60] even when-we bear-in-mind all-the facts-of[70]-the-case and acknowledge all-the difficulties, the time is[80] drawing nearer-and-nearer when-we-must-find ways-and[90]-means to-improve-the situation. Up-to-the-present nothing[100] has-been-done although attempts have-been made over-and[110]-over-again to-get-the Municipal-Council to-act. Our[120] town is dirty, east-and-west, north-and-south. It[130]-is growing faster-and-faster yet less-and-less houses[140] are being erected. It-is out-of-the-question to[150] continue in-this-manner indefinitely, and-in-accordance-with-the[160] decision of-the Committee I-am putting before-you today[170] for-your-consideration some-measures that I-think-we-must[180]-take in-connexion-with this sad state-of-affairs. (189)

(*b*) Ladies-and-Gentlemen, I-am happy to-be face-to[10]-face with-you this-afternoon and to-be-able-to[20] place before-you for-your-consideration a report which from[30]-first-to-last shows satisfactory-results. As-a-matter-of[40]-fact, we-have-grown accustomed to-satisfactory-reports, and-we[50]-are-inclined to-take-them as-a-matter-of-course.[60] Having-regard-to-the difficulties we-have-experienced during-the[70]-year, particularly in-the-early-part-of-the year, it[80]-is-satisfactory to-report better-results at-the-present-time[90] than for-the past-few-years. In-my-opinion this[100]-is a necessary-consequence of-the conservative-policy we-have[110] followed in the past, and-for-the-first-time our[120] profit figure, which-has-been higher-and-higher each year,[130] has exceeded £100,000. All-over-the-world[140] today there-is severe-competition in-consequence-of-the growing[150]-ability of-countries to-meet their-own-requirements, and-we[160]-cannot expect-to-receive orders as easily as-we-have[170]-done in-the past. Notwithstanding-the-fact of-this-competition,[180] however, we-have in a short-space-of-time increased[190] our sales by two-or-three per-cent. (198)

Some "Distinguishing" Phrases

It happens with phrases as with single outlines that in some cases the consonantal structure of two forms is similar, or nearly so, and position writing affords no guidance. In the case of separate outlines this difficulty is overcome by the insertion of a vowel-sign (e.g. .... *amusing*, ... *amazing*) or by the adoption of special outlines (e.g. .... *fatal*, ... *futile*). Possible clashes may be avoided in phrase writing by the same means, and examples are given here. It must be added, however, that the speed writer is not *compelled* to make these distinctions. The extent to which a writer seeks to distinguish between pairs of outlines or pairs of phrases is purely a personal matter. The experienced and alert shorthand writer will know when it is necessary to make some distinction to prevent error. In many cases the context prevents error, but context is not always a sure guide, particularly for the younger and less experienced writer. For this reason the following examples should be studied carefully, and the underlying principles understood and applied.

1. Distinction by Vowel-sign

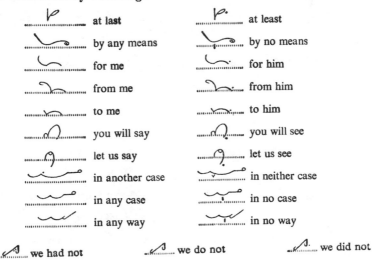

at last		at least	
by any means		by no means	
for me		for him	
from me		from him	
to me		to him	
you will say		you will see	
let us say		let us see	
in another case		in neither case	
in any case		in no case	
in any way		in no way	

we had not   we do not   we did not

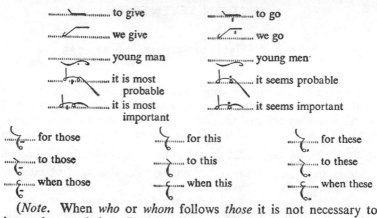

to give		to go	
we give		we go	
young man		young men	
it is most probable		it seems probable	
it is most important		it seems important	

for those   for this   for these

to those   to this   to these

when those   when this   when these

(*Note.* When *who* or *whom* follows *those* it is not necessary to insert the vowel-sign. In many cases position is sufficient distinction and the vowel-sign is unnecessary, as _____ in *those,* _____ in *this,* _____ in *these;* _____ with *those,* _____ with *this,* _____ with *these.*

2. Distinction by Disjoining

I know		I note	
we know		we note	
know this		note this	
I may		I might	
it may		it might	
in all cases		in two cases	
it can be		it could be	
I can be		I could be	
who can be		who could be	
for the year		in the year	
very well		very ill	
it is unnecessary		it is not necessary	
it is unnatural		it is not natural	
it is unknown		it is not known	

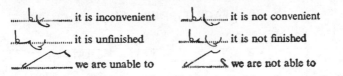

it is inconvenient	it is not convenient
it is unfinished	it is not finished
we are unable to	we are not able to

(*Note.* Disjoining after *not* should be applied in all cases similar to those given above.)

3. Miscellaneous Examples

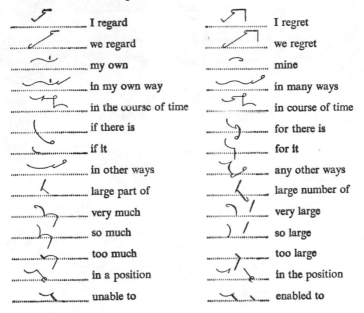

I regard	I regret
we regard	we regret
my own	mine
in my own way	in many ways
in the course of time	in course of time
if there is	for there is
if it	for it
in other ways	any other ways
large part of	large number of
very much	very large
so much	so large
too much	too large
in a position	in the position
unable to	enabled to

4. Past Tenses

The past tense of a contracted form may be indicated where considered necessary by writing a small disjoined tick after the contraction, as in the following examples—

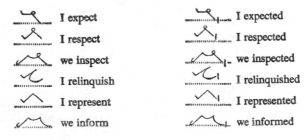

I expect	I expected
I respect	I respected
we inspect	we inspected
I relinquish	I relinquished
I represent	I represented
we inform	we informed

FACILITY DRILL 17

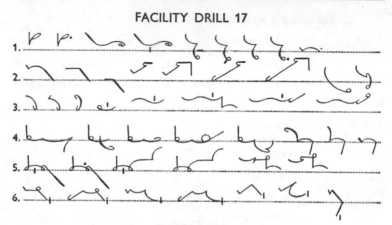

EXERCISE 17A
Read, and Write from Dictation

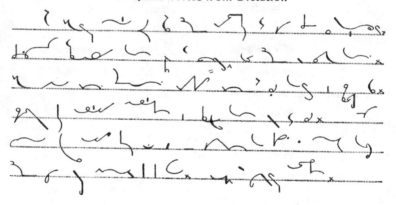

EXERCISE 17B
Write from Dictation Several Times

(Phrasing is suggested by hyphenation)

You-will note with pleasure that-the-profit for-the[10]-year is much higher-than-the profit made in-the[20] year before. It-is-not necessary for-me to-go[30] into great detail here regarding-the accounts but it-can[40]-be stated that-we-have in-all-cases done better[50]-than we-expected. I-regret-that-the accounts reached-you[60] rather later-than usual but-you all know-the reason,[70] and it-is-unnecessary to-repeat it here. You-will[80]-see from-the figures that-we-have in-no-way[90] suffered as-a-result of-the shipping difficulties. We-did[100]-not expect to-feel the full effects of-those-difficulties[110] at-once but-we-expected to-feel them to-some[120]-extent. (121)

APPENDIXES

APPENDIX ONE

Classified Phrases

IN the preceding sections the student has been taught the principles of phrasing and has been shown how to apply them. As has been pointed out, the application of the principles should not be narrow or stereotyped: there must be an intelligent application of the various devices to meet both the familiar and the changing needs of the individual shorthand writer.

There are fashions in speech just as there are fashions in clothes and, with the continuing extension of knowledge and the steady development of science and industry, the terms used by speakers and writers change. The shorthand writer has to adopt new phrases to meet the new conditions.

The following lists of phrases (which have been selected from the lists given in the *Shorthand Reporter*) show standard phrases for various fields of interest. Shorthand writers are not asked to practise and memorize all these phrases, but to select and practise those that are likely to be useful in their particular spheres of activity.

General Business

account sales
additional cost
additional expense
annual general meeting
any other business
at your earliest convenience
bill of exchange
bill of lading
board of directors
by passenger train
by return of post
declare a dividend
directors' report
discount for cash
faithfully yours
I am directed to inform you
I am directed to state
I am in receipt of your letter
I am instructed to inform you
I am instructed to state

I am requested to inform you
I beg to acknowledge receipt of your letter
I beg to call attention
I beg to enclose herewith
I have to acknowledge receipt of your letter
in reply to your letter
in your reply to my letter
ordinary rates
postal order
profit and loss account
referring to our invoice
referring to your letter
referring to yours
registered letter
respectfully yours
under bill of sale
we beg to quote
we respectfully request
your obedient servant

yours faithfully   *yours respectfully*

yours obediently   *yours sincerely*

Banking

accepted for the honour of

accepted payable in London

ad valorem stamp

advance against a life policy

arbitration of exchange

bank note

bank post bill

British Government Securities

cable remittance

cancel the cheque

circular note

clearing house

country cheque

course of exchange

date of the maturity of the bill

deed of transfer

draft on demand

form of indemnity

in case of need

Joint Stock Bank

last indorser

London clearing bankers

long exchange

memorandum of deposit

metropolitan cheque

negotiable instrument

negotiable security

nominal consideration

not negotiable cheque

orders to retire acceptances

paying-in slip

per procuration acceptance

rate of exchange

refer to drawer

restrictive indorsement

short exchange

specially indorsed

telegraphic transfer

town cheque

without recourse

written authority of the drawer

Stockbroking

bearer shares

blank transfer

buying for control

capital liabilities

carry-over facilities

concentrating plant

consolidated annuities

convertible gold bonds

cum dividend

cumulative preference shares

day to day money

demoralized markets

directors' qualification

dwts. per ton

ex-dividend

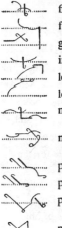
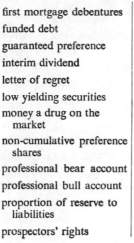

first mortgage debentures	reduction plant
funded debt	second preference shares
guaranteed preference	sinking fund
interim dividend	sinking operations
letter of regret	special settlement
low yielding securities	stock and share market
money a drug on the market	stocks and shares
non-cumulative preference shares	Stock Exchange
professional bear account	subscribed capital
professional bull account	surplus profits
proportion of reserve to liabilities	Treasury bills
	upward movement
prospectors' rights	yield per cent
	yield per ton

Insurance

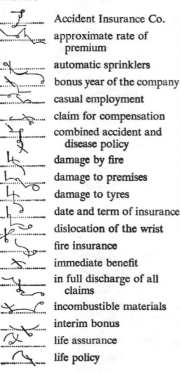
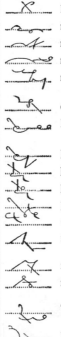
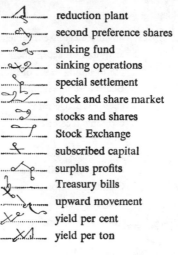

Accident Insurance Co.	loan on the policy
approximate rate of premium	medical examination
automatic sprinklers	morale of the risk
bonus year of the company	motor-car insurance
casual employment	negligence of the chief engineer
claim for compensation	ordinary accident policy
combined accident and disease policy	Personal Accident Insurance
damage by fire	personal injury
damage to premises	policy is declared void
damage to tyres	policies are declared void
date and term of insurance	proposal form received
dislocation of the wrist	quinquennial valuation
fire insurance	registered number of the car
immediate benefit	renewal of the policy
in full discharge of all claims	responsibility of the company
incombustible materials	Third Party Indemnity Insurance
interim bonus	Workmen's Compensation Act
life assurance	
life policy	

Shipping

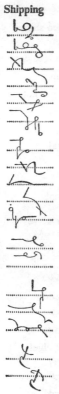

- advances against shipment
- advances on acceptances
- bill of lading in set of four
- Board of Trade regulations
- cable exchange rate
- captain's receipt for documents
- case of total loss
- cash against bill of lading
- Chamber of Commerce
- charter party
- constructive total loss of cargo
- consular invoice
- cost, insurance and freight (*c.i.f.*)
- documents of title
- indorsed and confirmed
- errors and omissions excepted (*e. & o. e.*)
- foreign general average
- free of general average

- free on rail (*f.o.r.*)
- free on board (*f.o.b.*)
- London office of the bank
- Marine Insurance Act
- marine insurance policy
- Merchant Shipping Act
- nature and cause of damage
- not responsible for the damage
- Port of London Authority
- remit draft on Paris
- remit proceeds of bill
- salvage charges
- shipping documents enclosed
- telegraphic codes
- to be approved by the underwriters
- value to be declared
- voyage policy
- weight subject to correction
- York-Antwerp Rules

Political

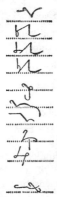

- Act of Parliament
- at the first reading
- at the second reading
- at the third reading
- British Constitution
- British Empire
- Cabinet meeting
- Chairman of Committee
- Chancellor of the Exchequer
- colonial preference

- Commissioner of Works
- Conservative Party
- First Lord
- freedom of the press
- freedom of trade
- hon. and learned member
- hon. gentleman
- hon. member
- hon. member for Preston
- House of Commons
- House of Lords

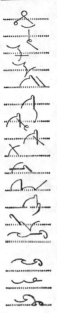

	Houses of Parliament	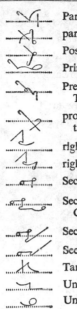	Parliamentary Committee
	in committee of supply		party leaders
	in the House of Commons		Postmaster-General
	in the House of Lords		Prime Minister
	Labour Party		President of the Board of Trade
	Leader of the House		
	Leader of the Opposition		proportional representation
	Leader of the Party		
	Liberal Party		right honourable
	Local Government Board		right hon. gentleman
	Lord of the Admiralty		Secretary of State
	Lord of the Treasury		Secretary of State for the Colonies
	Member of Parliament		Secretary of State for War
	my hon. and gallant friend		Secretary for War
	my hon. friend		Tariff Reform
	National Insurance Act		United Kingdom
	naval estimates		United States

Electrical and Engineering

	alternating current		free charge
	automatic apparatus		heating apparatus
	Bessemer steel		high resistance
	block signal		high voltage
	civil engineer		induction coil
	combustion chamber		lever and weight safety valve
	current density		
	discharge chamber		low pressure cylinder
	discharge resistance		low voltage
	earth currents		mechanical stokers
	eddy currents		monophase generator
	electric current		no voltage attachment
	electrical engineer		pressure gauge
	energy current		primary battery
	energy resistance		primary coil
	exhaust valve		primary currents

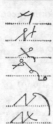 railway engineer
residual charge
resistance board
resistance of copper circuits
rotary converter
rotary transformer

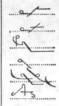 secondary coil
secondary current
sight feed lubricator
spring balance safety valve
vacuum brake
water cooling plant

Railway

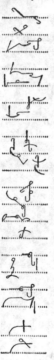 break down plant
British Railways
Charing Cross Station
chief mechanical engineer
defective signal
diesel engine
dining car
district traffic manager
driver's report
engine driver
Euston Station
fast passenger train
first class compartment
general manager
goods traffic committee
high pressure of steam
King's Cross Station
locomotive and engineering committee
locomotive department
locomotive superintendent

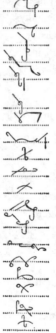 loss in transit
main line
Paddington Station
passenger brake van
passenger traffic committee
passenger train
passengers' luggage
permanent way committee
railway directors
railway executive
railway manager
railway receiving station
St. Pancras Station
second class compartment
sleeping saloon
Station Master
superintendent of the line
telegraph superintendent
traffic manager

Legal

 Articles of Association
breach of promise of marriage
Central Criminal Court

 Chancery Division
circumstantial evidence
counsel for the defence
counsel for the defendant

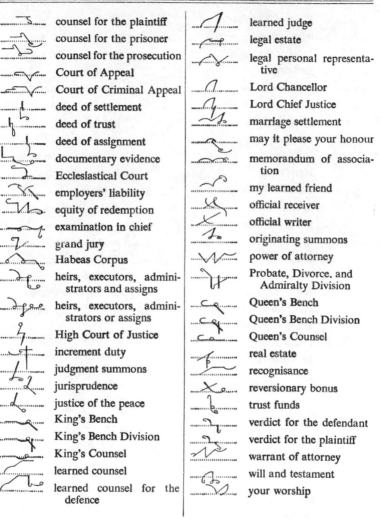

counsel for the plaintiff
counsel for the prisoner
counsel for the prosecution
Court of Appeal
Court of Criminal Appeal
deed of settlement
deed of trust
deed of assignment
documentary evidence
Ecclesiastical Court
employers' liability
equity of redemption
examination in chief
grand jury
Habeas Corpus
heirs, executors, administrators and assigns
heirs, executors, administrators or assigns
High Court of Justice
increment duty
judgment summons
jurisprudence
justice of the peace
King's Bench
King's Bench Division
King's Counsel
learned counsel
learned counsel for the defence

learned judge
legal estate
legal personal representative
Lord Chancellor
Lord Chief Justice
marriage settlement
may it please your honour
memorandum of association
my learned friend
official receiver
official writer
originating summons
power of attorney
Probate, Divorce, and Admiralty Division
Queen's Bench
Queen's Bench Division
Queen's Counsel
real estate
recognisance
reversionary bonus
trust funds
verdict for the defendant
verdict for the plaintiff
warrant of attorney
will and testament
your worship

Religious

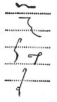

Almighty God
Catholic faith
Children of Israel
Christ Jesus
Church and State

Church of England
Episcopal Church
Epistle to the Corinthians
Established Church
everlasting life

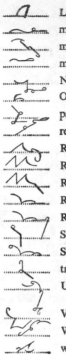

Feast of Tabernacles
fellow-creature
fruits of the Spirit
glad tidings
goodness of God
gospel of peace
Greek Church
Heavenly Father
Holy Scripture
Holy Word
House of Israel
in Jesus Christ
in the presence of God
in the providence of God
in the sight of God
in the words of the text
Jewish dispensation
kingdom of Christ
kingdom of God
kingdom of heaven
knowledge of Christ
Lord and Saviour Jesus Christ

Lord Jesus
minister of the gospel
my beloved brethren
my text
New Testament Scriptures
Old Testament
passage of Scripture
resurrection of Christ
Revised Version
Right Reverend
Right Rev. Bishop
Roman Catholic
Roman Catholic Church
Sabbath day
Sermon on the Mount
transubstantiation
United Free Church of Scotland
Virgin Mary
Wesleyan Methodist
world without end

APPENDIX TWO

Figures; A Few Further Devices

1. Figures

In general, numbers containing three or more digits are represented in shorthand writing by the ordinary numerals. It is, however, a serious waste of time to write a series of noughts when representing a round number. The following method should be employed—

HUNDRED:	....✓.... as	5	500	9	900
THOUSAND:	....(.... as	5(	5,000	9(	9,000
MILLION:	....⌐.... as	5	5,000,000	9	9,000,000
		5	500,000	950(	950,000
		5(⌐	5,000,000,000		

When a series of figures is "complete" there is no need to insert the sign for *hundred, thousand,* etc. If one or more noughts occur in the course of the number, however, it is useful to use the sign, as shown in the following examples—

5621 for 5,621 *but* 5(1 for 5,001

5321678 for 5,321,678 *but* 5 26 for 5,000,026

Care must be taken when using stroke *ith* for *thousand* to ensure that it is properly formed and does not resemble either ‘he figure one or the figure six—

5126   5626   5(26

The following devices are often used by high-speed writers—

...1.... one and a half

...1.... one and a quarter

...1.... one and three-quarters

2. A Few Further Devices

The following phrases are not all "textbook" forms, and are not necessarily intended for the use of beginners. They will, however, be found useful in the recording of company report material and in business letters.

ADOPTION: _____+___ in moving the adoption, __+△___ in moving the adoption of the report and accounts, __+___ I am glad to move the adoption

AFRAID: ___⌒___ I am afraid, __⌒___ we are afraid

ALREADY: __✗___ we have already, __✗___ we have already said, __✗___ as I have already said, __△___ it has already been

AMOUNT: __∿___ certain amount

CALLED: __⌐___ so called, __⌐___ what is called

CAN WE: __⌐___ can we, __⌐___ can we have your, __⌐___ can we say, __⌐___ can we do

CAPITAL: __⊬___ paid up capital, __≢___ paid up capital of the company

COME: __◿___ we shall come to the matter, __∿___ I hope you will come next week, __⌐___ can you come along, __⌐___ if you will come over

CONCERNED: __⌐___ I am concerned, __⌐___ we are concerned

DISTRIBUTION: __⌐___ available for distribution, __⌐___ to make a distribution

DIVIDEND: __⌐___ declare a dividend, __⌐___ preference dividend, __⌐___ yearly dividend

FULL: __⌐___ is it full, __⌐___ it is full

HAVE: __⌐___ we have, __⌐___ can we have, __⌐___ we can have, __⌐___ you can have

KINDLY:	........⌐........ will you kindly, ...⌐........ will you kindly let me know, ...⌐........ if you will kindly
MAY BE:	........⌐........ it may be, ... they may be, ... which may be
OFFICE:	.... head office, ... branch office
PER CENT:	.... five per cent, ... five per cent per annum
PURPOSE:	.... for the purpose, ... for your purpose, ... for my purposes, ... for this purpose
REPORT:	.... annual report, ... monthly report
SHALL:	.... we shall be glad, ... we shall be glad if you will, ... we shall have pleasure, ... we shall look forward
SHARE:	.... preference shares, ... cumulative preference shares, ... deferred shares, ... ordinary shares
SHAREHOLDER:	.... preference shareholders, ... ordinary shareholders
SUBSIDIARY:	.... subsidiary companies
TO BE-	.... to belong, ... to behave
TURN/ING:	.... turn/ing to the balance-sheet, ... turn/ing to the profit and loss account
WISHES:	.... best wishes, ... with best wishes

APPENDIX THREE

An Alphabetically Arranged List of Phrases

THIS list formerly appeared in the *Phonographic Phrase Book*. While some additions and deletions have been made, the list remains essentially the same. No list of phrases can be exhaustive as the variety of speech-patterns, and therefore the possibilities for the joining of outlines, are almost without limit. The use of the list will, however, help the shorthand writer to build further phrases. Under *have* in this list, for instance, the student will find ⟨outline⟩ *have been*.

It is obvious that from this phrase can be built up: ⟨outline⟩ *I have been,* ⟨outline⟩ *we have been,* ⟨outline⟩ *as we have been,* ⟨outline⟩ *I have been there,* ⟨outline⟩ *we have been there,* ⟨outline⟩ *as we have been there,* and so on.

Under *tell* is given ⟨outline⟩ *tell him.* It is a simple matter to add ⟨outline⟩ *to* and write the phrase ⟨outline⟩ *to tell him.*

Under *large* is given ⟨outline⟩ *large measure.* From what has been taught in the section on omissions the writer will know that ⟨outline⟩ *in a large measure* is a permitted derived phrase.

From the three thousand or so phrases listed here, therefore, the shorthand writer can derive tens of thousands.

The index should be used when it is desired to refer to a specific principle of phrasing, while the section on classified phrases should be consulted for specialized phrases.

Finally, it may be repeated here that it is not possible to be dogmatic about the use of phrasing in shorthand writing. It is, for instance, equally correct to write ⟨outline⟩ or ⟨outline⟩ for *number of them,* and it is satisfactory to write either ⟨outline⟩ or ⟨outline⟩ for *I think that it is.* On the whole, a good general rule is to use the phrase that occurs *first.* For example, ⟨outline⟩ would be written, *provided* that the writer had not already lifted the pen after ⟨outline⟩; and to join ⟨outline⟩ to ⟨outline⟩ in *I think that it is* is to be preferred because it is the *first* of the possible joinings. It is not, however, wrong to join ⟨outline⟩ to ⟨outline⟩ instead of to ⟨outline⟩. Freedom of choice must remain in the writing of phrases, and slight variations are not serious.

able to agree		all members	
able to deal		all my brethren	
able to read		all my life	
able to take		all my time	
able to think		all one	
about the		all other classes	
above their		all our own	
absolutely certain		all over the country	
according to my		all over the world	
according to the		all particulars	
Act of Parliament		all persons	
after a time		all places	
after he is (has)		all proceedings	
after that		all questions	
after they (them)		all respects	
after we have		all right	
after which the		all situations	
against us		all sorts of	
agreed that		all states	
all classes		all such	
all directions		all that day	
all friends		all that is necessary	
all great		all that one	
all his (is)		all the matters	
all his countrymen		all the men	
all his endeavours		all the work	
all his interests		all the world	
all his life		all the year round	
all his own		all their own	
all his purposes		all these circumstances	
all its clauses		all these occasions	
all mankind		all these parts	
all manner		all these questions	
all manner of ways		all these reasons	
all matters		all this time	
all means		all those who are	

all those who may be		and if this is	
all very well		and if such	
all we can		and if you will	
all we want		and in all probability	
all were (we are)		and in all the circumstances	
all which		and in my opinion	
all worlds		and in some cases	
all you can		and in some respects	
almost always		and in their	
almost any		and in this way	
almost certain		and is (his)	
almost immediately		and of the	
almost impossible		and such	
already been		and that they were	
also state		and the Government	
always been		and the rest	
always excepting		and there were	
among themselves		and they were told	
among the most		and under the present	
among the same		circumstances	
among those who have not		and we shall be pleased	
among those who were		another affair	
amongst them		another instance	
and after that		another nation	
and afterwards		another opinion	
and have since		another point	
and his country		another question	
and I am		another situation	
and I have the honour		another station	
and I hope		another subject	
and I notice		another time	
and I only		any business	
and I take this		any more	
and I took		any other	
and I trust		any person	
and if it is to be		any word	

anything else	as it is
anywhere else	as it really
apart from	as it seems to me
are not entitled	as it sometimes was
are not found	as it surely
are you	as it was
army and navy	as it were
as a general rule	as it will
as a result	as it would
as a rule	as little as possible
as compared with last year	as long as it is
as early as possible	as long as it may
as far as	as long as necessary
as far as can	as long as possible
as far as may be	as long as they
as far as our	as long as will
as far as regarded	as many as are
as far as regards	as many as can be
as far as the	as many as choose
as far as usual	as much as before
as far as was	as much as can be
as far as will	as much as ever
as far as you can	as much as it is
as fast as	as much as may
as good as	as much as our (are)
as good as before	as much as possible
as good as ever	as much as they
as good as if	as much as was
as good as it	as much as will
as good as need be	as much as your
as good as possible	as per
as he is (has)	as promised
as if the most	as provided
as in the case of	as regards
as is (his)	as satisfactory
as it certainly	as soon as convenient

as soon as possible	at some time
as soon as they were	at such
as soon as we have	at the end
as the	at the present time
as this is	at the request (of)
as to	at the same moment
as usual	at the same time
as we have not	at the time
as we have said	at times
as we have suggested	Atlantic Ocean
as we trust	
as well as it can be	be able to
as well as most	be assured
as well as our	be called upon
as well as your	be certain
as will be observed	be clearly
as will be seen	be considered
at a glance	be done
at a loss	be gratified
at all events	be greatly
at all times	be it so
at any rate	be made
at any time	be pleased
at church	be received
at first	be said
at home	be satisfied
at home and abroad	be saved
at last	be seen
at least	be such
at length	be supposed
at once	be sure
at one another	be sure their (there)
at one time	be the case
at present	be their (there)
at right angles	be this
at sight	be thought

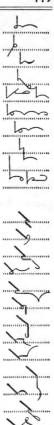

be told that		before the war	
be your		before us	
bear in mind		before you	
because he		being the case	
because he could not		being the same	
because he is now		believe that	
because he was		best of my recollection	
because it cannot be		best of our ability	
because it is		best possible	
because it was		best time	
because it will be		best way	
because of		best wishes	
because of their		better and better	
because such		better still	
because they have		better than	
because this		between his (us)	
because we		between our	
because we are		between which	
because we have		blacker and blacker	
been able to		both sides	
been answered		bound to say	
been done		boys and girls	
been enabled		breach of faith	
been known		break up	
been observed		bring forward	
been received		bring up	
been required		British Empire	
been said		British Museum	
been so		British railways	
been taken		British ships	
been told		broken up	
been understood		business experience	
before Christ		business letter	
before him		business man	
before his		but can	
before my (me)		but may	

but one		by land and sea	
but so		by many	
but such		by me (my)	
but surely		by means of	
but tell		by no means	
but that		by one	
but their (there *or* they are)		by our	
but they will		by people	
but this		by permission	
but we have received		by reason (of)	
but we have taken		by several	
but we may		by some means	
but when		by some other means	
but whenever		by something	
but whether		by such	
but would		by that	
but you will have		by the by	
by all means		by the Chairman	
by and by		by the Government	
by as many		by the House	
by certain		by the means	
by circumstances		by the same	
by considering		by the way	
by every		by their	
by far the least		by their means	
by far the most		by their own	
by far the worse		by this	
by him		by this nation	
by his (us)		by this time	
by his own		by those who are	
by his own statement		by those who are not	
by his own supposition		by way of	
by it		by which it appears	
by its (itself)		by which it can	
by its means		by which it has (is)	
		by which it may	

by which it seems		cannot hope	
by which it would		cannot make	
by which many		cannot receive	
by which means		cannot regard	
by which you		cannot say	
by you		cannot see	
by your		cannot take	
by your own		capital and labour	
by your request		care of	
		carried on	
call attention to the matter		carried on their	
call that		carried out	
called upon		carry on	
came to the conclusion		Catholic religion	
can be found		cause and effect	
can be said		celestial regions	
can be seen		certain circumstances	
can become		certainly been	
can do		certainly not	
can have		Christian friends	
can it		Christian principles	
can it appear		Church of God	
can it be		City of Manchester	
can it bring		City of Norwich	
can never		City of Westminster	
can only assume		civil servant	
can you have		Civil Service	
cannot be		civil war	
cannot be considered		civilized world	
cannot be said		clearly shown	
cannot be there (their)		Colonial Office	
cannot become		come forward	
cannot do		come to the conclusion	
cannot expect		comes forward	
cannot give		Commander-in-Chief	
cannot go		considerable time	

Constitution of the United States

cost of production

could be

could have

could have been

could have done

could never

could nevertheless

could not be

could not be the case

could not have

could they

could you have

country place

country town

courts of law

custom houses

dead letter office

depend upon it

depend upon us

did not

did not know

difference of opinion

distinctly understood

divine love

divine providence

divine wisdom

do assure

do not

do not be

do not entirely

do not know

do not necessarily

do not say

do not see

do not understand

do not wish

do so

do something

do sometimes

do such

do that

do they

do this

do you mean to say

do you mean to suggest

do your

does appear

does he

does it

does not

does nothing

does one

does that

does this

duly qualified

during the month

each of them

each other

each was

early closing

East and West

East Indies

electric light

enclose herewith

end of next week

end of the month

England and Wales

English language

enter into		following words	
ever been		for (a) consideration	
ever since		for a few days	
every appearance		for a long time	
every consideration		for a moment	
every day		for a time	
every direction		for another	
every morning		for even	
every one		for ever	
every other		for fear	
every station		for further particulars	
everywhere else		for great	
existing circumstances		for he was	
expect to receive		for he would have the	
expression of opinion		for he would not	
extremely sorry		for his account	
		for his advantage	
fact of the matter		for his appearance	
fair and reasonable		for his country	
far and wide		for his interest	
favourable circumstances		for his opinion	
fear of God		for his own good	
fear of death		for his own interest	
fear of the world		for his part	
fellow citizens		for his purpose	
few more		for his sake	
few weeks		for instance	
few words		for it will be	
fewer than		for many	
first and foremost		for me	
first class		for months	
first, second and third		for my friends	
first time		for my own sake	
five or six		for no one	
five pound note		for one	
following points		for perhaps	

for possibly		for this time	
for sale		for those who	
for services rendered		for us	
for some considerable time		for we are told	
for some reason or other		for we had	
for some time past		for we were	
for some years		for where	
for something		for which we are obliged	
for such matters		for which you are	
for the account		for your information	
for the advantage		foreign affairs	
for the Government		foundation stone	
for the main		free library	
for the management		free of charge	
for the matter of that		freehold property	
for the moment		from among	
for the most part		from as many	
for the pleasure		from beginning to end	
for the present		from certain	
for the progress		from church	
for the rest		from every	
for the sake of		from first to last	
for the same reason		from him	
for the Word of God		from its	
for the work		from many	
for their opinion		from month to month	
for their satisfaction		from principle	
for their support		from some cause	
for them (they)		from the fact that	
for there has been		from the first	
for there is		from the other	
for there were		from the place	
for they were		from time immemorial	
for this		from time to time	
for this bill		from us	
for this country		from whom	

from year to year	
from you	
from your	
full particulars	
further consideration	
further instructions	
further than (on)	
future advantage	
future time	
General Election	
general manager	
generally speaking	
generation to generation	
get rid of	
get rid of their	
give me	
give him	
glory everlasting	
God is just	
God is love	
good deal	
good enough	
good fortune	
good many	
good men	
great advantage	
great affairs	
great applause	
Great Britain	
great danger	
great difference	
great difficulty	
great events	
great favour	
great interest	

great men	
great nation	
great opportunities	
great pleasure	
great principles	
great respect	
great value	
Great War	
greater part (of)	
greater than	
had been	
had not	
had not been	
had not known	
had their	
had you	
hard and fast	
hard and fast rule	
has been	
has been considered	
has been done	
has been issued	
has been received	
has he	
has it	
has it ever been	
has not been	
has that	
has this	
have also	
have another	
have become	
have been	
have been able to	
have been expecting	

have been given to understand	
have been known	
have been received	
have been told	
have believed	
have calculated	
have called	
have closely	
have come to the conclusion	
have decided	
have demanded	
have done	
have endeavoured	
have every	
have found	
have frequently	
have great hopes	
have greatly	
have heard	
have indeed	
have it	
have just	
have just been	
have known	
have lately	
have likewise	
have long	
have mentioned	
have much pleasure	
have never been	
have no doubt	
have no objection	
have no time	
have not been able to	
have one	

have only	
have only just	
have perhaps	
have pleasure	
have possibly	
have probably	
have said	
have seen	
have sent	
have shown	
have some	
have sometimes	
have spoken	
have such	
have suggested	
have supposed	
have taken	
have the honour	
have their (there)	
have this (these or those)	
have thought	
have to be	
have told	
have tried	
have understood	
have we	
having heard	
he cannot be	
he has (is)	
he has (is) never	
he has (is) not	
he has received	
he must be	
he seems	
he seems to be able to	
he should be	

he will be		how much	
he will never		how the	
he will not be		how the matter	
he would have		human being	
he would have been		human character	
he would make		human kind	
hear, hear		human life	
hear you		human mind	
heart and soul		human nature	
heavy expenses		human race	
Her Majesty		Hyde Park	
here and there			
high pressure		I agree	
high state of		I agree with	
His Majesty		I am	
his own		I am able to	
his own interests		I am afraid	
history of the world		I am also	
hither and thither		I am aware	
Holy Scriptures		I am certain that you will	
Home Office		I am concerned	
Home Secretary		I am convinced	
honourable and gallant member		I am, Dear Sir	
		I am extremely sorry	
hon. senator		I am free	
House of Commons		I am going to speak to you	
House of God		I am gratified	
house of prayer		I am greatly	
House of Representatives		I am in doubt	
house to house		I am instructed	
how can		I am most	
how can there be		I am never	
how can we		I am not	
how far		I am not quite sure	
how is it		I am persuaded	
how long		I am pleased	

I am quite sure	I hope there will be	
I am ready	I intended	
I am sorry	I know nothing	
I am sorry to say	I know there is	
I am therefore	I like	
I am told	I may say	
I am truly	I mentioned	
I am very sorry	I must	
I am, Yours truly	I must not be	
I assure you	I must now	
I became	I must take	
I become	I need hardly say	
I believe	I need not say	
I bequeath	I observed	
I beseech you	I presume	
I call	I propose	
I can assure you	I purpose	
I can never	I referred	
I cannot expect	I remember	
I consider	I see no objection	
I could not have	I shall never	
I dare	I shall take	
I dare not	I shall therefore	
I desire	I speak	
I do not say	I spoke	
I do not see	I suppose	
I do not think that	I take	
I do not wish it to be	I take this	
I feel	I tell him	
I feel sure	I thank	
I gave	I think so	
I have no objection	I think that we	
I have suggested	I thought that	
I have the honour to remain	I told him	
	I took	
I hope that	I trust you will	

I understood		if there/their	
I want		if there is one	
I was never		if there is one thing	
I was there		if there were	
I was under the impression		if therefore	
I will endeavour		if they	
I will tell you		if they had	
I wish it were not		if they must be	
I would		if this country	
I would like to know		if this gentleman	
if convenient		if this is the case	
if he		if those who are	
if he can		if we are	
if he has been		if we believe	
if he were		if we have seen	
if he would		if we may	
if his		if we take	
if it		if we understand	
if it become		if you are successful	
if it did not		if you like	
if it has (is)		if you mean	
if it has (is) never		if you please	
if it is found		if you require	
if it please		if you would	
if it possibly		in a day or two	
if it prove		in a few days	
if it was		in a large number of cases	
if it were		in a month's time	
if it would		in a position	
if necessary		in accordance with	
if only		in addition to the	
if possible		in all cases	
if that is not the case		in all matters	
if that is possible		in all parts of the country	
if the matter		in all probability	
if the present		in another case	

in another sense		in his own way	
in another world		in his own words	
in any affair		in his situation	
in any case		in his station	
in any instance		in his time	
in any position		in it	
in any respect		in its own	
in any situation		in its place	
in any station		in judgment	
in any way		in many	
in appearance		in many cases	
in as far as		in me	
in behalf		in mine	
in charge		in more	
in (the) circumstances		in most	
in comparison with that		in most cases	
in conclusion		in my own	
in conformity with		in nine cases out of ten	
in connexion with their		in no case	
in contempt		in one form or another	
in course of		in one word	
in effect		in order that the	
in every way		in order to	
in favour		in other directions	
in him		in other places	
in his		in other respects	
in his account		in other ways	
in his behalf		in other words	
in his case		in our opinion	
in his day		in person	
in his face		in place of the	
in his hands		in possession	
in his interest		in questions	
in his opinion		in reality	
in his own case		in regard to that	
in his own interest		in regard to this subject	

in relation to the		in the ordinary course of events	
in reply to the		in the ordinary way	
in some		in the other	
in some cases		in the same way	
in some countries		in the shape of	
in some respects		in the street	
in some way		in the truth	
in spite of		in the word	
in spite of the fact		in the world	
in succession		in the year	
in such matters		in their case	
in such places		in their interest	
in that day		in their own case	
in that direction		in their own interests	
in that matter		in their place	
in that way		in their position	
in the account		in their stead	
in the case of		in themselves	
in the circumstances		in these	
in the city of God		in these times	
in the conviction		in these words	
in the country		in this	
in the course of		in this affair	
in the dark		in this age	
in the direction		in this century	
in the early part (of)		in this city	
in the event (of)		in this difficulty	
in the first place		in this direction	
in the House		in this manner	
in the land		in this place	
in the manner (of)		in this respect	
in the matter (of)		in this world	
in the meantime		in those	
in the morning		in time	
in the name (of)		in vain	
in the nature of things			

in which event

in which it has been

in which it is

in which there are

in which we have been

in which you are engaged

in which you require

in your last letter

in your letter

inasmuch as

including their

income tax

income tax payers

instead of the

into effect

into most

into that

into their

into this country

is as

is it

is it likely

is it not

is it possible

is it the

is it true

is it worth while

is necessary

is no doubt

is not one

is not only

is not this

is that the wisest

is the

is the matter

is the most

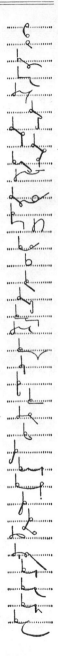

is this

is to

it appears to me

it can have

it certainly

it has been done

it has been said

it has been suggested

it has not been

it is a well-known fact

it is absolutely necessary

it is admitted

it is also

it is answered

it is as (his)

it is believed

it is better than

it is calculated

it is certain that

it is clearly

it is considered

it is difficult

it is equal

it is expected

it is found

it is generally

it is intended

it is interesting

it is just

it is just possible

it is most

it is most probable

it is needed (indeed)

it is never

it is no doubt

it is no longer

it is not the first time		it makes	
it is nothing		it may not be	
it is now		it may seem	
it is one		it may well be	
it is only		it means	
it is plain		it must	
it is possible		it must certainly	
it is rather		it seems impossible	
it is ready		it seems probable	
it is really		it should not be	
it is seen		it sometimes	
it is shown		it sometimes seems	
it is so		it stands to reason	
it is something		it surely	
it is sometimes		it was impossible	
it is such		it was known	
it is sufficient		it was nothing	
it is suggested		it will also be found	
it is taken		it will appear	
it is the case		it will be found	
it is this		it will be impossible	
it is thought		it will be observed	
it is time		it will be seen	
it is to be		it will never be	
it is true		it will not be	
it is truly		it will take	
it is unnecessary		it would appear	
it is unworthy		it would be something	
it is well known		it would have been	
it is worth while		it would only	
it is worthy			
it is written		just a few	
it is wrong		just after	
it is your own		just as	
it is yours		just been	
it looks		just enough	

just finished		let us remember	
just in time		let us see	
just now		let us try	
		let you have	
ladies and gentlemen		like to have	
laid down		little advantage	
land tax		little consideration	
large measure		little more	
large number		little more than	
large number of cases		little time	
large number of men		local board	
larger and larger		local option	
last moment		logical conclusion	
last month		London County Council	
last time		London mails	
last week		long before	
last year		long enough	
later than (on)		long one	
latter part (of)		long since	
law court		long standing	
laws of God		long time ago	
lay down their		long way	
leading article		longer and longer	
learned friend		longer than	
learned gentleman		looking forward	
learned member		Lord Mayor	
leasehold property		Lord President	
leave the matter		Lord Provost	
leave us		Lord's Day	
legal representative		Lord's house	
let us		loss of life	
let us be		lower and lower	
let us consider			
let us have		Magna Charta	
let us hope		make it clear	
let us know		make their way	

make way		may sometimes	
manner in which		may therefore	
man's estate		may you	
many feel		Medical Board	
many have		medical corps	
many instances		medical examination	
many more		medical journal	
many nations		medical student	
many of these		Member of Parliament	
many of those who		Members of Parliament	
many of you		men and women	
many people		middle ages	
many persons		middle classes	
many such		modern times	
many things		Monday morning	
many think that		more and more	
mark of respect		more certain	
may also		more favourable	
may as well		more freely	
may be able to		more frequent	
may be called		more frequently	
may be considered		more important	
may be made		more likely	
may be used		more or less	
may bring		more than another	
may certainly		more than their	
may consider		more time	
may greatly		most amiable	
may have been		most anxious	
may mention		most certainly	
may never		most difficult	
may not		most excellent	
may not be		most important	
may only		most learned	
may probably		most likely	
may serve		most men	

most naturally		must prove	
most necessary		must receive	
most probable/y		must say	
most undoubtedly		must see	
Mr. and Mrs.		must take	
Mr. Chairman		must try	
Mr. Mayor		must undoubtedly	
Mr. President		my Christian brethren	
Mr. Speaker		my dear brother	
much as		my dear friend	
much as it is		my dear hearers	
much more		my dear madam	
much more than		my dear mother	
much obliged		my father	
much pleasure		my fellow Christians	
musical instrument		my fellow creatures	
must admit		my fellow subjects	
must also		my good friend	
must appear		my good sir	
must ask		my hon. and learned friend	
must bring		my kind regards	
must come		my life	
must consider		my love	
must do		my mind	
must expect		my noble and learned friend	
must generally		my noble and rev. friend	
must have		my noble and right rev. friend	
must have been			
must hope		my noble friend	
must make		my only friend	
must mean		my opinion	
must necessarily		my own	
must needs be		my own account	
must never		my own advantage	
must not		my own belief	
must not be			

my own circumstances		next week	
my own conclusion		no advantage	
my own endeavours		no alternative	
my own experience		no appearance	
my own feeling		no doubt	
my own interest		no fewer than	
my own part		no instance	
my own sake		no interest	
my own sentiments		no knowledge	
my own things		no less than	
my own time		no longer than	
my own understanding		no more than	
my partner		no necessity	
my respected friend		no objection	
my servant		no part	
my son		no such	
my time		no worse than	
		noble lord	
national affairs		nor can	
national regeneration		nor did	
national representation		nor do	
need appear		nor have	
need be		nor in	
need necessarily		nor is it	
need never		nor is this	
need not		nor need	
needless to say		nor such	
neither instance		nor was	
neither more nor less		nor were they	
neither of them		nor will	
never been		north, south, east and west	
never said		not absolutely	
never was		not been	
new ships		not enough	
news agency		not even	
next month		not excepting	

not generally		of him	
not in vain		of his own	
not less		of his time	
not less than		of itself	
not more		of many things	
not necessarily		of one of his	
not necessary		of several	
not one		of some	
not only		of some importance	
not possible		of such matters	
not so		of such men	
not such		of the case	
not that		of the matter	
not these		of the way	
not this		of this Bill	
not those		of this century	
not understood		of this country	
not we		of those who are	
nothing else		of us	
nothing is less		of very great	
nothing more		of which it must be said	
notwithstanding such		of which we are now	
notwithstanding that		of your letter	
notwithstanding the fact that		of yours	
		official assignee	
now and then		official receiver	
number of		old age	
		old man	
of advantage		old men	
of as few		on account of many	
of as many		on account of the	
of course this is (has)		on account of your	
of every one		on every	
of grace		on his behalf	
of great advantage		on his face	
of her own		on his part	

on many occasions		one or two	
on me (my)		one point (pound)	
on most		one thing	
on one		one understands	
on one side		one way	
on some		one word	
on such		or not	
on the one hand		or perhaps	
on the other hand		or rather	
on the other side		or some other	
on the present occasion		or something	
on the subject		or sometimes	
on this occasion		or surely	
on this question		or there	
on this side		ordinary circumstances	
on your part		other circumstances	
once again		other classes	
once more		other people	
once or twice		other questions	
one and all		other side	
one another		other times	
one another's interest		other way	
one by one		ought never	
one cannot expect		ought not	
one instance		ought not to	
one knows not		ought not to be	
one man		ought not to have	
one may		ought to be considered	
one month		ought to be made	
one more		ought to have	
one must		Our Father	
one of his		our own	
one of our		our part	
one of the most important		out of	
one of these days		out of doors	
one or other		out of the question	

out of the way		present and future	
over and above		present instance	
over and over again		present interest	
over them		present month	
over there		present state of things	
over which the		present question	
owing to the fact		present time	
		President of the United States	
part and parcel		price lists	
part of		Prince of Wales	
pass away		Princess of Wales	
past year		printing press	
peculiar people		private and confidential	
pen and ink		public house	
per annum		public library	
per cent		public meeting	
per day		public service	
per dozen		purchase agreement	
per head		purchase money	
per month			
perfectly clear			
perfectly satisfactory		quite agree	
personal experience		quite certain	
personal representative		quite correct	
personal service			
Pitman writer		Railway Company	
please give me		rate of	
point at issue		reason to suppose	
political advantage		reasonable time	
political association		right or wrong	
political opinion		round and round	
political power		rules and regulations	
postage stamp			
postal services		sanitary inspector	
present advantage		satisfactory conclusion	
present age		satisfactory manner	

satisfactory report		she can	
Saturday afternoon		she cannot	
Saturday evening		she did not	
Saturday next		she had	
say so		she has (is)	
second time		she has been	
secondary education		she has (is) not	
secondary schools		she has nothing	
seeing you		she may	
seems to have		she never	
seems to have been		she says	
seems to me		she seems	
sent to you		she shall	
set apart		she sometimes	
set aside		she was	
set forth		shillings in the £	
set off		short space of time	
several times		short time	
shall be glad		short time ago	
shall be served		shorthand student	
shall do		shorthand writer	
shall endeavour		shorthand writing	
shall expect		should be considered	
shall give		should be said	
shall go		should become	
shall make		should fear	
shall most likely		should feel	
shall never		should have seen	
shall not be able to		should have told you	
shall receive		should instance	
shall require		should know	
shall say		should never	
shall see		should nevertheless	
shall take		should not be made	
shall there		should only	
shall there be		should these	

should this		so much as	
should those		so soon as	
should understand		so sure	
shoulder to shoulder		so that we may	
side by side		so to speak	
significant fact		so was	
signs of the times		so well (will)	
since it		so would	
since no doubt		so you are	
since nothing		so you must	
since that		solar system	
since that time		some account	
since they		some amount	
since this is the case		some care	
since which		some consideration	
Sir Isaac Pitman		some may	
Sir James		some man	
six months		some men	
six months ago		some means	
smaller than		some measure	
so are		some months	
so are they		some of them	
so be it		some of you will probably remember	
so called			
so do		some one	
so far		some one or other	
so far as the		some other	
so good		some people	
so good as to		some people seem to imagine	
so has (is)			
so he		some perhaps	
so it seems		some probability	
so little		some reason or other	
so long as		some reference	
so may		some regard	
so must		some seem inclined	

some such		such as may	
some there are		such as must be	
some there may be		such as need not	
some time		such as that	
some time ago		such as this	
some time or other		such as were	
some time since		such can	
something has been said		such cannot	
something like		such cases	
something to his advantage		such considerations	
somewhere else		such has been	
sons of men		such has (is) never	
sort of		such has no doubt	
South Africa		such has (is) not	
spare time		such have been	
speaking from memory		such is his	
special circumstances		such is not the case	
spirit of prayer		such is the case	
spirit world		such matters	
spiritual world		such may not be	
St. Paul		such men	
steam engine		such principles	
steps are being taken		such was	
still more		such were	
stronger than		such will	
struggle for existence		such would	
such a manner		Sunday closing	
such a manner as to			
such a plan		take care	
such and such		take care of	
such are they		take charge	
such as are		take courage	
such as can		take down	
such as can be		take exception	
such as he		take it for granted	
such as it is		take out	

take part (of)		that does	
take(n) place		that does not	
take some time		that has been	
take steps		that has (is) never	
take such		that has not been	
take that		that he can have	
take the case (of)		that he has been	
take the chair		that he may	
take the place (of)		that he must be	
take them		that is a question	
taken into account		that is another	
taken part		that is intended	
takes away		that is it	
takes notes		that is necessary	
taking part		that is not the	
technical education		that is nothing	
technical terms		that is now	
telegraph office		that is one	
telegraph wire		that is one point	
telegraphic communication		that is only	
tell him		that is possible	
tell it		that is so	
tell me		that is thought	
tell such		that is to be	
tell that		that is to say	
tell them		that is understood	
tell us		that is where	
tell you		that is worse	
tell your		that is worth	
tells me		that it has (is)	
tells us		that it may be	
than the other		that it must be done	
thank you		that may be	
that circumstance		that perhaps	
that day		that plan	
that difficulty		that question	

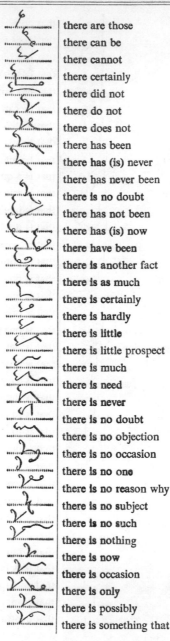

that such	there are those
that supposition	there can be
that the country	there cannot
that the directors	there certainly
that the matter	there did not
that there are	there do not
that there are several	there does not
that there must be	there has been
that there should be	there has (is) never
that there should have been	there has never been
	there is no doubt
that they were	there has not been
that this affair	there has (is) now
that this was	there have been
that those nations	there is another fact
that thought	there is as much
that time	there is certainly
that was	there is hardly
that way (we)	there is little
that we are able to	there is little prospect
that we could not	there is much
that we have made	there is need
that which will be	there is never
that will do	there is no doubt
that you should not be	there is no objection
their measures	there is no occasion
their own	there is no one
their reasons	there is no reason why
there and then	there is no subject
there are	there is no such
there are a great many	there is nothing
there are not	there is now
there are now	there is occasion
there are persons	there is only
there are several	there is possibly
there are some	there is something that

there is sometimes		they said that	
there is still		they speak	
there is undoubtedly		they state	
there may not		they suppose	
there must		they that	
there must have been		they themselves	
there seemed		they think that	
there sometimes		they thought	
there was another		they were	
there were		they will not	
there will have been		they would	
there would have been		think he	
these circumstances		think him	
these gentlemen		think it	
these questions		think me (my)	
these things		think perhaps	
they appear		think that	
they are certain that		think their (there)	
they are expecting		think them (they)	
they are not		think there has (is)	
they are perhaps		think there has been	
they are possibly		think there has (is) never	
they are required		think there has (is) not	
they believe		think they may	
they care		think this	
they did not		think this is	
they do		think you may	
they do not		this account	
they have been		this advantage	
they have not seen		this appears	
they have received		this bill	
they made		this cannot	
they may		this circumstance	
they must		this conclusion	
they must not be		this could not	
they probably		this country	

this day		this knowledge	
this department		this letter	
this did not		this month	
this difficulty		this morning	
this discussion		this need	
this does		this no doubt	
this done		this notice	
this evening		this now	
this generally		this one	
this generation		this one thing	
this had		this opinion	
this has become		this part	
this has been		this party	
this has never		this period	
this has no doubt		this place	
this has not		this point	
this has nothing to do		this purpose	
this has the		this question	
this he		this reason	
this instance		this statement	
this intention		this subject	
this interest		this supposition	
this is done		this thing	
this is intended		this time	
this is it		this understanding	
this is known		this vote	
this is never		this was	
this is no doubt		this week	
this is no time		this will	
this is not		this will not	
this is not the case		this world	
this is nothing		those accounts	
this is noticed		those advantages	
this is now		those appearances	
this is the case		those countries	
this is where		those days	

those did not		through as many	
those difficulties		through his interest	
those discussions		through his means	
those faculties		through his own	
those have		through it	
those nations		through many	
those parts		through me	
those places		through the world	
those that		through their	
those things		through their own	
those which		through you	
those which we are now		throughout the world	
those which we have		Thursday morning	
those who have		till his	
those who were		till his own	
though he		till his own time	
though it		till it can	
though that		till my	
though their (there)		till some	
though then		till such	
though there had		till that	
though there has been		till their	
though there has (is) not		till then	
though there was		till these (this)	
though there were		till they	
though there will		till we	
though these (this)		till you	
though they		to a certain extent	
thought he		to a great degree	
thought it		to a great extent	
thought that		to a less extent	
thought them		to account	
thought this		to advantage	
thought we were		to amount	
three months		to appear	
three or four		to assure	

to be made	to many of them
to be served	to me
to become	to mention
to behave	to my part
to believe	to one another
to belong	to our friends
to blame	to prevent
to bring the matter	to propose
to bring up	to receive
to call	to satisfy
to certain	to say a few words
to choose	to seek
to do	to serve
to every	to some extent
to expect	to speak to you
to give	to state
to give an expression of opinion	to such
	to suppose
to give and take	to take
to go	to that which you
to have the same	to the account of
to have their	to the amount
to him	to the best advantage
to his advantage	to the truth
to his knowledge	to their
to His Majesty	to these
to His Majesty's Government	to these institutions
	to these places
to his memory	to this
to his notice	to those
to his own advantage	to try
to his own interest	to us
to its (itself)	to which it appears
to love them	to which it can
to make the most	to which it has (is)
to make way	to which it may

to which it may not		United States of America	
to which it must		up to date	
to which it was		up to the present	
to which you can		up to the time of writing	
to whom		upon us	
to your		upon which	
to-morrow morning			
too far		valuable time	
too great		various parts	
too late		very bad	
too little		very best	
too long		very certain	
too many		very far	
too much		very first	
too short		very freely	
too true		very frequently	
towards it		very good	
towards one another		very late	
towards that		very likely	
towards this		very many of them	
trade union		very much more	
twelve months		very pleased indeed	
two or three		very rare	
two years ago		very serious	
		very short	
unable to find		very short time	
under no		very similar	
under no circumstances		very soon	
under such		very sure	
under the circumstances		very true	
under these circumstances		very truly yours	
under this		very well	
under way		vice versa	
under which		viva voce	
Union Jack		voluntary system	
United Kingdom		vote of thanks	

was another		we are entitled	
was as		we are glad	
was as much		we are in receipt of your letter	
was better			
was done		we are not	
was expected		we can do	
was he		we could not be	
was issued		we did	
was it right		we did not	
was it so		we do (had)	
was known		we do not	
was lately		we do not think	
was made		we find	
was meant		we had not	
was mentioned		we have also	
was necessary		we have no time	
was never		we have some	
was no doubt		we hope	
was not		we may be certain	
was not aware		we may be sure	
was not found		we must	
was nothing		we must not	
was received		we propose	
was said		we regret	
was seen		we regret to state	
was so		we reply	
was some		we shall expect	
was sometimes		we shall not	
was soon		we shall require	
was there		we spend	
was therefore		we take	
was to be received		we then	
was understood		we thought	
waste of time		we trust that you will	
ways and means		we were	
we are afraid		we were not	

we would	when do you go	
we would be	when does	
we would not be	when shall	
we write	when these	
well aware	when this	
well-known	when those	
well-known fact	when we are (when were)	
well then	when we are not	
well there is	when we are told	
were you	when you	
West End	whenever he	
West End of London	whenever his	
West Indies	whenever it may	
what amount	whenever that	
what can be done	whenever there has (is)	
what cannot	whenever there has been	
what do	whenever there is found	
what do not	whenever there occurs	
what does	whenever there were	
what has happened	whenever they	
what in the world	whenever this	
what is called	where were	
what is it	whereas it is	
what is the matter	whereby you may	
what is the reason	wherefore there is	
what it has (is)	wherever there is	
what matter	whether certain	
what must	whether it is	
what position	whether it is or not	
what was	whether it will be	
what was the matter	whether or not	
what were the	whether there are	
what would be	whether they	
what you	whether we believe	
whatever be	which appear	
when do	which are not	

which could not be		which we may have	
which do (had)		which will not	
which has never been		which you may require	
which has (is) no doubt		while there is	
which has (is) now		while they	
which has (is) possibly		while this	
which has (is) your		who are never	
which have been		who are they	
which have the		who cannot	
which have their (there)		who come	
which is believed		who could not	
which is certainly		who has done	
which is intended		who has (is) the	
which is known		who have not	
which is no		who has (is) it	
which is not only		who has (is) this	
which is often		who said	
which is sometimes		who seems to me	
which is thus		who suppose that	
which is understood		who were	
which it is understood		will be able to make	
which made		will be glad to know	
which makes		will be the case	
which many		will have	
which may be considered		will have no alternative	
which may not		will have their	
which must be		will it be	
which one		will it not	
which our		will not	
which perhaps		will only be	
which probably		will perhaps	
which represent-ed		will probably	
which seems		will their (there)	
which seems to me		will therefore	
which some		will you	
which was necessary		will you please	

with advantage		witness-box	
with each		word for word	
with equal advantage		words a minute	
with equal effect		words of my text	
with equal honour		words of our text	
with equal satisfaction		words of Scripture	
with one		working classes	
with one another		working man	
with one consent		world to come	
with one thing		worse and worse	
with reference to it		worst thing	
with reference to that		worth while	
with reference to this		would be something	
with regard to him		would expect	
with regard to it		would give	
with regard to this		would go	
with the present		would happen	
with the same		would have been	
with this country		would hope	
with this end in view		would indeed	
with those whom		would instance	
with us		would interest	
with which we have sent		would it not be	
with you		would know	
within necessary		would mention	
without doubt		would never	
without his		would not have	
without his knowledge		would not have been	
without it		would possibly	
without one		would rather	
without such		would receive	
without that		would say	
without their		would see	
without them		would understand	
without this		would you	
without which		would your	

wrong way		you may rest assured	
		you must certainly	
year ago		you must consider	
year by year		you must have been	
year of grace		you refer	
year since		you should have seen	
years ago		you were not	
years and years		you will consider	
year's lease		you will not	
years of age		you will probably agree	
year's rent		you will remember	
yes, if you please		you will say	
yes or no		you will see	
yes, sir		young man	
yesterday afternoon		young person	
yesterday evening		your favour	
yesterday morning		your letter	
you appear		your own	
you are not		your reply	
you cannot		your station	
you make		yours faithfully	
you may as well		yours sincerely	
you may consider		yours very truly	

KEY

Facility Drill 1

1. of-much, of-which, of-each, with-much, with-which, with-each, that-those, that-this, that-these, in-those, in-this, in-these
2. for-you, have-you, if-you, for-you-are, if-you-are, of-you, to-you, tell-you, to-tell-you, we-can-tell-you
3. we-shall, we-shall-be, we-shall-be-glad, I-shall, I-shall-be, I-shall-be-glad, we-think, we-think-you-are, I-think, I-think-you-are
4. you-are, that-you-are, you-may, if-you-may, I-think-you-may, we-think-you-may, I-think-you-may-be, we-think-you-may-be
5. we-are, we-are-glad, we-are-glad-that, we-are-glad-that-you-are, we-are-glad-that-you-can, we-are-very-glad-that-you-can
6. we-are, we-are-not, we-are-sure, we-are-pleased, we-regret, we-regret-that, we-know, we-know-that

※ ※ ※

7. it-is (-has), it-is (-has)-not, it-has-not-been, which-is (-has), which-is (-has)-not, which-has-not-been, that-is (-has), that-is (-has)-not, that-has-not-been, he-is (-has), he-is (-has)-not, he-has-not-been
8. we-have, we-have-done, I-have, I-have-done, they-have, they-have-done, we-have-not-done, I-have-not-done, they-have-not-done
9. for-your, for-your-letter, for-your-letters, for-your-receipt, for-your-receipts, for-years (-yours), for-several-years, for-many-years
10. last-year, last-years, two-years, three-years, three-months, two-months, those-days, in-those-days, these-days, in-these-days
11. we-must, you-must, they-must, she-must, he-must, we-may, he-may, they-may, she-may, he-may
12. as-to, as-it, as-it-is (-has), as-it-is (-has)-not, as-it-has-not-been, as-it-seems, as-it-seems-to-be, there-seems, there-seems-to-be, he-seems, he-seems-to-be

※ ※ ※

13. dear-sir, dear-sirs, dear-madam, dear-Miss-Brown, yours-truly, truly-yours, very-truly-yours, we-have-pleasure, we-have-much-pleasure
14. we-can, can-we, we-may, may-we, we-can-have, can-we-have, we-can-see, can-we-see
15. no-doubt, there-is, there-is-no-doubt, there-was, there-was-no-doubt, there-are, there-are-several, no-more, there-is-no-more
16. good-enough, it-is-enough, long-enough, long-time, very-long-time, very-slow, very-fast
17. to-make, to-take, to-tell, to-run, to-jump, to-laugh, to-win, to-fight, to-look, to-master, to-live
18. we-are-told, we-are-told-that, we-are-informed, we-are-informed-that, inform-you, this-afternoon, this-evening

Exercise 1A

(*a*) Dear-Sirs, We-thank-you for-your-letter of-yesterday,[10] and-we-have to inform-you that-we-shall-be[20]-glad to-do everything we-can to assist you. Our[30]

157

Mr.-Morris proposes to-call-upon you next Friday at[40] about ten o'clock in-the-morning and he-will-bring[50]-with him a wide selection of-samples of-our products[60] so-that-you-may-have a fair opportunity to-examine[70] them in-some detail and to-make satisfactory decisions.

We[80]-are-sending today copies of-our various catalogues. We-think[90]-that there-is-no-doubt that after examination of-the[100]-catalogues you-will-agree-that our prices are very-competitive,[110] and-compare favourably with-those of-our principal rivals. When[120] our Mr.-Morris calls-upon you he-will-be-glad[130] to-offer-you any-more information you-may-like to[140]-have and to point-out to-you any special uses[150] to-which our products can-be put. We-shall-be[160]-glad to-hear from-you in-confirmation of-day and[170] time of-his suggested visit. Yours truly,   (177)

＊   ＊   ＊

(b) Dear-Sirs, This-is to-tell-you that-we-enjoyed[10] meeting your Mr.-Morris, and-we-feel that-his visit[20] was very useful. As you no-doubt know, he-left[30] a large-amount of-material here, and it-has taken[40] a rather long-time to-look through it and to[50]-examine it with care. We-have-now-completed this task,[60] however, and-we-are today sending an order to-you[70] for goods valued at £250. We[80]-are-placing-this order with your firm because you state[90] it-can-be dealt-with without-delay. It-is-important[100] that-there-is-no delay in dispatching the goods as[110] their-receipt will-enable our factory to-finish several orders[120] that-have remained uncompleted for-some weeks. We-are-therefore[130] depending-upon you to-carry out your-promise of-early[140]-delivery. We-are, Yours-truly,   (145)

Exercise 1B

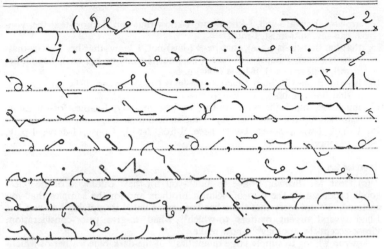

Facility Drill 2

1. pay-the, by-the, can-the, give-the, for-the, if-the, have-the, think-the, in-the, are-the, weigh-the
2. at-the, add-the, try-the, may-the, lay-the, which-the, touch-the, say-the, was-the, show-the, enjoy-the
3. address-the, makes-the, pass-the, choose-the, says-the, face-the, influence-the, raise-the, lose-the, guess-the, thinks-the
4. in-the-year, for-the-year, over-the-year, in-the-same, for-the-same, over-the-same, at-the-same, at-the-time, by-the-by
5. in-the-course, in-the-course-of-the, in-the-meantime, take-the-matter, give(n)-the-matter, all-over-the-country
6. of-the, to-the, on-the, but-the, with-the, when-the, what-the, would-the, how-the, why-the, that-the, beyond-the, and-the

※ ※ ※

7. I-have-the, I-have-not-the, I-have-had-the, I-have-not-had-the, I-think-the, I-think-that-the, I-think-that-you-will, I-think-that-you-are. I-see-the, I-wish-the
8. I-know, I-know-that, I-know-that-it-is (-has), I-know-that-it-is (-has)-not. I-took, I-took-the, I-took-the-matter, I-shall, I-shall-be
9. I-am, I-may, I-can, I-cannot, I-cannot-see, I-will, I-will-be, I-ran, I-went, I-trust, I-believe-that
10. you-will, you-will-be, you-are, you-can, you-can-be, you-could-not, you-could-not-be, you-may, you-may-be
11. if-you, if-you-will, if-you-will-be, if-you-are, if-you-can, if-you-can-be, tell-you, do-you, have-you
12. are-you, to-let-you, to-let-you-know-the, to-let-you-have, to-let-you-have-the, can-you, to-give-you, to-make-you, to-take-you

※ ※ ※

13. with-you, when-you, what-you, would-you, would-you-take, to-agree-with-you, when-you-think, what-you-do, would-you-go, to-go-with-you, to-take-with-you

14. are-you, how-are-you, I-know-you, I-know-that-you, I-know-that-the, you-can-say, you-must, I-must
15. that-he, that-he-is (-has), that-he-is (-has)-not, I-know-that-he, I-know-that-he-is (-has), I-know-that-he-is (-has)-not, I-think-he-is (-has), I-think-he-will, if-he-is (-has), if-he-is (-has)-not
16. he-will, if-he-will, he-is (-has), when-he-is (-has), he-can, if-he-can, he-says, that-he-says, he-seems, if-he-seems
17. much-the, much-the-same, in-the, in-the-same-way, for-the, for-the-same, to-take-up-the, by-the-same, by-the-same-means
18. I-shall, I-wish, I-was, I-say, I-see, I-feel, I-will, I-raise, I-draw, I-play, I-glance

Exercise 2A

(a) Dear Mr.-Brown, I-have to-thank-you for-the[10] catalogue of-the latest goods produced by-the firm of[20]-Smith Brothers and-for-the samples that-you enclosed. I[30]-am-sorry-that-there-has-been some delay in replying[40] to-you but I-had several urgent matters to-which[50] I-had to-give prior-consideration. Please-accept-the apology[60] I-now make.

Are-you willing to supply large quantities[70] of-the-dark-blue leather of-which-you sent me[80] a sample? I-am at-present preparing-the plans for[90] furnishing-the lounges of-the large hotel in-the-course[100]-of erection in New Street, and-I-am suggesting-that[110]-the predominant colour shall-be blue. Can-you telephone me[120] and let-me-know whether-you can supply at-least[130] 150 yards of-the leather? If-you[140]-can I-shall call-upon you and-inspect-the leather,[150] and-if-the quality is equal to-that of-the[160]-sample I-shall place-the order with-you immediately. Very[170]-truly-yours,   (172)

❋   ❋   ❋

(b) You asked-me recently to-give-you a list of[10]-some of-the latest books that I-recommend-you to[20]-read. You-are no-doubt aware that vast numbers of[30] books are published each year and-that to-do what[40]-you suggest is difficult. I-am, however, doing what I[50]-can for-you, and-I trust I-shall-have-the[60] list ready in-the-course-of a day or-two.[70] Would-you care to-come along and-have tea with[80] me towards-the end of-the week? I-can then[90] show-you-the list and discuss with-you all-the[100] points of interest. Let-me-know when-you can come[110] so-that I-can-have-the tea ready and-the[120] fire stoked up. In-the-meantime you-may-like to[130] buy-the recent issue of *Book Reviews for-the-Year*[140] as-this publication-contains reprints of-the-important reviews published[150] in-the leading newspapers and magazines.   (156)

Exercise 2B

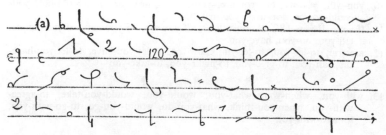

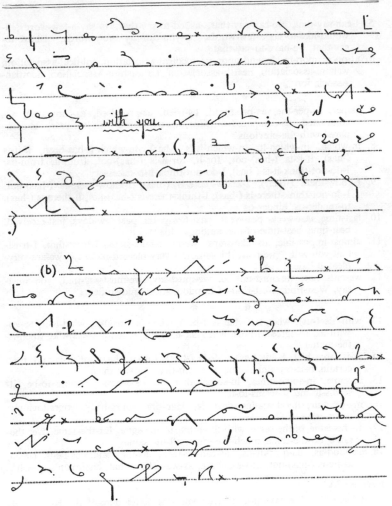

Facility Drill 3

1. it-can-be-seen, it-will-be-seen-that, in-those-days, in-these-days, please-inform, please-inform-me, please-make, please-accept, it-is-really
2. in-his, in-his-opinion, in-his-view, in-his-interests, it-is (-has), is-it, which-is (-has), which-is (-has)-not, it-has-been, it-has-not-been, which-has-been, which-has-not-been
3. as-to, as-to-the, as (-has)-the, as-much, as-much-as, as-far-as, as-far-as-the, as-early-as, as-long-as, as-fast-as, just-as
4. of-his (-us), to-his (-us), with-his (-us), for-his (-us), in-his (-us), from-his (-us), to-give-us, let-us, let-us-say, let-us-see, against-us

5. I-can-say-that, we-can-say-that, asked-to-say-that, to-say-a-few-words, I-would-like-to-say-a-few-words, if-you-can-say-a-few-words, I-have-to-say-that, we-have-to-say-that

6. at-once, upon-us, depend-upon-us, medical-association, political-association, welfare-association, health-association, Lancashire-Association, Scottish-Association

✻   ✻   ✻

7. as-per, as-per-the, as-produced, as-tried, as-promised, as-compared, as-contrasted, as-compared-with-the, as-compared-with-last-year, as-compared-with-the-previous

8. in-which, in-which-it, in-which-it-is (-has), in-which-it-has-been, if-it-is (-has), if-it-is (-has)-not, for-it, for-it-is (-has)-not, from-it, from-its, I-do-not-think-it-is (-has), I-do-not-think-it-is-necessary

9. I-know-there (-their), I-know-there-is (-has), I-know-there-is (-has)-not, I-do-not-think-there-is (-has), I-think-there-is (-has)-not, if-there-is (-has), to-render-us, hinder-us

10. last-time, last-week, past-year, past-few-years, past-few-days, just-received, best-time, best-time-of-life, amongst-this

11. almost-impossible, to-take-steps, we-must-take-steps, I-trust-that, I-trust-that-you-will, we-trust-this-is-not, very-pleased-indeed, we-are-very-pleased-indeed

12. we-must-not, we-must-not-be, we-must-say, we-must-say-that, you-must-say, West-End, West-End-of-London, shorthand-students

✻   ✻   ✻

13. with-his (-us), when-is, what-is (-has), when-is (-has)-it, what-is-it, to-go-with-us, to-agree-with-us, what-is (-has)-the, when-is (-has)-the, when-is-the-matter

14. as-is (-has-his), is-his (-as), this-is (-has), this-is (-has)-not, it-is-said, it-is-certain, it-is-certainly, almost-certain-that, as-we-can

15. in-some, in-some-other, in-some-other-way, it-seems, it-seems-to-be, it-seems-to-me, it-seems-to-us

16. my-dear-sir, my-dear-sirs, dear-sir, dear-sirs, yours-truly, yours-lovingly, yours-respectfully

17. at-the-same, in-the-same, with-the-same, to-the-same, for-the-same, over-the-same, do-the-same, much-the-same, all-the-same

18. as-good-as, as-quickly-as, as-can-be-seen, as-they-said, as-he-is (-has), as-he-is (-has)-not, as-we-believe, as-we-believe-that, chairman's-speech

Exercise 3A

(a) Dear-Sir, We-have-just-received your-last-letter dated[10] the last-day of-last-month setting out your trading[20] figures for-the last-week of-January. We-notice-that[30]-there-is a considerable drop in-these figures as-compared[40]-with-those for-the-same week of-the past-year,[50] and-we-trust-that-you-will give-us your-reasons[60] for-this decrease. As-far-as we-can-see, there[70]-has-been a serious fall during-the past-few-weeks,[80] and you-must-take-steps to-improve your figures. It[90]-is almost-impossible for-us at-this distance to-suggest[100] the right-steps for-you to-take, and-we-do[110]-not-think-it-is-necessary for-us to-do-so[120] in-view-of-your past-experience in-this field. We[130]-must-say, however, that-there-is-no-time to-lose,[140] and-we-trust-that-you-will write to-us again[150] next-week as-promised, and tell-us-the areas in[160]-which-it-has-been decided to operate intensively. Yours-truly,   (170) (*b*) Gentlemen, I-would-like-to-say-a-few-words to[10]-you this-afternoon on-the-subject-of-the accounts for[20]-the past-year. In-some-respects these-are very-satisfactory[30] but it-seems-to-me that in-some-other-respects[40] there-has-been an unsatisfactory trend during-the-past-few[50]-months. As-can-be-seen at-once, the profit figure[60] is favourable as-compared-with-last-year, and-we-must[70]-not-be led into taking-steps to-change our organization[80] until we-can-be-certain-that immediate-steps are required.[90] In-my-last-report I-said that-it-was almost[100]-certain-that Government-controls would continue to hinder-us and[110]-there-seems-little hope of-their removal for-some-time.[120] However, we-trust-that something will-be-done in-this[130]-respect within-the-next-few-months, and-if-it-is[140] we-shall-be very-pleased-indeed. (146)

* * *

(*c*) Last-week I-spent a day in-the West-End[10]-of-London. Generally I walk as-fast-as I-can[20] and-spend just-as little time as-is reasonable inside[30] shops, but in-the West-End I-took-steps that[40]-were slow. I-spent as-much-as I-dared of[50]-the-money in-my purse, and-I stayed out as[60]-long-as I could. (64)

Exercise 3B

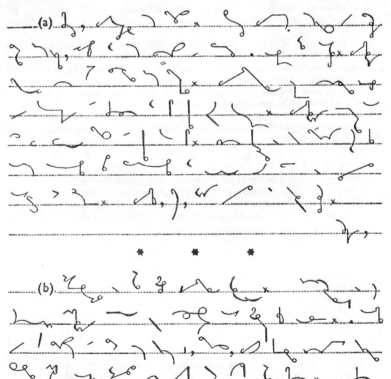

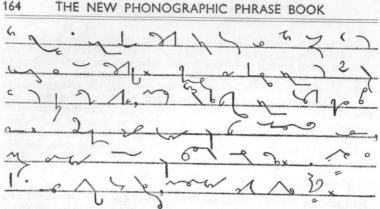

Facility Drill 4

1. we-can, as-we-can, as-we-can-be, as-we-can-be-there, as-we-cannot, as-we-cannot-be, as-we-cannot-be-there, as-we-have, as-we-have-been, as-we-have-been-there
2. as-we-know, as-we-know-there-is, as-we-know-there-is-not, as-we-are, as-we-think, as-we-hope, as-we-hope-that-you-are, as-we-feel, as-we-say, as-we-wish
3. as-well (-will), as-well-as, as-well-as-possible, as-well-as-can-be, as-well-as-usual, as-will-be, as-will-be-seen, as-will-be-known, as-will-be-said
4. as-soon-as, as-soon-as-possible, as-soon-as-we-know, as-soon-as-we-know-there-is, as-soon-as-they-have, as-soon-as-they-have-been
5. as-said, as-satisfactory, as-satisfactory-as, as-certain, as-certain-as, as-has (-is), is-as (-his), as-is-usual, as-is-known
6. as-we-had, as-we-had-not, as-we-do, as-we-do-not, as-we-did, as-we-did-not, as-we-shall, as-we-shall-not, as-we-shall-be, as-we-shall-not-be, as-we-shall-not-be-there

❋　　　❋　　　❋

7. this-city, in-this-city, in-these-cities, this-side, on-this-side, on-these-sides, this-subject, on-this-subject, on-these-subjects, in-these-subjects
8. this-is (-has), this-has-been, this-has-not-been, this-is (-has)-done, it-is (-has)-seen, it-is (-has)-seen-that, is-satisfactory, it-is-satisfactory, it-is-satisfactory-that, it-is-certain, it-is-certain-that
9. it-is-simple, it-is-simply, it-is-suggested, this-section, these-sections, in-these-sections, these-sentences, in-these-sentences, for-his-sake
10. we-trust, as-we-trust, we-promised, as-we-promised, as-we-tried, as-we-brought, as-we-bring, as-we-produce, as-we-provide
11. we-are, as-we-are, we-are-not, as-we-are-not, we-do-not, as-we-do-not, we-do-not-think, as-we-do-not-think, we-feel, as-we-feel, as-we-felt
12. will-be, will-be-seen, as-will-be, as-will-be-seen, well, as-well-as, as-well-as-possible, as-well-as-can-be, as-well-as-last-time

❋　　　❋　　　❋

13. certain-that, it-is-certain-that, certainly-not, it-is (-has)-certainly-not, it-has-certainly-not-been, seen, it-is -(has)-seen, it-is (-has)-seen-that

14. soon, as-soon, as-soon-as, as-soon-as-possible, as-soon-as-they, as-soon-as-we, as-soon-as-he, as-soon-as-it-is (-has), as-soon-as-it-is-possible.

15. we-trust, as-we-trust, we-trusted, as-we-trusted, we-crossed, as-we-crossed, we-appreciate, as-we-appreciate, we-drove, as-we-drove

16. in-such-cases, in-these-cases, in-the-circumstances, in-these-circumstances, in-all-these-sections, in-all-these-subjects, all-these-days, this-site, these-sites

17. is-his (-as), it-is-his (-as) as-is (-has), as-is-the, as-is-the-case, as-has-been, as-has-been-said, as-is-done, which-is-his

18. as-we-have-been, as-we-have-been-there, as-we-think, as-we-think-there-is, as-we-know, as-we-know-there-is, as-we-introduced, as-we-took

Exercise 4A

(a) Dear-Sirs, As-we-promised that-we-would let-you[10] see-the plans for-the new hotel as-soon-as[20]-possible, we-are-sending-you this-section of-the sketch,[30] as-we-think it-will-interest-you. As-will-be[40]-seen, this-sketch is for-the east wing, and-is[50] a rough draft only. As-we-wish to-have-your[60] views it-is-suggested that-you-examine this-sketch carefully[70] and give-us your opinion. This-suggestion is made as[80]-we-do-not-wish to complete-the whole work only[90] to-find that-it-is-simply wasted as-we-have[100]-not fully understood your ideas. We-shall proceed with-the[110] work on-the basis of-the enclosed sketch as-soon[120]-as-we hear that-it-is-satisfactory. Yours-truly,   (129)

✤   ✤   ✤

(b) As-will-be-seen from this-section of-the book,[10] it-is-certainly an advantage to-us to-phrase as[20]-much-as-possible. It-is almost-certain-that many of[30]-us do-not make as-much use of-phrasing as[40]-we-might, as-we-have-not studied this-subject sufficiently,[50] and it-is-suggested that all-these-sections should-be[60] studied and-practised as-soon-as-possible and as-well[70]-as-possible. As-we-do-not-wish to-lose-time[80] when writing shorthand, and as-we-know-that phrases save[90]-time, it-is-clear that-we should spend as-much[100] time as-we-can on-the mastery of-the-principles[110] of-phrasing, as-we-shall in-this-way be-able[120]-to apply-the principles whenever it-is-satisfactory to-do[130]-so.   (131)

✤   ✤   ✤

(c) It-is-satisfactory for-us to-be-able-to inform[10]-you that-we-are doing as-well-as-can-be[20] expected in-the-present-circumstances. Trade in-this-city has[30]-not-been as steady as-is customary but-this-is[40]-not a matter within-our-control, and it-is-certain[50]-that-we-are getting our full share of-such trade[60] as-has-been available. As-we-do-not-think-there[70]-is any justification for alarm and as-we-trust that[80] trade will improve shortly, we-are-proposing to-pay-the[90]-same dividend as-last-year.   (95)

Exercise 4B

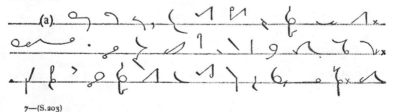

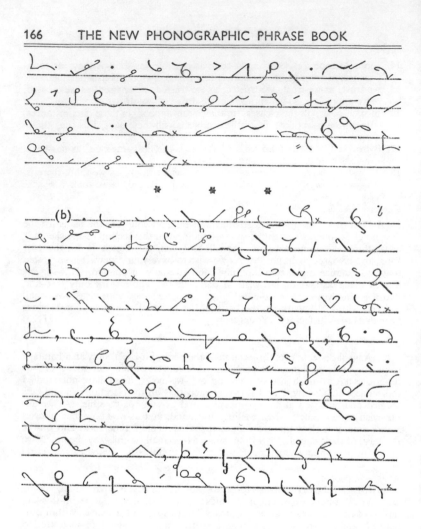

Facility Drill 5

1. first, first-time, for-the-first-time, first-thing, first-things, first-hand, first-hand-information, first-class first-class-quality
2. first-instance, in-the-first-instance, first-information, first-news, first-cost, first-costs, at-first-cost, first-prize, first-prizes
3. at-first, at-first-hand, at-first-appearance, at-first-appearances, for-the-first, in-the-first, in-the-first-case, first-place, in-the-first-place, very-first
4. Sunday-next, Monday-next, Tuesday-next, Wednesday-next, Thursday-next, Friday-next, Saturday-next
5. fast, fast-as, as-fast-as, just, just-as, as-just-as, just-now, against-us
6. at-last, at-least, last-year, last-few, last-few-years, for-last-year, during-the-last-year, over-the-last-year, last-few-days, last-few-months

Exercise 5A

At-last I-am-able-to give-you first-hand[10]-information regarding-the first-class organization in-which-you-are[20]-interested. At-first-appearance the results of-the last-few[30]-years do-not seem to-be as-good-as might[40] be hoped, but further investigation shows that-the business has[50] progressed as-fast-as could-be expected, and-is just[60]-now in a very-satisfactory-position. The profits for-last[70]-year show that for-the-first-time this-company has[80] made a large-profit, and-the results are at-least[90] as-satisfactory-as those for any similar-company. I-suggest[100] that-the first-thing for-you to-do is-to[110]-call in and see me at-my office on-Monday[120]-next when I-can show-you at-first-hand some[130] trading figures for-the last-few-months.   (137)

Exercise 5B

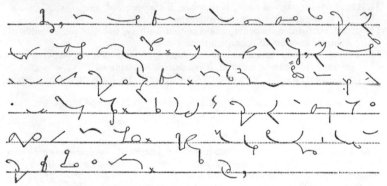

Facility Drill 6

1. it-appears, it-appears-that, it-appears-to-me, it-appeared, it-appeared-that, it-appeared-to-me, will-appear, it-will-appear, it-will-appear-that, to-appear, it-would-appear
2. per-minute, per-month, per-term, as-per, per-cent, per-annum, per-day per-head
3. Hyde-Park, Central-Park, Municipal-Park, local-parks, St.-James'-Park, Green-Park
4. part-of, great-part, great-part-of-the, all-parts, all-parts-of-the-country, all-parts-of-the-world, various-parts, various-parts-of-the-country, various-parts-of-the-world
5. your-part, my-part, for-your-part, for-my-part, some-parts, several-parts, for-the-most-part, to-part-with, to-part-with-the
6. Colonel-James, Lieut.-Colonel-Thomson, Water-Corporation, Electricity-Corporation, Professor-Robinson, Professor-of-English, Superintendent-Rees, Superintendent-of-Mines

       *   *   *

7. they-are, they-are-not, that-they-are, that-they-are-not, I-know-that-they-are, I-know-that-they-are-not, if-they-are, if-they-are-not, I-think-they-are, I-think-they-are-not
8. in-our, in-our-view, in-our-opinion, in-our-interests, in-our-conditions, in-our-circumstances, in-our-society, in-our-bank

9. in-order-to, in-order-to-have, in-order-to-be-there, in-order, in-order-that, in-order-that-they-are, in-order-that-we-may
10. to-assure, to-assure-you, I-assure-you, you-may-be-sure, you-may-rest-assured, I-can-assure-you, we-can-assure-you, if-you-can-assure-us, to-assure-us, they-assure-us
11. how-far, how-far-is-it, too-far, too-far-away, is-it-far, so-far, very-far, very-far-away, by-far-the-most, by-far-the-most-important
12. set-forth, to-set-forth, we-set-forth, put-forth, I-put-forth, we-put-forth, purchase-agreement, it-is-agreed

*　　*　　*

13. appear, appears, it-would-appear, it-appears, it-appears-that, it-appears-to-me, part, part-of, for-my-part, for-the-most-part, in-many-parts
14. are, they-are, they-are-not, if-they-are, if-they-are-not, our, in-our, in-our-view, in-our-opinion, in-our-interests
15. order, your-order, in-order, in-order-that-we-may, in-order-to, in-order-to-achieve, in-order-to-control, in-order-to-say
16. assure, assured, to-assure, to-be-assured, to-rest-assured, we-may-rest-assured, you-can-be-assured, it-is-assured, to-assure-us
17. far, how-far, too-far, very-far, by-far-the, forth, set-forth, to-set-forth, put-forth
18. park, school-park, car-park, several-parks, Local-Parks-Committee, two-parks

Exercise 6A

(a) Dear Professor-Martin, We-have-been-interested to-receive-your[10]-letter in-which-you set-forth details of-your visit[20] to-various-parts-of-the-world. We-can-assure-you[30] that-it-appeared to-us that a book based on[40]-your journey would-be most-interesting, and in-our-opinion[50] it-would enjoy large sales. In-order-that-we-may[60] recommend it with confidence to-the Travel Publishing-Corporation, however,[70] it-is-necessary for-us to-have further details. If[80]-they-are to-be interested prior to-the actual writing[90] of-the book it-appears desirable for-you to-list[100] for-us how-far you penetrated into hitherto unknown regions[110] and how-many-parts-of-the-world you propose to[120] include in-one volume. The Travel Publishing-Corporation like to[130] include photographs of-various-parts-of-the-world in-their[140] books, and in-order-to-achieve this without making-the[150] publication too-large it-is-sometimes necessary to-restrict detailed[160] writing to-certain-parts and to-mention other-parts only[170] briefly. Kindly-therefore give-us further details, and-we-will[180] submit your scheme to-the Publishing-Corporation at-once. If[190]-they-are-not interested we-shall-contact other-companies. Very[200]-truly-yours,   (202)

*　　*　　*

(b) Dear-Sirs, We-thank-you for-your-letter-of-yesterday[10] in-which-you set-forth your-requirements per-month for[20]-each of-the next six-months. We-can-assure-you[30] that-we-shall-do everything in-our-power to-supply[40] goods to-your-order. How-far we-shall-be successful[50] in-this must-depend to-some-extent upon our receiving[60] regular supplies of-raw materials from-the Universal Metal-Corporation.[70] In-order-that-there-may-be no unexpected delay we[80]-have already written to-this-Corporation ordering ample supplies, and[90]-they-assure-us that-they-will-do their-part to[100]-keep-us well supplied. It-appears, therefore, that no-difficulties[110] should arise, and it-is-certainly in-our-interests to[120] ensure that-they-do-not.

Will-you-please inform-us[130] whether your factory is very-far from-the nearest railway[140]-station? It-may-be so-far away that road transport[150] is preferable.

You-may-rest-assured that your-order will[160]-have our best-attention. Yours-truly, (166)

Exercise 6B

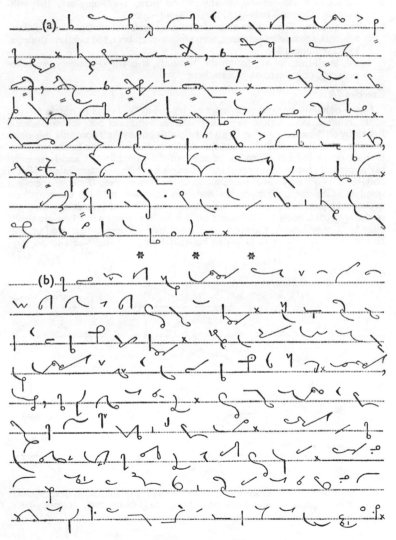

Facility Drill 7

1. at-all, at-all-costs, at-all-events, at-all-times, by-all, by-all-means, by-all-accounts, by-all-reports, by all-agreements, by-all-men
2. if-only, if-only-it-is (-has), if-only-it-is (-has)-not, it-is (-has)-only, that-it-is (-has)-only, that-it-has-only-been, only-just, it-is (-has)-only-just, that-it-is (-has)-only-just
3. we-can-only-be, I-have-only, I-have-only-been, I-have-only-just, I-have-only-just-been, I-may-only, they-may-only, they-may-only-have
4. it-will-only, it-will-only-be, it-will-only-be-there, I-will-only-say, they-will-only-say, they-will-only-sign, they-will-only-take
5. fellow-citizens, fellow-members, fellow-brothers, fellow-travellers, fellow-students, some-fellow-citizens, some-fellow-members, some-fellow-students, to-make-application
6. in-all, in-all-this, for-all, for-all-the, not-only, it-is (-has)-not-only, we-have-not-only, only-been, only-been-there

Exercise 7A

I-have-only-just-received your-letter asking-me at[10]-all-costs to obtain for-you some reliable information regarding[20]-the activities of-our fellow-students. I-shall by-all[30]-means do what I-can to help-you but by[40]-all-accounts it-is-only-the few who really know[50] what-the future activities of-the-Society will-be. I[60]-have-only-just-been elected a Member-of-the-Committee,[70] and-I-can-only-say at-present that certain important[80] changes are being-contemplated. I-may-only-be-able-to[90] let-you-have a few details for two-reasons. First,[100] there-is a small sub-Committee which-makes decisions unknown to[110]-the General-Committee and, secondly, most of what-takes-place[120] at-the meetings must-be-regarded as confidential at-all[130]-costs and not-to-be passed on to fellow-citizens[140] outside. I-can-only-say, therefore, that I-will by[150]-all-means that are fair and-honest do what I[160]-can to help-you but-that I-may-only-be[170]-able-to do very-little. (175)

Exercise 7B

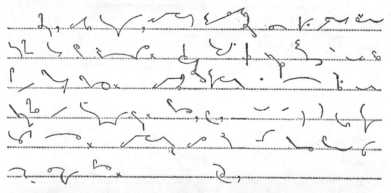

Facility Drill 8

1. I-have-been, I-have-been-there, we-had-been, we-had-been-there, already-been, already-been-there, only-been, only-been-there, recently-been, recently-been-there, previously-been

2. he-has-recently-been, he-has-recently-been-there, it-has-recently-been, he-has-not-been, he-has-not-been-there, they-have-been, they-have-been-there, it-has-been, it-has-been-there

3. better, better-than, fewer, fewer-than, higher, higher-than, harder, harder-than, smaller, smaller-than, bigger, bigger-than

4. longer, longer-than, shorter, shorter-than, farther, farther-than, more, more-than, nearer, nearer-than

5. carry-on, to-carry-on, carried-on, I-carried-on, he-carried-on, later-on, further-on

6. your-own, for-your-own, her-own, in-her-own, in-her-own-interests, our-own, their-own, their-own-interests, my-own, my-own-interests

*   *   *

7. I-am, I-am-not, you-are, you-are-not, you-will, you-will-not, you-will-not-be, you-will-not-be-there, we-do-not, we-do-not-know, we-do-not-know-that

8. you-may, you-may-not, you-may-not-be, you-may-not-be-there, he-may, he-may-not, he-may-not-be, he-may-not-be-there, they-may-not, they-may-not-be-there

9. I-will, I-will-not, I-may, I-may-not, you-will, you-will-not, you-are, you-are-not, you-can, you-cannot

10. certainly, certainly-been, certainly-not, it-is (-has)-certainly-not, almost-certainly-not, this-will-not, this-will-not-be, it-will-not-be

11. at-once, upon-us, depend-upon-us, against-us, Monday-next, Tuesday-next, Wednesday-next, Thursday-next, Friday-next, Saturday-next, Sunday-next

12. at-the-beginning, from-the-beginning, from-the-beginning-to-the-end, it-is-not-convenient, if-it-is-convenient, if-it-is-not-convenient, at-your-con-venience, at-my-convenience, it-will-not-be-convenient

*   *   *

13. have-been, I-have-been, I-have-been-there, I-have-not-been, I-have-not-been-there, I-had, I-had-been, I-had-not-been, I-had-not-been-there

14. your, your-own, in-your-own, for-your-own, to-your-own, of-your-own, on-your-own, in-your-own-interests

15. more, more-than, more-than-their, better, better-than, better-than-there, bigger, bigger-than, bigger-than-there

16. we-do-not, we-do-not-know, we-do-not-know-that, we-do-not-know-that-there-is, we-do-not-know-there-is, we-do-not-think-there-is, we-do-not-think-it-is

17. I-cannot, I-cannot-be, I-could-not, I-could-not-be, he-cannot-be, he-could-not-be, cannot-be, could-not-be, we-cannot-be, we-could-not-be

18. you-are, you-will, you-may, you-are-not, you-will-not, you-may-not, I-am, I-will, I-am-not, I-will-not

Exercise 8A

(a) Dear Mr.-Wood, The delay in-answering your-letter of[10]-the 1st May was certainly-not due to-lack-of[20] interest on-my-part. I-have recently-been on holiday[30] in-the-South of-France, and-while I-have-been[40]-there I-have-not attended to-mail. With-regard-to[50] your suggestion that I-make an early visit to-the[60]-proposed new factory site, I-can-only-say-that I[70]-have already-been-there. I-have-spoken to-our Mr.[80]-Simpson, and he informs me that-he-has-recently-been[90]-there also. Neither of-us feels that-the-proposed site[100] is-satis-factory. We-do-not-consider that-it-is any[110] better-than-the site that-had pre-viously-been proposed as[120]-it-is-rather smaller-than we-need, and it-is[130] more-than double-the price. We-are also informed-that,[140] due to-local labour-conditions, it-would-take longer-than[150] desired to-erect a factory there. We-shall, therefore, carry[160]-on with our-own plans, and make no changes other[170]-than those demanded by special-circumstances. Yours-faithfully,   (178)

❋   ❋   ❋

(b) Dear-Charles, We-have recently-been discussing with your tutor[10] the progress you-are making in-your studies. From what[20]-he-says we-think-that, for-your-own sake and[30]-in-your-own-interests, you-should work harder-than you[40] have-been doing during-the-last-few-months. We-know[50]-that-you could-do much better-than you have-been[60] doing. Your hours of work should-be longer-than they[70]-have-been, and your hours-of-play should-be shorter[80]-than they-have recently-been. If-you do-not act[90] at-once you-will-be very-sorry later-on when[100]-you find that others have-done much better-than you[110] have-done, and-that-they-have succeeded while you have[120] failed. Will-you come and see us on-Monday-next[130] if-it-is-convenient so-that-we-can discuss-the[140]-matter with-you? We-trust-that-you-will-not think[150] of-this visit as a punishment. We-wish to-do[160] as-much-as-we-can to help-you, and-we[170]-think-that-the best plan is-to-draw up a[180] strict scheme of work to operate from-the-beginning of[190] next term. If-you-are-not free on-Monday-next,[200] Wednesday-next will-be-convenient for-us. You-may depend[210]-upon-us to help-you in-any-way possible. Your[220]-loving Parents,   (222)

Exercise 8B

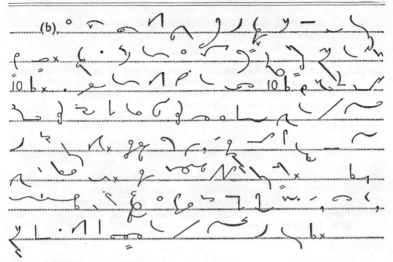

Facility Drill 9

1. I-have, I-have-had-the, I-have-done, I-have-been, I-have-been-there, we-have, we-have-been, we-have-been-there, they-have, they-have-been, they-have-been-there

2. which-have, which-have-not, which-have-been, which-have-not-been, which-have-their, which-have-been-there, which-have-not-been-there, who-have, who-have-not, who-have-been, who-have-not-been, who-have-not-been-there

3. set-of, set-of-the, state-of, state-of-the, state-of-things, state-of-affairs, out-of, out-of-the, out-of-touch, copy-of, copy-of-the, plenty-of, plenty-of-the

4. sort-of, in-spite-of, in-spite-of-the, instead-of, instead-of-the, part-of, part-of-the, present-state-of, present-state-of-things, report-of

5. take-off, to-take-off, to-take-off-the, make-off, to-make-off, wipe-off, to-wipe-off, to-wipe-off-the, better-off

6. which-have, which-have-been, who-have, who-have-been, set-of (-off), state-of, out-of, group-of, range-of, instead-of, shortage-of, present-state-of-affairs

❋ ❋ ❋

7. this-afternoon, this-evening, tomorrow-afternoon, tomorrow-evening, yesterday-afternoon, yesterday-evening

8. Monday-afternoon, Tuesday-afternoon, Wednesday-afternoon, Thursday-afternoon, Friday-afternoon, Saturday-afternoon, Sunday-afternoon

9. Monday-evening, Tuesday-evening, Wednesday-evening, Thursday-evening, Friday-evening, Saturday-evening, Sunday-evening

10. at-all, at-all-times, at-all-events, which-events, such-events, this-effect, effect-of, into-effect

11. those-who, those-who-have, those-who-have-been, those-who-have-not-been, those-who-have-been-there, those-who-have-not-been-there, those-who-have-had, those-who-have-not-had, those-who-have-done, those-who-have-not-done

12. instead, instead-of, instead-of-the, spite, in-spite, in-spite-of, in-spite-of-the, sort, sort-of, sort-of-the

* * *

13. part, part-of, part-of-the, part-of-the-arrangement, state, state-of, present-state, present-state-of, present-state-of-things, present-state-of-affairs
14. rate, rate-of, rate-of-interest, rate-of-exchange, rate-of-pay, rate-of-tax, rate-of-taxation, rate-of-Income-Tax
15. take, to-take, take-off, to-take-off, to-take-off-the, make, make-off, to-make-off
16. set, set-of (-off), set-of (-off)-their, set-of-things, set-of-books, set-of-requirements, to-set-off, to-set-off-the, I-set-off-the, they-set-off-the, we-set-off-the
17. out-of, out-of-the, out-of-doors, out-of-touch, out-of-their (-there), plenty-of, plenty-of-things, plenty-of-marks, plenty-of-insurance
18. which-have-been-there, who-have-been-there, have-been-there, I-have-been-there, they-have-been-there, those-who-have-been-there, he-has-been-there, I-have-not-been-there

Exercise 9A

(a) Ladies-and-Gentlemen, I-am happy this-afternoon to-be[10]-able-to put before-you trading results which-have-been[20] much better-than was hoped a year-ago. In-spite[30]-of all-the difficulties which-have-had to-be faced[40] during-the part-of-the year under-consideration your-Corporation[50] is able-to-report a small-profit instead-of-the[60] loss which-was feared. The credit for-this must-be[70] given to all-those-who-have-done-their work with[80]-such spirit and-enthusiasm throughout-the period. Out-of-their[90] work has come success. Not-only has-the undertaking made[100] a profit but it-has-been possible also to-wipe[110]-off a total-of £150,000[120] of-debts which-have accumulated throughout-the past three-years.[130] There-has-been an increase in-the rate-of-Income[140]-Tax but it-may-be possible to-set-off that[150] by reductions in-expenses elsewhere. As-for-the present-state[160]-of trade, I-may-say that-there-are plenty-of[170] encouraging-signs, and it-appears-that-the country has-now[180] passed out-of-the period-of depression into-one of[190]-prosperity. Last-year I-told-you that-we-had found[200] it necessary to postpone putting into-effect plans for-the[210] extension of-our factory, and it-gives me great-satisfaction[220] today to say that-these plans will-be put into[230]-effect early in-the coming year. Your-Directors are at[240]-all-times watchful of-expenditure and are prepared to-meet[250] all-such-events as-may occur in-the-course-of[260] operations. (261)

* * *

(b) Although-the present-state-of trade is-not entirely satisfactory[10] we-can at-all-events find-comfort in-the reflection[20] that in-spite-of-the effect-of-the adverse-conditions[30] which-have recently had to-be faced, we still find[40] our order books full. This-is a state-of-things[50] that-we-trust will-continue. You-will-be interested to[60] know-that on-Monday-evening last Mr. Wilson and-Mr.[70]-Brown, who-have-been on a prolonged tour of-inspection[80] of-our group-of-companies overseas, returned home. Those of[90]-us who-have-had-the opportunity of-speaking to-them[100] of-their experiences have-been greatly pleased to-hear of[110]-the rate-of progress that-has-been maintained in-spite[120]-of-conditions which-have-not always-been favourable. It-has[130]-been-arranged to hold a special meeting on-Thursday-afternoon[140] when-these two gentlemen will speak of-their experiences, and[150]-we-trust-that-you-will all-try to-be-present.[160] The meeting should-be of-particular interest to-those-who[170]-have-not-had-the opportunity to-visit-the countries in[180]-question.   (181)

Exercise 9B

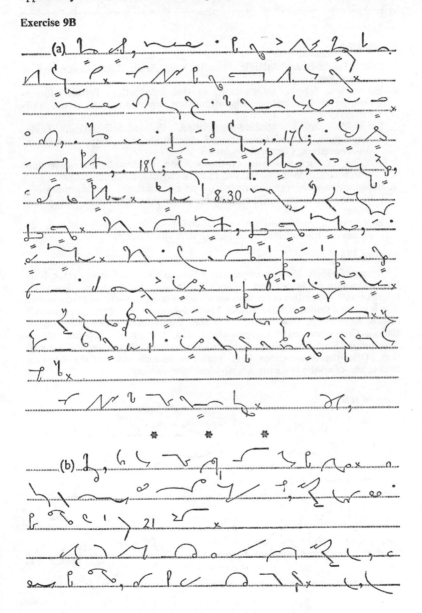

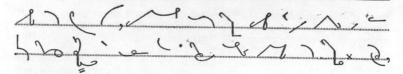

Facility Drill 10

1. Pacific, Pacific-Ocean, Atlantic, Atlantic-Ocean, Arctic, Arctic-Ocean, Indian, Indian-Ocean
2. information, for-your-information, for-their-information, further-information, for-his-information, this-information, any-information, recent-information
3. Empire-Association, Medical-Association, Political-Association, Trade-Association, Traders'-Association, Rubber-Association, Sugar-Association, Oil-Association, Copper-Association
4. occasion, on-such-occasions, on-this-occasion, on-these-occasions, section, in-this-section, in-these-sections, in-some-sections, in-which-section
5. in-connexion-with (any-connexion), your-connexions, trade-connexions, trading-conditions, world-conditions, under-these-conditions, in-any-conditions
6. in-possession, in-(a)-position, we-are-in-(a)-position, in-this-position, in-succession, no-decision, trade-recession, no-justification

Exercise 10A

Groups of-people who-are-interested in-the-same sort[10]-of things often form themselves into an association if-they[20]-are in-a-position to-do-so. For-your-information[30] and-in-this-connexion we list some of-the-associations[40]-connected with important trades and-industries: Medical-Association, Legal-Association,[50] Science-Association, Shorthand-Association, Rubber-Association, Sugar-Association, Oil-Association,[60] Copper-Association, Farmers'-Association, Metal-Association, Steel-Association, Bankers'-Association,[70] Book-keepers'-Association. Often-the Associations have branches on-each side[80]-of-the Atlantic-Ocean, and-often-the branches are divided[90] into-sections.   (92)

Exercise 10B

Facility Drill 11

1. it, for-it, for-it-is (-has), if-it, if-it-is (-has), if-it-is (-has)-not, if-it-has-been, if-it-was, if-it-was-not, if-it-were, if-it-were-not

2. in-which, in-which-it-is (-has), in-which-it-is (-has)-not, in-which-it-has-been, in-which-it-says, make-clear, to-make-it-clear, depend-upon, depend-upon-it, I-think-it-is, from-it

3. able, able-to, I-am-able-to, we-are-able-to, they-were-able-to, they-were-able-to-make, we-were-able-to-make-it-clear

4. unable, unable-to, I-am-unable-to, I-am-unable-to-find, we-are-unable-to, they-were-unable-to, we-were-unable-to-control-the

5. I-am-not, I-will-not, I-will-not-be, you-are-not, you-will-not, you-will-not-be-able-to, we-will-not, we-will-not-be, we-will-not-be-there, we-will-not-say, they-are-not

6. I-do-not, I-do-not-think, I-do-not-think-there-is, we-did-not, we-did-not-know, certainly-not, almost-certainly-not, it-is (-has)-certainly-not, this-will-not, is-it-not

＊   ＊   ＊

7. I-would, I-would-not, I-would-not be, I-would-not-be-there, we-would-not-be-there, they-would-not-be-there, this-would-not-be-the, they-would-not-consider-the-matter

8. these-words, in-these-words, in-their- (-other)-words, in-his-own-words, few-words, in-a-few-words, to-say-a-few-words, how-many-words

9. this-time, some-time, at-some-time, at-the-same-time, for-some-time, for-some-time-past, some-time-or-other, at-some-time-or-other, for-some-time-to-come

10. from-time-to-time, at-all-times, modern-times, valuable-time, lunch-time, at-one-time, more-time, there-is-no-more-time

11. set-out, to-set-out, we-set-out, they-set-out, carried-out, I-carried-out, if-you-carried-out, brought-out, I-brought-out, we-brought-out

12. to-state, this-state, this-statement, in-this-statement, present-state, present-state-of, present-state-of-things, present-state-of-affairs, in-their-statement, high-state-of

＊   ＊   ＊

13. in-this-part, part-of, in-all-parts, in-all-parts-of-the-world, in-all-parts-of-the-country, various-parts, various-parts-of-the-world

14. for-my-part, part-and-parcel, sort-of, this-sort-of, in-this-sort-of, in-spite, in-spite-of, in-spite-of-the, instead-of, instead-of-the

15. we-will, we-will-not, we-will-not-consider, we-will-not-consider-the, we-will-not-consider-the-matter, I-do-not, I-do-not-think, I-do-not-think-it-is (-has), I-do-not-think-it-is-necessary, I-do-not-think-there-is

16. it-would, it-would-not-be, they-would, they-would-not-be, he-would-not-consider-the-matter, we-would-not-consider-the-matter, we-would-certainly-not

17. they-are, that-they-are, they-are-not, that-they-are-not, I-am, I-am-not, I-am-not-in-a-position, they-do (-had), they-do (-had)-not, they-do-not-know-that, they-do-not-know-that-we

18. in-these-times, in-our-time, several-times, more-time, no-more-time, at-times, at-all-times, in-the-meantime

Exercise 11A

(a) For-some-time-past I-have-not-been-able-to[10] ascertain-the present-state-of-affairs. I-have-spent much[20] of-my valuable-time in-conversation with-the-Directors of[30]-the-organization but, as-they-state in-their-own-words,[40] they-are short of staff and-they-are-not able[50]-to set-out in-full all-the details of-the[60] past-year's working. We-shall almost-certainly-not receive-the[70] accounts by-the date named, and-I-do-not-think[80]-there-is any action I-can take as I-am[90]-unable-to-control-the activities of-the-Directors. You-may[100] depend-upon-it that I-am at-the-same-time[110] doing my best to-make-it-clear that-the situation[120] is serious.   (122)

*   *   *

(b) For-some-time I-have-been-considering a scheme for[10] setting up branch offices in various-parts-of-the-country.[20] I-am-certainly-not ready to-give-you a complete[30] plan but I-am-able-to enclose a report in[40]-which-it-is set-out in broad outline. If-it[50]-were-not for-the present-state-of-the nation's finances[60] I-would-endeavour to put-the plan into operation some[70]-time this year, but I-do-not-think-there-is[80] anything to-gain by undertaking-the work for-some-time[90]-to-come in-view-of-present-circumstances. At-the-same[100]-time I-do-not-wish to abandon-the scheme. I[110]-shall-be-glad, therefore, if-you-will-be good-enough[120] to-state your opinion. If-you have any sort-of[130] criticism please-do-not hesitate to-let-me-know as[140] I-would-like-to-have-your views.   (147)

*   *   *

(c) We-see all-sorts-of developments and changes going-on[10] in-all-parts-of-the-world, and-we-state that[20]-we-are-proud to-live in-such modern-times. We[30]-do-not-think-that-the people of-times past were[40] modern because-they-did-not-know about television, radio, the[50] cinema, motor-cars or aeroplanes. Yet it-is-clear that all[60] of-us must-live in-the-present, and-the times[70] in-which men have lived have always represented modern-times[80] to-them.   (82)

Exercise 11B

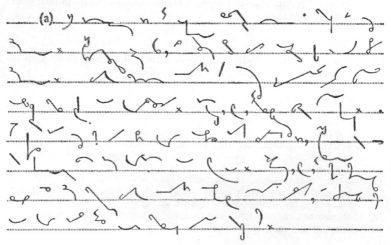

Facility Drill 12

1. in-which, in-which-there (-their), in-which-there-is, in-which-there-is-not, I-think, I-think-there (-their), I-think-there-is, I-think-there-is-not, I-have-been, I-have-been-there, I-have-not-been-there

2. making-their, making-their-way, making-their-own-way, taking-their, taking-their-own

3. I-believe, I-believe-there (-their), I-believe-there-is, I-believe-there-is-not, I-was, I-was-there, I-shall-be, I-shall-be-there, I-shall-not-be-there, although-there-is, although-there-is-not

4. in-there (-their), in-their-opinion, in-their-view, in-their-interests, in-their-own-opinion

5. upon-there (-their), depend-upon-their, had-been, had-been-there (-their), better-than, better-than-their, greater-than, greater-than-there (-their), more-than, more-than-there (-their)

6. out-of-there (-their), which-have-their, set-of-their, state-of-their, copy-of-their, range-of-their, group-of-their, exchange-of-their

✸   ✸   ✸

7. some-other, some-other-ways, in-some-other-ways, some-other-cases, in-some-other-cases, some-other-means

8. by-some, by-some-other, by-some-other-means, in-some-other-respects, in-other-times, in-other-ways, in-other-words

9. my-dear, my-dear-sir, my-dear-friend, my-dear-Mr.-Smith, my-dear-members, my-dear-mother

10. very-dear, my-very-dear-sir, my-very-dear-friends, my-very-dear-members, my-very-dear-mother

11. I-am-therefore, I-have-therefore, I-think-therefore, I-shall-therefore, we-shall-therefore, I-was-therefore, that-he-was-therefore
12. somehow, somehow-or-other, some-time, some-time-or-other, in-order, in-order-that

* * *

13. if-there-is, if-there-is-not, if-there-were-not, if-there-is-nothing, for-there-is-for-there-is-not, for-there-is-nothing
14. other-words, some-other-words, in-some-other-words, in-other-words, some-ways, in-some-other-ways
15. my-dear-sir, very-dear-sir, my-dear-friend, very-dear-friend, dear-Miss-Smith, my-dear-Miss-Smith, my-very-dear-Miss-Smith
16. out-of, out-of-there, which-have, which-have-there, set-of, set-of-their, state-of, state-of-their, sight-of, sight-of-their
17. I-shall-be-there, she-will-be-there, they-will-be-there, I-shall-not-be-there, they-will-not-be-there, he-will-not-be-there, let-us-be-there, if-you-can-be-there
18. finer-than, finer-than-their, higher-than, higher-than-their, larger-than, larger-than-their, bigger-than, bigger-than-their

Exercise 12A

(a) I-visited my-very-dear-friends the Browns yesterday-evening,[10] and-I-think-there-is-no garden better-than-their[20] garden. There-are many gardens bigger-than-their garden, and[30]-there-are many houses larger-than-their house, but I[40]-do-not-know any home in-which-there-has-been[50] so-much-attention paid to-getting the best out-of[60]-their available space. In-their-own-view the house is[70] better-than-their garden, but in-my-view the garden[80] is better-than-their house, which-is charming but rather[90] cramped. The grounds, however, are perfect. I-was amazed at[100]-the state-of-their lawns at-this dry season of[110]-the-year, but-the Browns tackle-the-matter in-their[120]-own-way, and-they-have little jets of-water that[130] periodically sprinkle-their lawns. In-spite-of our having-had[140] no rain for weeks the flower-beds were a riot[150] of-colour. I-was reminded of-Kew Gardens. Have-you[160] been-there this season? I-was recently-there, and-I[170]-found everything very lovely.   (174)

* * *

(b) My-dear-Sir, I-have submitted your samples to-some[10] experts for-their advice, and-they state-that in-their[20]-view you-are asking for-your goods more-than-their[30] true worth. I-know-there-is a good-deal of[40] work in-the-manufacture of-the articles, but in-other[50]-ways the costs are small.

I-shall-therefore be grateful[60] if-you-will let-me-know whether you-can quote[70] a reduced price. If-you-cannot I-shall-be-obliged[80] to-satisfy my-requirements by-some-other-means, and-I[90]-am today writing to-other manufacturers asking for details of[100]-the range-of-their products. I-think-there-is, therefore,[110] every chance of-our purchasing from-some-other manufacturer in[120]-the-circumstances. Yours-faithfully,   (124)

Exercise 12B

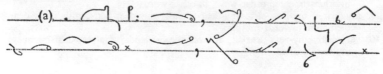
(a)

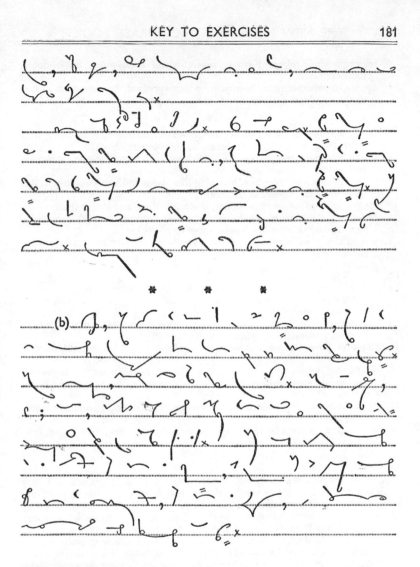

Facility Drill 13

1. were, you-were, if-you-were, if-you-were-not, they-were, and-they-were-not, we-were, if-we-were
2. world, this-world, in-this-world, in-the-world, throughout-the-world, all-over-the-world
3. war, during-the-war, after-the-war, before-the-war, throughout-the-war, if-there-is-war
4. per, per-day, per-head, per-ton, per-pound, per-cent, per-annum, Sir-James, yes-sir

5. telegraph-wire, telegraph-wires, several-wires, these-wires, out-of-doors, indoors
6. appear, it-would-appear, to-appear, which-appeared, in-some-parts-of-the-world, in-all-parts-of-the-world, in-various-parts-of-the-world

     ❋   ❋   ❋

7. let-us, let-us-have, please-let-us-have, let-us-know, please-let-us-know, this-letter, those-letters, business-letter, business-letters, for-sale
8. somewhere-else, everywhere-else, nowhere-else, anywhere-else, less-than, no-less-than, any-less-than
9. something-like, nothing-like, anything-like, I-would-like, I-would-not-like, we-would-like, we-would-not-like
10. longer-than, no-longer, any-longer, no-longer-than, any-longer-than
11. this-week, these-weeks, next-week, last-week, previous-week, few-weeks, past-few-weeks, next-few-weeks, for-several-weeks
12. you-will, you-will-remember, I-will, I-will-not-be, I-know-that-he-will-be, so-well, very-well, as-well-as, as-will-be-seen, as-we-know

     ❋   ❋   ❋

13. in-the-house, if-the-house, to-the-house, in-this-house, in-the-House-of-Commons, I-hope, I-hope-that, I-hope-there-is, I-hope-there-is-not, we-hope, we-hope-that-you-will
14. what-has-happened, what-is-happening, at-home, per-head, to-him, of-him, for-him, to-himself, for-himself, to-her
15. you-were, you-were-not, they-were, they-were-not, I-will, I-will-not, we-will, we-will-not
16. would-you, would-not, it-would, it-would-be, it-would-not-be, he-would, she-would, she-would-be-there, I-would-be-there, I-would-not-be-there, they-would-do
17. to-let-me-know, to-let-us-know, your-letter, two-letters, this-letter, these-letters, all-these-letters
18. week's-time, six-weeks'-time, several-weeks'-time, next-week, next-few-weeks, this-week, last-week

Exercise 13A

(a) First I-would-like-to-say-that I-hope-you[10]-will all be-pleased with-the-proposed dividend of 6[20] per-cent. Before-the-war we-were-able-to pay[30] as-much-as 13 per-cent for-several-years in[40]-succession. This-is no-longer possible. During-the-war the[50] dividend fell to only 2 per-cent but after-the[60]-war our position gradually improved, and-the dividend of 6[70] per-cent proposed today is-the highest paid since-the[80]-war. I-hope-there-is no-one here this-afternoon[90] who-will-not feel that-we-have-done very-well[100] to-reach this-position. I-do-not-think-there-is[110] any-longer any-need for-us to-be pessimistic about[120]-the prospects of-trade in-this-country or in-the[130]-world generally. There-are many-signs that trade throughout-the[140]-world is expanding in a remarkable-way. Many new types[150] of-product are offered for-sale, and-only last-week[160] I-was informed-that a new and quite revolutionary fibre[170] is-to-be-placed on-the-world market within-the[180]-next-few-weeks. (183)

     ❋   ❋   ❋

(b) Dear-Sir-James, We-thank-you for-your-inquiry, and[10]-we-have-the-pleasure to enclose a brochure which[20]-will give-you full details of-the latest fertilizer produced[20] by-this-House. We-would-like-to-mention that-this[40] fertilizer can-be obtained nowhere-else-in-the-world, and[50] that indeed there-is-nothing-like it anywhere-else so[60]-far-as-we-are aware. The fertilizer is of-great[70] strength and-efficacy, and our estimate is-that for crops[80] of-the-size you-mention you-will-not need more[90]-than 30 pounds of-it per-annum. The cost is[100] low at £3 per-pound. You-will-see from[110]-the directions that a small application per-day for-several[120]-weeks is likely to-have a better effect than one[130] large application, but-you-will-find either method very-satisfactory.[140] If-you-will let-us-know your needs we-will[150] let-you-have-the fertilizer immediately, and-we-hope-you[160]-will let-us-have-your opinion of-it at-the[170]-end of-the-season. Yours-truly, (176)

Exercise 13B

(a)

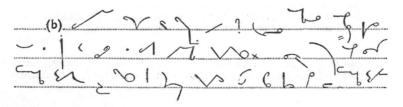

(b)

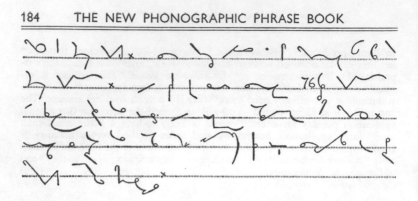

Facility Drill 14

1. in-control, I-am-in-control, you-will-control, It-is-controlled, unable-to-control, we-are-unable-to-control, can-you-control-the
2. in-the-contract, another-(in-their)-contract, in-this-contract, we-have-contracted, no-contractions, use-the-contractions, useful-contractions
3. this-competition, your-competition, unfair-competition, overseas-competition, we-must-compete, we-have-competed, we-cannot-compete, you-are-competing
4. we-must-complete-the, we-have-completed, It-is-completed, in-completion, in-contemplation, if-he-completes, are-you-completing, it-has-been-completed
5. in-connexion-(with), no-connexion-(with), no-connexions, you-should-control, on-the-committees, he-should-contact, if-the-committee, on-the-Continent, several-continents
6. it-is-considered, take-into-consideration, we-may-consider, you-may-consider, we-have-concluded, we-have-come-to-the-conclusion, come-to-the-conclusion, to-come-to-the-conclusion

* * *

7. your-ability, your-abilities, our-ability, their-abilities, these-abilities, best-of-my-ability, best-of-your-ability, best-of-their-ability, best-of-our-ability
8. in-reality, no-reality, there-is-no-reality, can-there-be-reality, to-face-reality, it-is-not-logical, if-we-are-logical, it-would-not-be-logical, they-are-not-logical
9. your-mentality, their-mentality, poor-mentality, high-mentality, low-mentality, of-this-mentality, undeveloped-mentality, well-developed-mentality
10. your-ships, our-ships, this-ship, these-ships, board-ship, several-ships, some-ships, for-shipment, last-shipment, several-shipments
11. in-the-fullness-of-time, some-yards, two-yards, many-yards, how-many-yards, several-yards, dozen-yards, half-a-dozen-yards
12. we-are-controlling-the-competition, we-shall-complete-the-contract, we-shall-consider-the-conclusion, we-may-consider-the-conclusions

* * *

13. they-consider-the, there-is-no-comfort, we-have-no-commitments, some-considerable-time, very-considerable-time, I-considered, I-considered-the-matter

14. no-connexion-(with), no-connexions, there-is-no-connexion-(with), these-connexions, it-is-connected, we-are-not-connected, in-contact
15. income, income-tax, income-tax-commitments, income-tax-control, clear-conscience, clear-consciences
16. we-have-no-ability, they-have-no-ability, your-ability, their-ability, best-abilities, poor-abilities, improve-the-ability, cultivate-the-ability
17. poor-shipment, poor-shipments, fine-shipment, large-shipment, large-ship-ments, small-shipment, small-shipments, big-shipment, big-shipments
18. we-have-yards, we-have-several-yards, dozen-yards, half-a-dozen-yards, some-yards, many-yards, two-yards

Exercise 14A

(a) Dear-Sirs, We-thank-you for-your-letter of-the[10] 1st May but-we-are-compelled to inform-you that[20]-we-cannot-control-the activities of-our-competitors. As you[30]-are-aware, there-is-no central-control in-this-connexion[40] and-all traders may freely-compete, using whatever means they[50]-consider most-likely to benefit themselves. In-reality, of-course,[60] they-constantly fail to benefit as-they enter-into-contracts[70] that-they cannot-continue to honour, and many-concerns go[90] bankrupt. If-the-concerns which-are-now-competing would form[90] a combination to control-the terms of-trade and to[100]-co-operate for-the-common good, we-consider-that such-combination[110] would-be useful. So-far, however, all attempts at-combination[120] have failed, as-the traders have-commitments for-some-considerable[130]-time ahead, and-they-have-been unable-to-agree on[140] a date when-such-commitments shall cease and-the-combination[150] come into-effect.

We-are-completely in-agreement with your[160]-comments, however, and-we-shall to-the best-of-our[170]-ability-consider what steps can-be-taken to-improve-matters.[180] Yours-faithfully, (182)

* * *

(b) Considering-the-combination of-circumstances that-have operated against the[10] interests of-this-concern throughout-the past-few-months, there[20]-are very-considerable grounds for-satisfaction. When-the-year-concluded[30] we-were-able-to show a profit of-some £57,000,[40] and-we-had several large-shipments pending.[50] We-are-not-conscious of any slackening in trade, and[60] it-seems-logical, therefore, to conclude that-we-shall-continue[70] to operate on-the most-completely satisfactory basis in-the[80] coming-months. The conclusion is further justified when-it-is[90]-considered that-we-have-no serious-commitments involving large-sums[100]-of-money. Uncontrolled expenditure upon expansion is prevalent just-now,[110] and-this-combined with lack-of-control of-credit to[120]-customers has endangered-the stability of-many-concerns. In-conclusion[130] I-must-say-that we-consider-the interests of-the[140] shareholders at-all-times. (144)

Exercise 14B

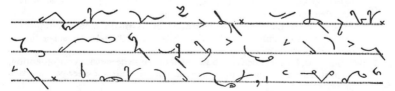

Facility Drill 15

1. political-party, political-parties, party-organization, party-leaders, life policy, cheap-money-policy, fiscal-policy, Professor-of-Chemistry, Superintendent-of-the-Line, capital-punishment
2. to-make-application, formal-application, Bank-of-England, commercial-banks, Treasury-bills, bill-of-lading, Thames-Embankment, sea-embankment, Bank-of-London
3. new-business, business-activity, business-letter, business-man, your-attention, your-attention-to-the-matter, close-attention, atomic-energy, atomic-power-plant

4. department-store, several-departments, Department-of-Commerce, com-mercial-department, lower-charges, increased-charges, free-of-charge, in-charge, Chancery-appeal, weekly-journal, Journal-of-Commerce
5. in-your-company, trading-companies, this-company, Urban-Council, Dis-trict-Council, County-Councils, issued-capital, issued-capital-of-the-com-pany, capital-expenditure, Captain Blythe, captain-of-the-ship
6. Smith-&-Co.,-Ltd., Mercantile-Co.,-Ltd., New-York-Corporation, Rubber-Corporation, Colonel-Johnson, government-orders, official-of-the-Govern-ment, French-Government, this-government, at-the-beginning

❋   ❋   ❋

7. several-forms, form-of-application, entry-forms, it-was-formed, to-call-forth, issue-forth, put-forth, set-forth, high-valuation, low-valuation, agents'-valuation
8. is-it-convenient, at-your-convenience, early-convenience, if-it-is-not-con-venient, local-authorities, to-claim-authority, some-authorities, Educa-tion-Authorities
9. for-several-months, five-months, past-few-months, this-month, next-month, six-months, three-months, three-months'-time, two-months
10. in-this-society, in-our-society, Commercial-Society, Teachers'-Society, Shorthand-Writers'-Society, life-assurance, new-assurance, trade-marks, water-marks, dirty-marks
11. Major-Williams, Major-Butler, tomorrow-morning, yesterday-morning, national-affair, national-interests, if-you-will-inquire, for-your-inquiry
12. similar-letters, similar-documents, your-communication, further-communi-cation, for-your-communication, motor-car-insurance, this-insurance

❋   ❋   ❋

13. liberal-measures, liberal-payments, Liberal-Party, Smith-&-Co.,-Ltd., West-minster-Co.,-Ltd., your-requirements, these-requirements, what-do-you-require, if-you-require
14. will-you-arrange, it-has-been-arranged, what-are-the-arrangements, excel-lent-arrangements, British-Railways, railway-nationalization, local-requirements, Conservative-Party, conservative-measures
15. will-you-kindly, if-you-will-kindly, if-you-will-kindly-let-us-have, we-have-already-seen, I-have-already-said, for-your-purpose, for-this-purpose, for-several-purposes
16. Royal-family, Royal-Charter, no-alternative, your-alternative, in-the-House-of-Commons, to-the-House-of-Commons, House-of-Commons, vote-of-thanks
17. South-America, North-and-South-America, limited-liability-company, in-pursuance (of), in-pursuance-of-the-policy, alternating-current, direct-current, resistance-coil
18. at-right-angles, best-of-my-recollection, best-of-our-recollection, Surveyor-of-Taxes, Surveyor-of-Roads, rank-and-file, from-time-immemorial, free-of-general-average

Exercise 15A

(a) Dear-Sirs, We-thank-you for-your-inquiry and-for[10]-your-application for a book of-order-forms. We-wish[20] to-draw-your-attention to-the offer made at-the[30]-beginning of-the book. For-the next six-months we[40]-shall supply free-of-charge one dozen packets of-our[50] Bubble Soap Powder to all retailers who order at-least[60] one gross. The retention of-this liberal-offer depends upon[70] our customers' meeting-bills promptly as credit facilities must-be[80]-limited. We-shall-be happy to-receive at-your-early[90]-convenience your-completed order-forms. We-can promise you prompt[100]-attention, and-we-shall at-all-times deal-with your[110]-requirements to-the best-of-our-ability. Yours-faithfully, Worth[120]-&-Co.,-Ltd.   (123)

✳   ✳   ✳

(b) Yesterday-morning it-was stated that-it-was expected that[10]-the Liberal-Party would-have a much better position in[20]-the-House-of-Commons in-the near-future than has[30]-been-the case for-some-months. The Conservative-Party is[40] still in a strong-position but it-is expected-that[50]-the Liberal-Party will-be-able-to call-forth-considerable[60] support from-the middle-classes who dislike-the taxation-policy[70] of-the Conservative-Government but who equally dislike-the nationalization[80]-policy of-the Labour-Party. Some-authorities-consider-that-the[90] Conservative-Party will-continue to-be-the leading political-party[100] with about three-hundred seats but-that-the Labour-Party[110] and-the Liberal-Party together could bring-down-the-Government.[120] It-is-not-considered very-likely, however, that-the official[130]-policy of-the Liberal-Party would-be to-unite with[140]-the Labour-Party. Their-policy is more-likely to-be[150] to-take an independent line.

It-is-certain-that-the[160] business-man will watch events with close-attention during-the[170]-next-few-months as what happens in-the-House-of[180]-Commons, particularly in-regard-to taxation-charges and-the monetary[190]-policy generally, is bound to-affect his business-activities and[200]-his business-dealings generally. Business-men would really like to[210]-be left alone to-run-their-businesses in-their-own[220]-way, and it-is-likely that-they-would indeed really[230] prefer to see no-party with a really powerful majority[240] and-with a specific-policy.   (245)

Exercise 15B

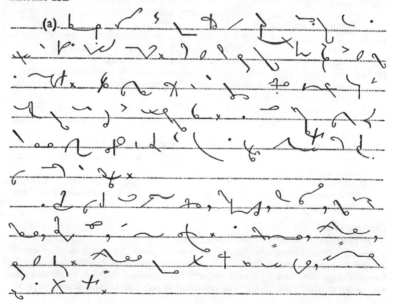

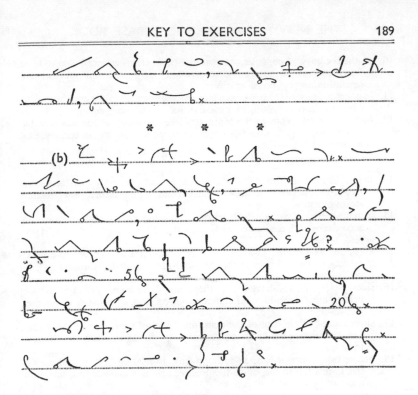

Facility Drill 16

1. last-week, last-month, just-received, most-probable, almost-certainly, must-be, it-must-be, it-must-not-be, it-must-be-there
2. very-pleased-indeed, we-are-very-pleased-indeed, industrial-life, animal-life, hardly-likely, telegraph-office, satisfactory-results, Prime-Minister
3. some-measures, most-measures, I-have-received, we-have-received, in-reply-(to), in-receipt-of, we-are-in-receipt-of, in-other-respects, worth-while
4. on-the-other, on-the-other-side, on-the-other-hand, any-other, no-other, to-look-forward, backwards-and-forwards, carry-forward, in-this-direction
5. Home-Secretary, Foreign-Secretary, one-thing, one-another, one-way, between-them, station-master, telegraph-wire
6. great-expense, large-expenses, heavy-expenses, take-exception, to-take-exception, personal-experience, personal-experiences, I-am-extremely-sorry

* * *

7. in-fact, as-a-matter-of-fact, another-fact, in-this-manner, in-the-manner, in-like-manner, in-such-a-manner
8. in-regard-(to), in-regard-to-the, having-regard-(to), having-regard-to-the, with-regard-(to), with-regard-to-the, as-regards, as-regards-the-matter
9. we-hope, we-hope-you-will, it-will-be, they-will-not-be-there, so-well, very-well, this-week, next-week, last-week

10. on-the-contrary, I-consider, to-consider-the-matter, cannot-be-considered, for-consideration, for-your-consideration, fully-considered, further-consideration, to-give-consideration

11. in-conclusion, satisfactory-conclusion, we-have-come-to-the-conclusion, to-come-to-the-conclusion, we-have-concluded, necessary-conclusion

12. I-am-instructed, your-instructions, enclose-herewith, as-soon-as-possible, as-well-as-possible, if-it-is-possible, as-much-as-possible, in-consequence, in-consequence-of-the

*   *   *

13. British-Empire, British-Association, Her-Majesty, Her-Majesty-the-Queen, Act-of-Parliament, Member-of-Parliament, high-pressure, low-pressure, steam-pressure

14. technical-terms, technical-education, I-am-requested-to-inform-you, in-accordance-with-the, in-connexion-(with), in-connexion-with-the, I-am-also, I-must-also

15. as-a-rule, as-a-result, at-a-loss, in-a-few-days, for-a-moment, to-a-great-extent, ladies-and-gentlemen, Mr.-and-Mrs., round-and-round, again-and-again

16. side-by-side, it-must-have-been, there-must-have-been, would-have-been, bear-in-mind, keep-in-mind, difference-of-opinion, as-a-matter-of-opinion, loss-of-life

17. short-space-of-time, out-of-the-question, point-of-view, fact-of-the-matter, notwithstanding-the-fact, on-the-subject, during-the-year, in-the-first-instance

18. one-or-two, more-or-less, in-addition-(to), in-relation-(to), in-addition-to-the, in-relation-to-the, up-to-the-present, neither-more-nor-less, take-into-account

Exercise 16A

(a) Dear-Sirs, In-accordance-with your-request we-send-you[10]-herewith samples of-our goods for-your-consideration, and-we[20]-trust-that-they-will reach-you safely. As-we-have[30]-just-received from-the manufacturers some new products with-which[40]-we-are-very-pleased-indeed, we-enclose-herewith samples of[50]-these also. The manufacturers state that-it-is just-possible[60] that-these new products will-be put on-the-market[70] for-sale to-the public next-month and-that-they[80]-are taking every-possible means to-expedite full production. As[90]-a-matter-of-fact, in-reply-to a request from[100]-us asking to-be informed of-the-most-probable date[110] of-delivery, we-have-received information that-it-is almost[120]-certain-that-the goods will-be in-full supply by[130]-the end of-this-month.   Having-regard-to-this, we[140]-consider-that it-would-be worth-while for-you to[150]-place an order with-us now for-the new product.[160] Will-you-please give-consideration to-the-matter and let[170]-us-have your-instructions as-soon-as-possible. Yours-faithfully,

(180)

*   *   *

(b) In-the-first-place I-wish to-draw-your-attention[10]-to-the-fact that-the-prices of all-the-materials[20] we-use have become higher-and-higher in recent-months,[30] and at-the-present-time they-are double what they[40]-were six-months-ago. In-the-second-place, labour-costs[50] also rise higher-and-higher, and-the number-of hours[60] worked grows less-and-less. To-a-great-extent this[70]-is a necessary-consequence of-present-day trends. Notwithstanding-the[80]-fact that rates-of-pay are excellent people have a[90] greater appreciation of-leisure. For-the-first-time in-their[100] history the working-classes can afford to buy leisure, and[110]-they-are-not at-a-loss for-ways of-using[120]-it. In-the-next-place, we-are face-to-face[130] with ever-growing-competition. Having-regard-to all-this, we[140]-have-found it necessary to-consider-the position very-carefully,[150] and-for-the-first-time for twenty years we-are[160]-considering a complete change in-our structure, and details of[170]-this change will-be put before-you in-a-few[180]-days' time.

(182)

Exercise 16B

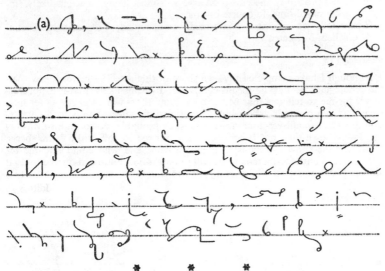

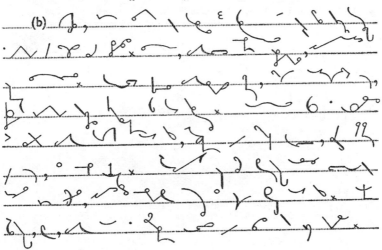

Facility Drill 17

1. at-last, at-least, by-any-means, by-no-means, for-those, for-those-who, for-this, for-these, to-him
2. I-may-be, can-be, could-be, I-regard, I-regret, we-regard, we-regret, if-there-is, for-there-is
3. your-own, her-own, their-own, his-own, my-own, in-my-own-time, in-my-own-way, in-many-ways
4. it-is-unnatural, it-is-inconvenient, it-is-unknown, it-is-unnecessary, it-is-unfinished, very-much, so-much, too-much
5. it-is-most-probable, it-seems-probable, it-is-most-likely, it-seems-likely, in-the-course-of-time, in-course-of-time
6. I-expected, we-inspected, I-informed, we-informed, I-represented, I-relinquished, I-objected

Exercise 17A

Although I-have-completed my-own share of-this work[10] I-regret-to-say that-the whole task is by[20]-no-means-complete. It-seems-likely that-it-is-unnecessary[30] for-me to-tell-you that Mr.-Brown found-the[40] work too heavy for-him. I-have written to-him[50] asking-him to-return to-me all-the sheets for[60]-completion but he-has-not-yet-done this. He-will[70]-probably do-so in-his-own-way and-in-his[80]-own-time but it-is-inconvenient for-me to-be[90] without-the sheets. Kindly let-me-know if-there-is[100] anyone at-your end who could help-me for at[110]-least a month for-there-is work still to-be[120]-done, and-I-am-unable-to do it alone. No[130]-doubt all will-be-completed in-course-of-time.   (139)

Exercise 17B

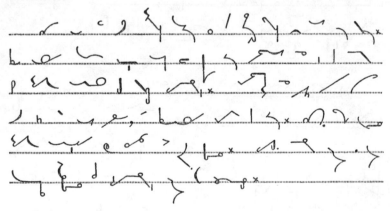

INDEX

"By thunder, sir!" he roared, "I voted for John C. Breckin-ridge, and you shall withdraw your comment, or we shall meet on the field of honor. Right here. Right now." The man had dropped both his spectacles and his dirty handkerchief and had gripped the handle of a big Bowie, looked more like a saber than a knife, belted across his waist.

That room turned real quiet. I forgot all about how heavy that coffee pot was I kept holding.

"I believe, sir," Mr. Reagan said, "that if you are challenging me to a duel, it is customary for me to choose weapons. So you might let go of that toothpick." I hadn't noticed, don't reckon nobody had, but that Indiana man had been eating with his right hand, keeping his left underneath the rough-hewn table, but now he brought up his left hand, which was holding a big-bore boot pistol, aimed at the Mississippian's belly.

That's when I dropped the coffee pot. Nobody seemed to notice, and I just froze there, letting the hot tar Pa brewed soak into the dirt floor.

"You. . . ." The Mississippi man glared.

Mr. Reagan cocked the single-shot pistol, and the Southerner jerked his hand off that knife handle like it was hotter than the coffee I'd just spilt. The Indiana gent didn't lower the cocked .50-caliber, not yet, nohow.

"All I said, sir," Reagan said, "was that the recent election was a godsend for the states, both North and South."

The Mississippi man had to bite back whatever he was think-ing about telling Mr. Reagan.

"Senator Douglas is a good man, but if you had heard one of the debates with President Lincoln a couple of years ago, as I had the honor of doing when, by fate, business took me to Galesburg, you would have had no doubt as to which man is the better candidate. But that Kentucky blow-hard, Breckin-ridge, is an atrocity, sir, and I will not withdraw what I said, respectfully." Slowly he lowered the hammer on the copper percussion cap, but didn't put away the pistol. "You have the floor, sir."

"You don't really know Senator Breckinridge," the Mississippi man said. "He's a good man, loyal, willing to serve his people. Not just Northern people, but *his* people."

"He never should have agreed to run, not on the terms you Southrons demanded. But you are correct. I do not know Senator Breckinridge. I know, however, what he stands for. Or, rather, what you fire-eaters stand for."

"You're a da- Abolitionist," the Mississippi man said. "Just like your Mr. Lincoln."

" 'Not an Abolitionist, hardly an anti-slavery man.' Those are the words from Wendell Phillips, an outspoken Abolitionist, about our new President. Nor am I. I am merely a humble Hoosier who fought in the war against Mexico, and who cherishes all about this nation. Mr. Phillips went on to say perhaps Lincoln is a 'pawn on the political chessboard.' I think he is far from that, but a great man, a great leader. I do not hold with slavery. But it's the South's institution, so let the South deal with it. Yet I will not see this blight of yours spread across the continent."

The Southern man tried to stand taller. "The South will deal with it, as we shall deal with you despots if you force our hand. Mayhap you already have. That farce of an election was just what we needed."

"You should remember Mr. Lincoln's words . . . 'A house divided against itself cannot stand.' "

"You Northerners have forced us into this. Remember that when the streets of Pennsylvania Avenue are 10 feet deep with blood, gore, and the mangled bodies of Northern dead. You shall see who wins your game of chess."

"Then it's your move, sir."

Well, I was sweating, and the Mississippi man started reaching for his knife, while the Hoosier gent again thumbed back the hammer on that cannon of a little pistol. That's when Pa walked in.

"If you're stumping, do it outside. This ain't Charleston. This ain't Washington City. And here's the law at Soldier's Farewell." Pa pointed at the coffee pot. "Both of you are paying extra for that."

One hand moved away from the Bowie knife, and the boot pistol finally returned to its home.

Pa's a big man. Powerful as a Missouri mule. One time, Marco Max said of him to me: "Your pa's the onliest man I know who can lift a Celerity wagon off the ground . . . while he's standing atop it."

Both the Indiana man and the Southerner fished out a coin from their vests, and dropped them on the table in front of their bowls.

"I'd put a muzzle on any political debates," Pa told them. "It's a long way to California. Now get out. Stage leaves in 5 minutes."

December 9, 1860

Abraham Lincoln got elected president of our nation back on Tuesday, November 6. I guess I should have knowed that before now, but I never had much interest in those kinds of things, not like I got in the stories of Mr. Dumas and Mr. Dickens and, especially, Mr. Scott. Stories, I like a whole lot. There's some good stories in the Bible, too.

Other than the Bible, we only own four books, not counting a couple of readers we brung from Missouri, along with two dictionaries—Noah Webster's American Dictionary of the English Language from 1852 and the Pronouncing Germany Dictionary, which Pa bought back in Missouri because there was so many Dutchies moving in that country and bartering for his mules, but we haven't had much need of such a book here at Soldier's Farewell. I've read the novels I don't know how many times. Julian, when he was passing through here two years ago, promised he'd send along some Shakespeare, but he ain't done it yet. But I can read *The Three Musketeers, Ivanhoe, The Adventures of Oliver Twist* and *The Yemassee* by William Gilmore Simms. Pa says Ma enjoyed that Simms fellow a lot, but I like Scott the best of all. And Pa makes me read the Bible. Says it's for Ma.

I'm not even sure who was President before him, but I think it must have been Andrew Jackson, because I've heard his name bandied around a lot. Anyway, from all I've heard recently, I'm not sure this President Lincoln is that popular. Mr. Reagan from Indiana, and the man with the glasses from Mississippi ain't the only passengers I've heard debating the elections, the prospects for war, the North, the South, Abolition and slavery.

The South is threatening to abolish the Union. That's what dominated most of the talk at supper tonight on the Westbound.

"If that happens, there will be war, sure enough," said a man in a silk hat.

"Won't last long," commented another, a tobacco chewer who spit oftener than anyone I ever seen. The talked civil, though, so I wasn't afraid that they might slash or shoot one another.

December 10, 1860
Where should I stand on all this talk about war, about the North and the South? Not even sure what I am. I mean, my family hails from South Carolina, and lived in Mississippi for a spell. That's South, and, from what I've heard in passing, those two states are the biggest talkers about quitting the Union, and preaching war, the rights of the individual states, things like

that. I wonder what Senator Davis and Senator Hampton are saying back in Washington. Wonder where Pa stands in this thing.

I'm a Missourian. I guess I am. Was born there, anyhow. But for the life of me, I can't figure out if Missouri is for the North or for the South. Slavery's a big part of the talk, but I hear more talk about the rights of the states, and the necessity that the Union survives, even if it costs lives. I saw a few slaves in Missouri, but Pa never did own none, and he ain't never talked about any rights, states or nothing.

It don't always even seem to be about the North and the South. A while back, these two gents from Ohio, which I'm right sure is in the North, was talking about this coming war, and the guy from Columbus was arguing one way, and the man from Cincinnati another. The Columbus fellow called the Cincinnati gent a "doughface"—which Marco Max explained to me later is what they call a Northern man who has sympathies for the South.

Big changes. Pa often says that change is one thing that a body has to realize is going to happen. And this family has been through plenty of changes, what with us moving first to Mississippi, then to Boone County, and finally the Territory. What with Ma dying like she done. What with Julian going off to West Point and now in California.

"Everything changes," Pa said, "except the wind and dust blowing."

Changes with the Overland Mail Company, too. Back in March of this year, John Butterfield had to quit the company he started. Seems he owed a passel of money to this Wells, Fargo, & Company, which is what's running the Overland now. That wasn't no real change, I warrant. After all, here at Soldier's Farewell, things seem about the same. I never considered Mr. Butterfield the boss of this operation. Land's sake, he ain't never been west of Fort Smith, Arkansas, from what I've heard, and I don't think Mr. Wells or Mr. Fargo runs things, neither. Nor Superintendent Hawley over in Tucson. At Soldier's Farewell, Pa's the boss.

Everybody knows it, too.

December 11, 1860

Rained today. Think it might be snowing in the mountains higher up north of here.

December 15, 1860

It finally happened. Fletcher said he seen it coming. Only I had no idea. Emmett Mills, who come by just to visit and bring some news to Pa from Cooke's Spring, he and Ben Jakes got into fisticuffs this afternoon. They was arguing about the war— like the war has already begun—and pretty soon they was trading blows. Emmett's a Union man. Ben Jakes is a Texican. North and South. Well, Ben Jakes threw the first punch, but that's about all he got to do because one thing I learned today is you never want to get Emmett Mills riled up. Beat the tar out of Mr. Jakes, he did. Might could have killed him if Pa hadn't stepped in, and sent Emmett a-sprawling. You also don't want Pa riled up.

December 16, 1860

Snowed. First time I've seen snow since Missouri, even if it was just a dusting. I finally got around to asking Pa about this war, and where we should stand if the fight come to us.

He didn't answer for a long time.

"Don't fret over that, Smith," he finally told me. "We're in New Mexico Territory, more than 1,000 miles from those fire-eaters. War, if there is a war, will not touch us."

But it already has.

That's what I wanted to tell Pa, thinking about that fellow from Mississippi and Mr. Reagan from Indiana. Closer than them two, just yesterday, it come to us, touched us, when Emmett and Ben Jakes had their row. But I just told Pa: "Yes, sir."

December 19, 1860

Been a trifle busy. Snow's all gone, but the wind ain't slowed down even a bit. Tonight, feeding the folks on the Westbound, this rich-looking gent from the California gold fields asked if we always seasoned our stew with dirt, instead of salt.

If he thought his supper was full of dirt, he should have sampled breakfast this morning.

Another man asked if it was possible somewhere along the Overland to have a fried egg. And that got me to thinking when was the last time I'd even seen an egg. Or even a chicken. By jingo, I don't reckon I've even spied nary a quail's nest to rob since we left the States.

Going to bed hungry, dreaming of something to eat other than slumgullion or bread that does its best to break your teeth.

December 20, 1860

Trouble. Bad trouble. Apaches run off about a dozen mules. Including Sweet Ainsley!

December 21, 1860

Eastbound come through. Pa ain't here. Went off yesterday to get the mules. No time to write.

December 22, 1860

No word from Pa.

December 23, 1860

Pa still ain't back. Hope he ain't dead. Praying he ain't dead.

Give Marco Max a letter to leave at Fort Tejon for Julian, explaining that Pa's off chasing Apaches.

December 24, 1860

Snowing again. On Christmas Eve. Should be singing carols or reading the Bible or something. But reckon I'll write.

Back on Thursday morn, we discovered the missing mules, and Pa was inclined to stove in Ben Jakes's head with a single-tree. Jakes—I ain't calling him Mr., not now, not after what he done—swore he wasn't asleep when he was supposed to be standing watch, but nobody believes him. Jakes is lucky the Apaches didn't slit his throat.

Well, we had enough mules for the Eastbound the next day, and I reckon the Missouri mules we stock on this part of the Overland is all tough enough to make it down the pike to the next station. Shucks, when the mail first started running back in '58, there wasn't no station betwixt Soldier's Farewell and Stein's. Them first stages had to go 42 miles west without water, but now there's Barney's Station.

Things could have been a lot worser. If them Indians had taken all of our livestock, we'd all be afoot. Nice of them to leave us some mules, and, especially, all of Pa's prime breeding stock.

We sent word east and west down the trail and over to *Señor* Vee, who come quick with a musket and a double-action Adams .36, and I hadn't never seen him with no pistol before. Wearing a brace of Colts and carrying his Mississippi Rifle, Pa said he was going after those thieves, and *Señor* Vee said he expected that, and that he was more than a fair hand at following a trail, even a trail left by Apaches. I quickly yelled that I'd be coming too, that no dirty Indian was going to steal my brother's mule, but Pa wouldn't let me come along.

Said I was too little.

I about to cried. That surely hurt my feelings, and I was about to argue with Pa, but he wasn't in no mood for arguing. Emmett Mills come along directly, said he'd be joining the party, and Mr. Barney sent along a fellow named Cooper. Pa threw a saddle on a big mule he calls Boss.

Reckon if Apaches was any judge of mule flesh they would have taken Boss with them. Boss was sired by a big old black Mammoth Jack, with a Percheron mare as the dam. Boss stands better than 16 hands tall and weighs about 1,400 pounds. Mule like that could have fed a whole Apache *rancheria*.

That makes me sick. Thinking how them Indians might have already eaten Sweet Ainsley.

Same day, after supper
Ain't sure of the time. Pa taken his watch with him. Still ain't back yet. *Señora* Dolores come along this evening with Alyvia and Tori, and even Tori was on good behavior. I bet her ma warned her not to act foolish or rotten what with all the stuff that has been going on.

She brung along supper. Wasn't hungry. Still worried about Pa.

Pa up and left Fletcher in charge whilst he's gone. And right before he rode off, he pointed a big finger at Ben Jakes and said any mule that wasn't returned would be coming out of that scalawag's pay. And if Sweet Ainsley wasn't returned. . . .

Well, Pa didn't finish that threat. Don't reckon he had to.

Surprised Ben Jakes ain't run off yet.

Señora Dolores left after supper. Took the girls with her. I thought they might stay this time, what with Apaches in the area and all, but they didn't. Just don't like this place after dark. She wished me a fine Christmas, said she'd come back tomorrow, and told me not to worry about Pa or her husband.

I told her I wasn't worried at all. Pa and *Señor* Vee knowed how to take care of themselves.

Lying, of course. Is that a bigger sin to lie on Christmas Eve? Hope Pa ain't dead.

December 25, 1860

Christmas. Eastbound come through almost three hours late. Pa would have raised Cain over that.

Bad worried.

December 26, 1860

Tomorrow it will be a week since Pa took off chasing the Apaches. A rider come through this afternoon, and when I seen him, I thought it might be Julian. But it was just some Mexican. Fletcher asked if he'd seen any sign of anything, but the Mexican said no, hadn't seen nobody hardly since he crossed the border on the Janos Road.

Warned him that Apaches had stolen some mules.

Fed him the last of the slumgullion, and didn't charge him nothing on account it was so near Christmas and he looked like he hadn't eaten since he'd left Janos.

December 27, 1860

Pa ain't back. Ain't none of us much a hand at cooking, and we're trying to figure out what to feed the Westbound when the stage comes through on Sunday. Not to mention what we can eat. Maybe *Señora* Dolores will bring us some chuck. Ain't seen her since Christmas.

Hope she ain't dead, neither.

December 28, 1860

Eastbound come through, late, with a wagon full of passengers. A fellow riding up top yelled down if we had any recent news

44

about South Carolina. Something big must be going on back yonder, but we ain't heard nothing. Nothing from the States. More importantly, nothing from Pa or *Señor* Vee.

December 29, 1860

Pa's back! He's alive. PRAISE GOD!

December 30, 1860

Pa and I wrote us a letter to Julian, which we're sending on the Westbound when it comes tonight, telling him not to fret none from my previous letter, that Pa was alive, that everybody was alive, that he come back with Sweet Ainsley, who the Apaches didn't eat after all, even if they is partial to mule meat.

Well, that was some story Pa told us. I practically cried when I saw him, his face covered with beard and dirt and grime. He give me a big hug, shook Fletcher's hand, even didn't act like he wanted to give Ben Jakes a good thrashing. It was evening when he come in, just before dusk.

"What's for supper?" he asked after he got all the mules— they brung back all but two, no three. I forgot all about Boss, the mule Pa rode out on. "What's for supper?" he asked again.

Bartolomé, Fletcher, and me just stared at our feet.

Same day, 7 o'clock

Pa said *Señor* Vee is a mighty fine tracker. Not that they needed some famous scout to follow the trail the mules and Apaches had left. It looked like, Pa said, those Indians didn't count on being followed.

They must have figured we was all yellow.

Them Apaches sure don't know Pa. Well, they didn't. They sure do now.

The trail led east and a bit north, through this little forest of

yucca, but not along the Overland, and for a while there Pa and
Señor Vee was struck with this gut-wrenching fear, on account it
looked like those Apaches was making a beeline for the
Velásquez place, but right before they hit the creek, which is dry
this time of year, and dry most times of the year, the Apaches
drove the mules down past Little Grandmother Mountain.

That's mighty miserable country. Like most of what they call
mountains down here, Little Grandmother ain't much of a hill,
and Grandmother Mountain, southwest of the little one, don't
rise a whole lot higher, and neither one's a real mountain, just
what they call a collection of plugs and flows. Looks like a cone,
both of them mountains. The wind kept blowing, and it a bitterly cold wind, too. Pa called it "a vengeful, Old Testament
wind" when he was telling us the story, his eyes shining and
him having a great time with his belly full off some of the mescal Mr. Fletcher had bought off some drummer a while back.

Not much for mules to graze on down there. About all that
grows is creosote and tarbush, and nary a thimble of water to
be had. They come upon a lava flow, and that's where they
found the carcass of the first mule. Wasn't one of them we'd
brung from Missouri, but a good brown jenny some other mule
man had sold Mr. Butterfield.

The poor animal had broke a leg, so the Apaches had
butchered her and had a veritable feast. The Indians had left
some meat behind, and it hadn't quite spoiled yet, it being so
cold and all, so *Señor* Vee cut off some meat, and they ate supper that night in that lava flow.

"First time I've ever had mule," Pa said. "Not bad to eat.
Apaches are fair smart, I've learned."

By then, Pa was in his cups pretty fair.

Well, from that old lava flow, the trail pretty much dried up,
and Pa said he didn't have an inkling how *Señor* Vee knowed
where to go. But they followed him. It was then, while Pa was

telling this story, that Bartolomé asked *Señor* Vee how he knew which way the Apaches was going when they wasn't leaving no trail.

"They left sign," he said real soft-like, grinning and pointing at his dark eyes. "You just have to be able to see it."

"You saw it, Alejondro," Pa told him. "Because we found some apples the next day and knew we were right behind those Apaches."

From there, the trail turned south and west, through some of the roughest draws a body's ever seen, and into the Cedar Mountains. That's another bad name. Makes me think the folks who give places in this territory names are the worst grafters this side of St. Louis. Cedars! You won't find a cedar in those mountains, not even many junipers.

What Pa and the men found was the Apaches.

"Those mountains are like a fort," Pa said. "Steep, mean cañons. I thought we'd be rubbed out, because that country is just prime for an ambush. We were out of the wind, though, cold as it was, I still found myself drenched with sweat. That's when I saw the savage."

"Chiricahua," *Señor* Vee said. *"Muy mal."*

The Apache, who said his name was Dasoda-hae, sat atop a big black pony, and he was a mean-looking Indian with a dark face peppered with scars, a dirty red bandanna tied around his head. Only wearing moccasins and some deerskin leggings, and this red calico shirt, faded to almost pink, and he come riding, old musket in his hands, barrel pointing skyward. Pa and the others stopped, and Emmett Mills started for his own six-shooter, but Pa told him to hold off.

"They'll kill us," Emmett said.

"They could have killed us an hour ago," Pa said. "This one has come to talk."

So they commenced to have a little parley, with the Apache

talking in bits of Spanish and *Señor* Vee translating what he could for Pa. When they couldn't savvy none of the words, those two would just talk with their hands. Pa said he'd heard about signing with Indians before, but that was the first time he'd ever seen it done.

The Indian, Pa said, looked older than dirt. In his 60s, Pa said, and maybe even older than that. Big chief of the Bedonkohes. Speaking through *Señor* Vee's hands, Pa told the Apache they was supposed to be at peace, but the Apache said that peace had done been broken.

"Tell him who it was, Mr. Munro!" Emmett Mills pleaded with Pa during Pa's storytelling, but we all told Emmett to hush up, enraptured as we was with this report.

Seems like, the way the Apache put it, some miners from around Burchville—that's up in the Pinos Altos region way north of Soldier's Farewell—had attacked the Bedonkohe camp on the Río Mimbres. That wasn't the first time them miners had done that old Apache wrong. Some eight, nine, maybe ten years back, miners had tied that Apache to a tree and whipped him. And Apaches ain't a forgetting or forgiving breed of man.

This time, them miners had killed four of his people, and stolen better than a dozen women and children. So the Apaches was at war.

"Your war is with the miners in the Santa Rita Mountains," Pa told him. "Not the Overland Mail."

Now it was plain that the Apache and *Señor* Vee had little use for one another, but the Chiricahua was an honorable man. That's what Pa said. Honorable. I never heard nobody call no Indian that before.

"He wanted to trade," Pa said. "We had us a little truce now. The Apache said mules were good, but a lot of trouble, so he was willing to trade. At first, I told him I wasn't about to trade for mules I owned."

The Apache grinned. "You do not own them," he said. I ain't sure if he said this in the Mexican lingo or with his hands. "I do."

"They belong to the Overland Mail Company, most of them." The other Apaches, about four or five, from what Pa could see, had paraded the stolen mules out for Pa and his posse to see. "The Tobiano belongs to me."

"They belong to me," the Apache said. "I stole them."

Well, as big a skinflint as Pa is, he wasn't about to trade for no mules that had been stole from him, and he told the Apache that, but the Indian didn't seem to be bothered. Must have thought it was part of the bartering.

"If you valued those mules," the Apache said, "you would not have let me take them from you. Now, they are mine. But I trade. Or we will fight, the way we fight the miners and all other pale eyes."

Pa said he cussed Ben Jakes a blue streak for letting those mules get stole.

"It's about then that I remembered it was Christmas." Pa was really in his cups by the time he got to this part of his story. I don't think he even knowed he had missed Christmas until he got back to Soldier's Farewell. Since the Apaches was mad at the miners, and not us, I think what Pa remembered in the Cedars was that, if he didn't negotiate some sort of trade, there was going to be shooting. Most likely, Pa and his friends would wind up dead.

That's when it struck me that big black mule Pa had been riding was gone.

"You traded him Boss?" I fired off at him.

Pa just nodded. "I traded him Boss, some Navy tobacco, my saddle, some bacon, coffee, all of our sugar, and Emmett Mills's hat."

"They wanted powder and shot, but we wasn't about to give

them that," Cooper, the man Mr. Barney had sent along, added.

"But Boss . . . ," I started.

"And what gold coin we had on us," Pa said. "And that sorrel jenny that was too noisy, hee-hawing all the time."

I shook my head. "But they was stole. You should have fought them Indians."

"It was Red Sleeves, Smith!" Emmett Mills blurted out. "Mangas Coloradas himself!"

That shut me up. Mangas had to be the biggest Apache among the Chiricahua. For close to 30 years, he had been killing Mexicans, and, from the stories I had heard, the onliest reason he signed a treaty with the United States back in '46 was because we had just whipped the Mexicans in that war Pa had fought in, and old Mangas respected anybody who'd killed off some Mexicans. Only now, them Burchville boys had turned him into an enemy of us whites, too.

"I got Sweet Ainsley back," Pa said. "For Julian."

"And bought us some time, some peace, with Red Sleeves himself," Cooper added.

"Still . . . I mean. . . ." Not rightly sure what I meant.

Pa rose from his chair. "I'm still starved," he said, and shot a long stare at Ben Jakes. "And what we paid to get those mules back will come out of your pay, Jakes. And if it happens again, I'm delivering you to Mangas Coloradas, personally."

Same Evening, 9:15
THE UNION IS DISSOLVED!
More later.

December 31, 1860
Back when I was a little kid of maybe five or six, I remember waking up and wondering if the lead soldiers I'd dreamt that

Julian had give me was for real, or, maybe once or twice, that Ma wasn't really dead at all. But then I'd realize my hopes were forlorn—that's the word Pa used last night—and that, no, I'd just been dreaming. Sometimes, of course, I'd wake up and scoff because the dream had been so stupid I knowed it wasn't true, but oftentimes the dream seemed real and I'd have to think on it and do some considering for a little spell. So when I woke up this morning, the first thing I wondered was if everything I'd heard and witnessed last night had been a dream.

It wasn't.

The Union is dissolved.

Only it ain't really all the Union, I reckon. Just South Carolina left it, although, from what I can gather, South Carolina ain't expected to be lonesome for long. "The Union is dissolved" is what some folks in Charleston wrote to say the state wasn't no part of the United States any more. Seems that a newspaper in Charleston printed those words in big letters with an exclamation mark at the end.

They brung the news on the Westbound last night, and it was all everybody talked about.

If what I heard and remember is correct, on December 20, South Carolina voted in a convention to withdraw from the United States. Voted "unanimously"—meaning that nobody there wanted to remain part of the Union. Last night's passengers, and Marco Max and Little Terry, had first heard rumors of what had happened down in Charleston when they reached Fort Chadbourne in West Texas. "Soldier boys wasn't sure what they would do, wondered what Governor Sam Houston would do down in Austin if it was true," Little Terry said. "Some didn't believe it. Marco, he wouldn't believe it, said it was just a big story."

Only that story got confirmed when they arrived at Franklin about four days later. Bunch of Texicans was firing their pistols

51

into the ceiling at the El Paso Saloon, celebrating as if Texas had quit the Union, not South Carolina. That's what Little Terry also said he witnessed, though he attributed the fandango to "too much tangle-foot."

"I can't believe they actually did it," Marco Max kept saying over and over. "I can't believe those fools would actually secede."

"High time!" Ben Jakes exclaimed. "High time, I say, that the South got herself a divorce. Won't be long before Texas joins her independence-minded sister. Yes, sir. High time."

Well, that Celerity coach was chock-full of folks, and every last one of them had an opinion on South Carolina's actions. One gent said it was an insult, another shouted out: "As Mr. Greeley wrote . . . 'Let them go!' " One man with a Van Dyke beard and well-greased mustache kept trying to say something about Senator John Crittenden's proposed amendment, how it could have prevented all this ruction. I ain't rightly sure what that amendment was, or what an amendment really is, or who this senator is, but it don't really matter because the guy did manage to get a word in that the dad-blasted Congress (he actually used right saltier language than that) had defeated the senator's measure.

"It's war," said a young drummer from Virginia, and then he grinned. "Glad I'll be in Sacramento."

"It might not come to war," the only woman in the coach said hopefully. Then closing her eyes, she said softly: "It mustn't." Her accent sounded like she was from Central Missouri.

"They say we can expect Louisiana and Mississippi to follow South Carolina," a man from St. Louis said. "Alabama and Florida, too."

"And Texas!" Ben Jakes hollered. "Texas and Texicans ain't never held much truck with 'em Yankee tyrants!"

I figured Pa would tell Ben Jakes to keep his trap shut, but he

didn't offer nothing, just let that reprobate have his say, like everyone else was having his or her say, though the lady didn't say much at all.

"And Texas was a republic, stood by herself a long time ago," Ben Jakes went on, as if nobody else knew the history of the Lone Star state. "And we Texicans ain't never been scared of no fight. We'll be right happy to fit as many Yanks as Mr. Lincoln thinks he can throw at us."

The man from St. Louis didn't pay Ben Jakes much mind. "Not sure about Virginia, and other states, I warrant, will wait to see what the Old Dominion does. But mark my words, Missouri will leave the Union, too, and bid a fond farewell."

The lady, her eyes still closed, just shook her head.

They'd been talking a bit about the news since they knew it wasn't false in Franklin, but just a bit on account of the dust in the stagecoach, so Soldier's Farewell was the first chance they really had to speak about all this. Big news, it was. Biggest to hit the territories in a coon's age.

A gent from Ohio called the St. Louis man something, but I couldn't hear what he said because he muttered it, out of respect for the lady in earshot, but it wasn't polite. The St. Louis man didn't hear him, neither, but the Virginia drummer, sitting next to him, turned redder than one of *Señora* Dolores's hottest chiles, so it had to be mighty vulgar. Wish I could have heard what he said.

All this time, I kept shooting glances in Pa's direction after he come in from changing the team of mules, kept hoping that he might have something to opine on the matter, but he didn't opine nothing. Just sipped his coffee, asked Marco Max about the run, asked about Apaches, normal things. He sure didn't act excited like the rest of folks at the station, just went about like it was any other day.

I couldn't believe it. I mean, South Carolina was the state he was born in—at least, that's where I've always figured he entered this world. I know for sure it's where he got married, where he lived for the longest time, and where his friend Wade Hampton was serving as a senator. And now, from what I can gather, South Carolina is an independent sovereign—I heard that word last night, too—country.

Marco Max said again how he never figured South Carolina would go through with what she'd done. Then: "I had hopes." Quietly. "I had hopes. . . ."

"Forlorn hopes," Pa told him. Then he walked outside.

January 1, 1861

A new year. Wonder what 1861 will bring to Soldier's Farewell.

January 2, 1861

More news from South Carolina came on the Westbound. The men at the secession convention in Charleston voted 169-0 to leave the Union. One of the passengers, a big, burly guy who said he was from Richmond, Virginia had a newspaper with him, and everyone—even Pa—gathered around him like he had a page from the first Bible that ever got printed. Don't know what newspaper it was, or where he bought it, because I never got close enough to see, so crowded it was. The man took the paper with him. I bet he'll be popular at every stop betwixt here and Yuma, where he said he was going.

There also was a guy from Albany, New York on the stage, and he said he figured South Carolina was not only right in leaving the Union, but other states would follow soon—far as we know, there ain't been no more states to dissolve yet—and he didn't think they would just be Southern states, too. No, he allowed he expected California might leave the Union. Even New York could find some sense in becoming independent, or so this man said.

This time Pa spoke up, after the Westbound had left. He said the man from New York was the biggest fool he'd ever seen since he come to Soldier's Farewell.

More important seems to be the question of what will happen at Fort Sumter. That's a place out in the harbor of Charleston. The commander had not surrendered it yet. Those Southrons who are spoiling for a fight down in Charleston hadn't opened fire, either, but something is bound to happen there. There was a whole article about that in the paper the burly man owned.

"Carolinians is some of the hardest fighters you'll ever tussle with," Ben Jakes said to nobody in particular. Like that was news to us. That fool Jakes must have forgot my Pa hails from South Carolina, though he left nigh 20 years ago. "Bunch of Carolinians come down to fight at the Alamo, by grab. Next news we get we'll hear that that fort ain't flying that flag of tyranny no more. And then we'll hear that Texas is free, too."

Pa spoke up again, harsher this time. "If Texas quits the Union," he said, "then you'll be out of a job."

Jakes looked up, his face white. "You'd fire me, Mr. Munro? Just because I'm for Texas?"

Pa grunted, straightened his back, and put both hands on his hips. "What do you think will happen to the Overland if Texas secedes?" He said this like he was speaking to some simpleton. Ha. I allow that he was. Ben Jakes ain't got no brains, and I ain't writing "Mr." before his name no more. I'll call him Mr., because Pa expects it, and I ain't wanting no part of one of Pa's switches, or his razor strop. No, sir.

"Well. . . ." Jakes didn't know what to say.

"The Overland has a contract with the United States," Pa informed him. "Not the Republic of South Carolina. Not the Republic of Texas. You think they'll let us keep sending mail and people to California? If Texas goes. . . ." Pa shook his head and spit. He didn't say no more. In fact, nobody said a thing after that.

January 3, 1861

Mr. D.N. Barney come by this morning, and so did Emmett Mills and Freeman Thomas from Cooke's Spring, and a tall, skinny man named S.K. Clayton from Mimbres Stand and Mr. Dawson from Ojo de la Vaca. *Señor* Vee showed up, too. Even though he wasn't employed by the company, he's still a big man in these parts, especially after he tracked down Red Sleeves and helped get our mules back. He didn't say anything during the big meeting, however. I reckon all the important folks on the Overland between Mesilla and Stein's was here.

Luckily, as they had me making coffee and serving slumgullion and hardtack, I got to hear a lot of what they was talking about.

"La Mesilla's full of hotheads with ties to the South," Pa said.

"Anyone who reads the *Times* knows that," Emmett said.

"Tucson ain't much better," Mr. Barney said. "I wouldn't be surprised to see the southern half of New Mexico Territory declare its independence and align with the slaveholding states."

"If you read the *Times,* that's why they call this part Arizona," Emmett said. He didn't think much of the Mesilla newspaper.

"Our immediate concern is Texas," Mr. Barney said, and he went on to say that state officials wrote up this petition, allowing how Mr. Lincoln's election was a threat to Southern rights, and they've called for a statewide election so they can send delegates to a convention this month in Austin.

Austin might be the next Charleston.

I wasn't really sure why anything that happened in Austin would do us harm at Soldier's Farewell one way or the other as we're closer to Tucson and Santa Fé than the Texas capital, but then I remembered what all Pa had said about if Texas quits the Union, then the Overland is in trouble.

"What happens to us then?" Pa looked around the table.

A couple men shook their heads. Mr. Barney drummed his fingers on the table. Finally Freeman Thomas cleared his throat. He hailed originally from New York. If you took a poll, I reckon you'd find that most of the conductors and jehus and superintendents and such come from New York. Even John Butterfield was a New Yorker. Pa once said it was on account there were so many hacks in New York, it was easy to hire men who knowed what they was doing aboard a Concord or Celerity wagon. Even Marco Max, who growed up in Vermont, learned his trade and all about stagecoaching in New York City.

"Congress wants to move the line north," Mr. Thomas said. "More of a central line, probably along the route that new Pony Express is taking."

Mr. Barney nodded his head in agreement. "Many wanted that route from the start."

"It'll be up to the Postmaster General," Mr. Thomas added.

"But he won't let the Overland's property get stole by these Rebels," Mr. Clayton said. "Will he?"

"Not likely," Pa said. "But if Texas follows South Carolina, I don't see how he can stop it."

"Be a shame," Mr. Thomas said, "to break John Butterfield's heart, to see everything he worked so hard to build fall to ruin. Southern ruin."

"John Butterfield's heart's already busted," Mr. Barney said. "Since Wells, Fargo, and Company took over the Overland."

"Well . . . what happens to us?" Mr. Dawson asked.

"The Overland can't run without stagecoaches," Pa said. "Without livestock. Can't run without men, either. I reckon they'll move us north, too."

Clayton shook his head. "Never had much desire to live in

Kansas," he said.

"Let's wait and see what happens," Pa said. "It's all we can do. Just wait, and be ready."

They sipped some coffee and slurped the slumgullion, and then Emmett Mills asked Pa if he had heard from Julian. Pa just shook his head, and I recalled what Little Terry had said about the soldier boys down at Fort Chadbourne in Texas, how they wasn't sure what they would do, and I wondered if Julian and the soldiers at Fort Yuma was wondering the same, worrying.

Same day, 5:30

Pa riled me, though I didn't let on. At supper I asked him about South Carolina, and the Union being dissolved, and what this might mean to us, and he told me not to fret none, that this was a problem between the North and the South, and not New Mexico. Especially not Soldier's Farewell.

Sometimes I believe he thinks I'm just some dumb kid with no more brains than Ben Jakes.

Pa, I was inside with y'all most of the time this morn whilst y'all was talking about these things! I heard practically everything said!

That's what I wanted to yell at him, but I'm good at holding my tongue.

What about Julian? How's these events going to affect him? He's in the U.S. Dragoons! And he's our family.

I didn't say none of that, neither.

Too mad to sleep right now. Too mad to write any more, also.

I ain't stupid, Pa!

January 4, 1861

Got a letter from Julian. Well, it wasn't much of a letter. Only

one page, with him saying he was glad to hear Pa hadn't gotten
kilt by Apaches, and he thanked us for saving Sweet Ainsley,
apologized for not writing us sooner, and, finally, he closed with
a sentence about everything happening back East.

I guess you have heard about South Carolina.

That was it. Figured he'd have more to say on all the goings
on. Hoped he would, as maybe that would spark some comment from Pa. No luck, though. Well, I suspect Julian's right
busy. Probably tired.

As for Pa, well, he ain't been talking much about anything
lately.

January 5, 1861
The Velásquez family come over, and *Señora* Dolores brung us
some *menudo*. It's a soup. I ain't one to complain, and I managed to get my bowl full down, but I'm certain sure I don't
want to know what she puts in that soup, because it's about the
only thing I've ever tasted that makes me long for Pa's slumgullion.

Tori didn't act up none during the short visit. Alyvia asked
about Julian, and Pa read his letter, not that it was much of a
letter. Alyvia just nodded silently as Pa read. I wonder where
Señor Vee and his family stands in this whole mess, if they are
for the Union or for Southern rights.

Same day, quarter past 8, evening
Reread what I wrote about *Señor* Vee this morning, and that has
me thinking, and writing, again as it brings to mind stories Pa
and Julian every now and then would tell me about the Revolu-
tion, where we won our independence from King George and
England. Some of it was wrote about in one of those books by
Mr. Simms, but we ain't got but one of Simms's books no more

and it ain't about the war against the British. During that fracas, they say there was a lot of wild happenings in Camden, South Carolina, and that area, that folks would question neighbors if they was for the Patriots or on the King's side, and if you answered wrong, you might get tarred and feathered, whipped, burned out, or even killed.

I wonder if it'll ever come to that with this confrontation between North and South.

January 6, 1861
From listening to the grown-ups talk about things, it seems that South Carolina and any other states that decide to dissolve won't be sovereign countries. A lot of folks think when Mr. Lincoln replaces James Buchanan (Andrew Jackson ain't President, after all), he'll fight to preserve the Union. So the South will band together as a Confederacy. I heard that word mentioned on the Westbound.

Still no word on anything happening at Fort Sumter. South Carolina wants the Federal troops to get out, but President Buchanan says he ain't doing no such thing.

January 9, 1861
Don't reckon Texas will be the next state to secede, after all. Word from the Westbound is that there's a big meeting in Mississippi. Florida, Alabama, Georgia, and Louisiana have all called for conventions, too.

January 10, 1861
Rained this morning. Cold and windy.

January 11, 1861
Eastbound stage was about as crowded as I can remember ever seeing it, and that's saying something because there appears to

be a lot of folks going East now, or have been since news about South Carolina reached the territories and California. Only this time, there was a soldier boy, a baldheaded captain in the Navy who had left San Francisco and had resigned his commission. He got out to stretch his legs whilst we was changing the team of mules—Pa didn't like that none, but let it go, this time—and struck up a conversation with Ben Jakes, who was shirking his duties as usual, and said he could not protect the interests of the Union no more when his family and friends and home state were being threatened.

He's from South Carolina, and he talked a lot until a Yankee inside the stage yelled that he'd best shut up.

Thought there might be a fight, but the sailor tightened his lips and said nothing more, and Pa told the former captain that he'd best climb back inside the coach. Right about then there come up a little shower.

Pa just looked real sad at that sailor as he got back inside. Jakes hollered at him to kill a score of Yankees at Fort Sumter for him. The Navy captain said he prayed it wouldn't never come to that.

Then the stagecoach took off, and we turned in.

Rain stopped. Can't sleep.

January 12, 1861
Apaches killed two men traveling to the Pinos Altos mines from Mowry City. *Señor* Vee discovered their bodies, and lit a shuck back here to tell us the news. Pa rode out with Ben Jakes and *Señor* Vee to bury those guys. They got back as quick as they could, then *Señor* Vee rode off at a high lope to get back to his family. Can't blame him none for that.

Nobody's talking about South Carolina and the South and Mr. Lincoln any more. Got enough troubles. Pa ordered an extra guard each night to protect our mules. Don't want Sweet

Ainsley stole again.

January 13, 1861

No sign of any Apaches. Mules and livestock all safe here.

January 16, 1861

Mississippi has joined South Carolina. Word come quicker this time. But not many people talked about it. Those deaths of those two men must have reminded everyone that the Apaches are a bigger concern in New Mexico Territory, or Arizona Territory if you want to call it that, than what's going on in South Carolina and Mississippi.

Still no sign of Apaches. Wonder if those two guys who got killed were done in by Red Sleeves, old Mangas Coloradas himself. If so, he's keeping his peace with the Overland.

Glad I ain't a miner.

January 17, 1861

Ben Jakes says he heard Apaches while he was on guard duty last night, but he run them off. Nobody believes him.

January 18, 1861

Latest Apache scare seems to be fading away. Or was, at least, for me, until the Eastbound come in. Pa give the jehu a leather bundle, asked him if he'd see it got delivered to a Mrs. Luz Blanco in La Mesilla.

I asked him what it was and who was Luz Blanco, and he frowned, then said it was a letter and some personal belongings that he and *Señor* Vee had discovered on one of the fellows the Apaches had killed. Stuff the Indians hadn't stole off him.

"What about the other dead man?" I asked.

Pa shook his head. "Nothing," he said.

That got me to fretting. I mean, Pa and *Señor* Vee didn't find nothing that could tell them who this dead man was. Maybe Mrs. Blanco knows who her husband was traveling to the mines with, but what if she don't? Then this man, he's going to be buried for all eternity with not even a name over his grave. His wife, or his ma and pa might not ever know what become of him. That's sad.

Sometimes Soldier's Farewell seems to be the loneliest spot in the whole world.

January 19, 1861
Snowed. Just another dusting. Wind's blowing like a hurricane, and it's bitter, bitter cold. Don't think we have to worry about Apaches, not in this weather. Ain't fit to be outside.

January 20, 1861
More news from the South from the Westbound. Florida and Alabama are gone, Georgia's expected to secede—might already have done so by the time I write this—and there's a meeting in Louisiana later this month. Rumors are that the Southern states will meet in Montgomery, Alabama, and form a new nation. Plus Governor Sam Houston has called for a big meeting of the legislature tomorrow in Austin, Texas.

Mr. Lincoln, it is said, might not even live long enough to become President. Since he got elected, maybe even before then, folks have been saying how they'll kill him.

One man from Baton Rouge on the stagecoach tonight said only Lincoln's death could prevent a war. He said it would be a just death, too.

"Would that be enough to reunite North and South?" a schoolteacher bound for San Felipe asked.

"It's too late for reconciliation, sir," the Baton Rouge fire-eater fired back. "Much too late."

Also, learned that, on the 9th of this month, shots were fired

63

on this ship called the *Star of the West* that President Buchanan had sent to help the garrison at Fort Sumter. The ship wasn't damaged none, but now folks are saying there will surely be a war.

Thinking a lot about Julian.

So's Pa. Only he won't say it. He don't say much these days. But today, long before the Westbound stage come through, I watched him, whittling, leaning against the tall stone wall, staring at that old ragged flag that was popping like musketry in the wind. Cold as it was, windy as tarnation he didn't notice none of that. He just looked at that flag.

'Course, he might have been thinking about the first two states he called home, South Carolina and Mississippi, and how they ain't part of the United States any more, but I reckon I know he was thinking about Brother Jules. About the war folks say can't be stopped now.

Was I to ask him about it, Pa'd just tell me that no war between North and South would ever come to the territory, but he'd be lying.

It's Sunday, so Pa made me recite some Scripture today. He just stared at me as I spoke the words of Jesus from The Gospel According to St. Matthew.

" 'And ye shall hear of wars and rumors of wars; see that ye be not troubled. . . .' "

Before I could finish, Pa joined in. He'd never done that before. Sometimes I didn't think he knowed one verse from the Bible, but this time he started talking, just a whisper, but he was speaking with me, then, when I quit after just a few words, he finished the whole verse by himself.

" 'For all these things must come to pass, but the end is not yet.' "

January 21, 1861

Quiet day of chores. While Pa and the boys worked on the stables, repairing some fence, I had to head to the spring and fix the dam, pile on some more stones.

Good day, if cold. Nobody talking about the North, nobody talking about the South, nobody talking about Apaches.

Nobody talking, but I warrant all them things are heavy on most grown-ups' minds. Heavy on my mind, too.

January 22, 1861

Tuesday Eastbound came in an hour behind schedule, and Pa was hopping mad. Wind blowing like a gale, kicking up dust in the darkness. Couldn't see hardly a thing, and cold as it kept getting, that wind would suck the life out of you.

Mules begun balking—that no-account gray jenny even tried to sit on her hindquarters, but she wasn't the only one acting stubborn, stubborner than Pa, meaning both the teams we was unhitching and the fresh ones Bartolomé and Ben Jakes was bringing out of the stables. Couldn't blame them none. Nobody wanted to be out in this weather.

"Come on! Quit lollygagging!" Pa barked. "We can't afford to lose more time!"

Some folks say a jackman must be as patient as an oyster and that you almost got to be if you want to raise mules, and Pa is oftener tolerant when he's working with his animals. By jingo, I've knowed him to let a stallion run along with a jenny for upwards of six years before that jenny ever got in the family way and delivered us another mule. But ain't no station boss forgiving when working on the Overland, and when one of the passengers jumped down from the top off the Celerity wagon, Pa just about bust his gut.

Soon as the gent landed with a grunt, Pa had whirled around from the mules Bartolomé and Ben Jakes was bringing to the wagon tongue. When the newcomer called up for one of the other passengers unfortunate enough to have to ride up top if he'd toss down his carpetbag, Pa had had enough.

"What in blazes are you doing?" Pa yelled to the fellow in the shadows. "This ain't no leg-stretching stop. Get back on board, Mr., or you'll be walking to wherever you're going!"

He turned back, and shouted at me to give a hand, so I run from helping Mr. Fletcher, and conductor Donnie O'Donnell put the tired team in the stables, and started harnessing the fresh team to the coach.

My lips was cracked from the wind and cold, my fingers felt frozed, and I could barely breathe from the dust and weather.

When we got the team all hitched, Ben Jakes and me, working the right side of the coach, stepped back. Above the wind, I heard Pa yelling at the man that had jumped down off the coach to get back up, *muy pronto,* and then Big Terry, who was driving the Eastbound, just let out a belly laugh before firing out a stream of cusses as he popped that whip of his. The Celerity took off, kicking up more dust that I had to swallow, and disappeared in the blackness of the night.

The man in the shadows just stood there, holding a bag in one hand and what looked to be a rifle in the other.

"Mr., this better be your stop, you blamed idiot," Pa told the passenger who'd just got left behind, "because the only way you can get aboard another Eastbound is if there's room. And there ain't been a whole lot of room on any Eastbound coach the past two weeks."

With a nonchalant attitude, the man just flipped his carpetbag toward our little home. He took a couple of steps so that the light from the lantern on the post hit him.

"Maybe now," he said, "you can see a little better."

He wasn't dressed nothing like when I had last seen him. Even in the dark, I allow I would have recognized him had he been wearing that cloth shako of the dragoons. Atop Julian's head was a black slouch hat, dusty, battered and ripped in a couple of places along the front with a patch of crossed sabers—which had become regulation back in 1850—sewn into the crown. None of which I really seen till later. Instead of the blue woolen jacket with orange trim and brass epaulettes, he wore what we called back in Missouri a hunter's shirt, long, heavy gray flannel with the scales sewn on the shoulders to reveal his rank. His blue britches of kersey wool were stuffed in black boots, and he wore brass spurs and a black belt over his waist with a Colt revolver in the holster. No saber on him, although, later, I spotted it sheathed in its scabbard and tied to the bag he had tossed toward the door, but he held a 1847 musketoon in his left hand.

Nobody moved, not at first, just stood staring at the young man standing in the light.

Pa whispered my brother's name, and took a tentative step forward, then stopped, just staring while the wind blew so hard it bent one side of Julian's black hat up against the crown, and kept at it till Julian had to press the hat down on his head with his free hand to keep it from blowing all the way to old Mexico.

"Julian," Pa said again, only he still hadn't got his legs to working.

He looked different, my brother did, and it wasn't just all the makeshift uniform either. He wasn't a cadet fresh off the Hudson no more. Older, I reckon. Wiser. Maybe even harder. Chasing Paiutes will do that to any fellow. He had started growing this mustache before he took off to Fort Tejon, but back then it had looked mostly like dirty peach fuzz. Emmett Mills had even joked that Jules wouldn't need no razor to shave that thing off, that warm water would do the job. Now the mustache wasn't fuzz. I ain't writing that it was as big and brushy as Mr. Fletcher's, although Julian's wasn't yet so stained by tobacco juice and my brother hadn't grown a beard to go with it and Julian's hair was brown, not the color of sandstone like Mr. Fletcher's, but Julian's dark mustache wasn't something you'd overlook or joke about, neither.

It struck me then, in the dark, staring at my big brother.

Julian Munro had growed into a man.

I'm sitting here, scratching this while the memories are still in my head, waiting for Pa and Julian to finish talking about things so my brother, Lieutenant Munro, can come to bed. I'm supposed to be asleep, but it's too exciting to sleep now with my brother back home.

Home.

Never figured I'd call Soldier's Farewell home, but it is. Especially now that our family is back together again.

With the sight of Julian registering at last, I shouted out something, a cheer, maybe, I really don't know, but Pa came forward first, moving at last, holding out his right hand, as if he were going to shake Julian's hand, then rushing the final few rods, extending his left hand, and grasping my brother in a bear hug, laughing, twisting his first-born son around in a circle.

Calling Julian a dirty name, Pa finally released his grip and dropped Julian back to his feet and yelled: "Don't you know how to write? Why didn't you let us know you was coming?"

"Thought I'd surprise y'all."

"Uhn-huh." Pa stood there, sizing Julian up. "I knew a man back in Mississippi, decided he'd surprise his father and mother. Went home, walked in the door, and got his arm blowed off at the elbow by his daddy's shotgun. Yes, sir, that turned out to be quite a surprise."

"I'm glad you don't greet passengers with a shotgun."

"No. No, I reckon we're a tad less nervous, and a whole lot friendlier here."

"Uhn-huh." Julian grinned. "I've seen and heard how friendly you are here." He puffed out his chest, put his hands on his hips, and gave a right fair imitation of Pa's boisterous voice: "Mr., this better be your stop, you blamed idiot. . . . This ain't no leg-stretching stop, what in Sam Hill are you doing? . . . Quit lollygagging! We can't afford to lose any more time!"

Mr. Fletcher let out a chuckle over that, adding: "That's about the size of it." Which got Ben Jakes, Bartolomé, and Julian laughing like coyotes, and I soon joined in. After the longest while, Pa started cackling, too. Then we all stopped, but only for a second before Pa roared out again, slapping his thighs, and we joined him a-laughing and a-laughing till at last Pa stopped and said: "Let's get out of the wind."

Everyone come inside, shaking my brother's hand, telling him it was good to see him, how fine he looked, all that kind of stuff, while I hauled in my brother's grip—that's when I noticed the saber in its silver scabbard tied to the carpetbag—and Pa fetched a jug. I set Julian's bag in the corner and took the musketoon from him without comment, which I leaned against the wall beside his flowery carpetbag and shiny saber. As my brother unbuckled his gun belt, Pa poured Julian a glass, but he wasn't about to dirty up dishes for the rest of us, so the jug got passed around. He even let Ben Jakes have a snort, but snatched it from my hands when Ben Jakes passed it to me.

"Ah, Pa . . . ," I said, but not too loud on account I didn't want to spoil his mood.

"How long you here?" Mr. Fletcher asked. "You on leave?"

"New orders." Julian done some smacking and wiped his lips. "That'll age you." He studied the glass.

"Fort Tejon whiskey's better?" Pa inquired, as if he had just been insulted.

"Well," Julian said, "I ain't blind."

Eyes sparkling, Mr. Fletcher added: "Yet."

Which started them all guffawing again.

Pa asked Jules if he was hungry, and we warmed up some stew and coffee and ate us a late meal, with Mr. Fletcher, Ben Jakes, and Bartolomé calling it a night after they'd all had themselves a snort, telling Julian it was good to see him again, and then they filed out into the dark and went to their own bunks, leaving us Munros alone.

Nobody spoke while Jules filled his belly—we just stared at him, noticing how he looked, how he had changed, maybe just marveling at the sight of him, speechless the whole time—although I was right eager to pepper him with questions, and finally he slid the empty bowl away from him and said: "You're awful quiet, Smith. Cat got your tongue?"

"You going to see Alyvia?" Dumb. Just plain ignorant, but that's the only thing I could think of to ask right then and there, even though I was loaded up with questions, good questions, and stories I wanted to hear him tell.

"Now?" he asked, all surprised, and Pa tried not to laugh but couldn't hold it in his mouth. "It's a bit late to go. . . ."

Pa finished for him. "Courting?" He laughed at the following silence, which I broke.

"Well . . . what are you doing here?" I asked Julian. Then I got a little frightened. "You didn't run off, did you?"

Raking his rough hands through my hair, Julian shook his head and shot Pa a wink. "You're afraid I'm going to steal your bunk and make you sleep on the floor? Is that it?"

"No." I started to tell him that the floor would probably be more comfortable than my bed, but decided against that.

"You look different," I said.

"I feel different," he said, only he said it different, too, but I don't think Pa, or even Julian, noticed the change in his voice.

"You must be tired," Pa said.

"A Celerity wagon isn't the most comfortable conveyance," Julian agreed.

70

"Uhn-huh. You didn't answer Smith's question," Pa said. "Did you run off?" I spotted a glitter in Pa's eye.

"It's like I told Fletcher," Julian replied. "New orders."

"Can you tell me about fighting Paiutes?" I asked. I'd interrupted them, and Pa didn't like it none.

"Time for bed," he told me. "Don't worry. Julian can feed your appetite for war stories. . . ." He turned to my brother. "For how long?"

"I have plenty of time to tell some windies," he said. "I have two months' leave before reporting for assignment. Thought I'd stay here."

"You can ride Sweet Ainsley!" I suggested.

"I'd love to ride her."

Pa asked: "Where will you be going from here?"

Julian didn't answer for a while. He drummed his fingers, staring at them, and it looked to me like he started to reach for the jug Bartolomé had set on the table, but slowly withdrew that hand, and looked up at Pa.

"East," was all he said.

About then's when Pa sent me to bed, which ain't fair, however Pa wasn't in any mood for delays so I didn't tarry. It ain't like I could sleep, knowing Julian was back home, that he and Pa were probably drinking more from that jug of mescal and talking about important matters. Writing these words, I can still hear him and Julian talking, although I can't make out none of their words.

I got a good notion what the conversation's about.

The war. The shooting war that's coming about on account of the South pulling out of the Union. Julian's heading East, and that means he won't be fighting Paiutes, or Apaches, or some other red Indian. He won't be fighting the Mexicans, like Pa done in the big war before I was born. I recall one of those conversations I'd overheard here at the station after we got word about South Carolina dissolving the Union, although I can't remember who said it or when, but it strikes me that it must have been just a couple of days ago and from that schoolteacher who had taken a job in San Felipe, California.

"My fear is that you are correct, and that there will be war, unavoidable war, and this war will be like none we have ever seen on this continent. It will be a war of fathers fighting sons, brothers fighting brothers. I tremble at the thought."

I'm trembling now.

Same night, later, not sure of the time

Julian come in, the sharp stink of mescal on his breath. I wonder if there's any of that liquor left in the jug. He was pulling off his boots when I rolled over.

"Didn't mean to wake you, Smith," he whispered.

"I wasn't sleeping."

"Well, that's good." He tossed his boots, spurs still on, into the corner. "Pa says I can have your bed. You can sleep on the floor." He slapped my thigh. "Might as well move now. I'm tuckered out."

"You're in your cups."

"A tad. If you want to sleep in the bed. . . ."

"No." I sat up. "It's all right." I didn't tell him about the floor being more comfortable. He tossed his hat toward his boots, and started unbuttoning his hunter's shirt.

"You and Pa talked quite a bit."

"Too much," Julian said. "I'm worn out."

"You're going East?"

He left his hand on the heavy flannel, just looking out at nothing. "Yeah," he said after the longest while, and pulled off the garment.

"They say there will be a war," I said. "Between the North

and the South."

"I'd say they're right." He still wasn't looking at me. Now he started on his pants.

"Reckon that troubles Pa," I said.

He laughed, but it wasn't nothing like the laughs from earlier this night. In fact, it sounded more bitter than anything else. "I told Pa that I got just as much chance of getting killed by a Paiute arrow as I do from a white man back . . . wherever."

"Maybe not," I said hopefully. "There was this fellow from Baton Rouge on the stage, and he was saying that, if there was a war, it wouldn't be much of a war, that it would only last a week or two, a month at the most. You might still be here by the time all the shooting is stopped."

He didn't say a thing, just pulled off them soldier pants of his.

"You don't believe that?" I asked. I had to repeat the question before he answered me.

Now he turned, holding folded pants and shirt in his hands, sitting on the bunk in his winter drawers and socks. He just looked at me, looked at me the longest while, and I wasn't sure he had an answer. In fact, for a little bit I thought he might start to crying, but it was fairly dark in the room, and I was pretty tired myself.

"I . . . I don't know what to believe, Smith," he said. "Not any more."

Well, I couldn't come up with words to all that. Didn't even try.

"You keep the bed tonight," Julian told me. "Chasing Indians with Captain Carleton, I'm used to sleeping on hard ground."

He crossed the room, weaving some, didn't even bother taking a blanket with him, and laid down in the corner, using his folded clothes for a pillow, not even covering himself.

"This one fellow," I said, still sitting, "he said it would be a war like nothing we'd ever seen in America. He said it would be a war of brothers fighting brothers."

He rolled over, dark eyes locked on me.

"That scares you?" he asked.

I shrugged.

"I wouldn't fight you, Smith," he said.

"Good," I said, trying to make him laugh again. I mean, this was supposed to be a happy reunion, and here we were talking about war, and not all the glory of fighting in the Army and stuff, but bad thoughts. Seems that everyone traveling along the Overland had nothing but bad thoughts, or mean thoughts about other Americans. "Because I'd hate to have to whup you, Jules."

He laughed. "I won't give you the chance, baby Brother. Now go to sleep."

"Pa says he don't think the war will ever come to New Mexico Territory," I said. I didn't tell him about how, in some ways, the war had already come this way, with people fighting amongst each other, didn't tell him that there was a chance the Overland would even move the route out of New Mexico and up into Kansas or some place like that.

"Go to sleep," he said again, rolling over. Pretty soon, all I heard was the snores of Julian. Then it seemed like I heard footsteps, as if Pa had been listening to us talking, spying on us, and now he was walking away. Maybe that was my imagination.

Now I can hear the snores of both my father and my brother. I'm sitting here on my bed, writing in this bunk, although it's blasted hard to see right now.

Can't sleep.

January 30, 1861

By jacks, more than a week has passed since I last wrote in this diary. Guess that shows how busy things have been around here. Stagecoaches, both them heading east and those going west, have all been full of passengers and lots of mail. It brings to mind this story from a San Antonio newspaper—the *Herald* was its name, I think—that a passenger showed us when we first got here and the Overland started running in '58.

To make excellent jam; squeeze six or eight women, now-a-days, into a common stagecoach.

I thought about that, also, on account of the jam *Señora* Dolores brung. It ain't all been work, you see. On Monday, the 28th, Pa throwed a *baile* for Julian, and the whole Velásquez gang come. Emmett Mills, he was there, too, and *Señora* Dolores brought enough food to fill a whole brigade's bellies. The jam she made out of prickly pear, and I don't reckon I've ever had anything so tasty, at least, not since leaving Missouri. Julian kept teasing me after I'd spread some jam on one of her *tortillas* and was eating it all up, saying that I'd better watch for the cactus spines as I might get one stuck in my tongue.

Things couldn't get no finer.

Things couldn't get any finer than that party, or the past week.

Julian has been working with me some on my grammar— how I talk, how I write, teaching me things like subject and verb agreement, avoiding the usage of double negatives like I started to write just above. It's hard, but when he opened his carpetbag the day after he arrived, he pulled out a *McGuffey's New Fourth Ecletic Reader,* even though I never saw a *Third Reader* but had read the first two of those books before we left Missouri, and we've been practicing and reading it each night. Julian's a pretty good teacher, and patient.

He's also one mighty fine dancer. Everybody at the *baile* marveled about how he could dance. He and Alyvia danced just about every dance there was with *Señor* Vee sawing his fiddle and Emmett Mills banging out a tune on his jaw's harp while

Ben Jakes proved he ain't totally worthless as he brought out his spoons and kept time. Sounded good, too.

We played, sang, and danced to just about everything, from minstrel tunes like "Darling Nelly Gray" and "The Flag of Our Union" to songs I could belt out real loud like "Do They Miss Me at Home?", "Pop Goes the Weasel", and "Buffalo Gals". We danced to "Woodman, Spare That Tree", which Pa said is his favorite (I never knew that, never even heard him sing till that day), and "From Greenland's Icy Mountains", "Old Folks at Home"—a lot of Stephen Foster songs, I'd say—and some California songs Julian had learned at Fort Tejon, though I couldn't tell you what they were called, and at least two were in Spanish. They even played some songs by this fellow named Chopin. Tried to, anyhow.

The best part happened when Julian brought out a protesting *Señora* Dolores to cut the rug one time to Virginia reel. *Señor* Vee laughed and laughed as his wife pleaded, in Spanish and English, with Julian not to make her dance, but finally, with her girls urging her, she bowed graciously, and her husband sawed that fiddle.

Laughing herself after a while, the *señora* showed us all that she knew how to dance mighty fine, too, and when the reel ended, she was sweating. Sweating in January! Well, it has warmed up a mite, but not that much.

"Is that what they taught you at Fort Tejon?" Emmett Mills asked my brother, who had yet to sit out one dance.

"He didn't learn to dance from the Paiutes, I warrant," Mr. Fletcher said.

"Polkas, waltzes, quadrilles, mazurkas," Julian said. "An officer and a gentleman should know them all, although I had to teach my superiors the Carolina promenade."

Twice, I danced with Tori, and she wasn't no . . . wasn't a nuisance.

Everyone had worked up an appetite by the time we'd

finished dancing, and while we will usually eat some of *Señora* Dolores's leftovers after she brings us some grub, a body would have been pressed mighty hard to find even a crumb after we had eaten second and third helpings. Dancing makes you hungry.

Just about the most fun we've had at Soldier's Farewell in a coon's age.

Westbound's due tonight. Back to work.

January 31, 1861
Julian has gone off to see Alyvia, but told me to practice my writing in my diary, and that he wanted to see what I wrote when he got home. I thought about writing nothing. That would teach him a lesson. However, I guess I should practice, show my brother that he's a good teacher, and write about how great things have been now that he has come home.

Maybe he will feel guilty and I'll get my bed back.

February 2, 1861
I didn't write last night after the Eastbound left. Mainly because I was troubled. Still feel troubled. As pleasant as things have been since my brother returned home, last night turned downright savage. Now, I ain't . . . I'm not one to feel sorry for Ben Jakes, but. . . .

It happened like this.

The Eastbound pulled in right on time, and Julian helped out, bringing the fresh team of mules from the stables, and this fellow, riding atop the coach on account it was crowded with people, he called out: "Julian Munro, by the saints, is that you?"

Julian looked up, but on account of the dark, couldn't make out the fellow's face.

"Bucky Sullivan!" He stood up, wobbling atop the stage, and I thought he might step down, which would really rile Pa, but he didn't. He wore a shako and what looked like a striking military jacket, so I knew he was in the Army before he called out his rank. Seems that he had been serving in the dragoons as an officer at Fort Yuma, and I guess he and Julian had fought Paiutes together.

"Captain. . . ." Julian stopped, unsure, and stepped away from the mules.

"It's no longer, Captain, Mr. Munro," the passenger said, "but it will be Colonel Sullivan when I return home to Savannah." He sat down, and the stagecoach started with a jolt, heading into the night as Sullivan yelled out: "Georgia will never yield to tyrants! Huh-rah! Huh-rah for Southern liberty!"

Well, Julian just stood there, brushing off the dust, watching the darkness swallow the Celerity wagon, and Ben Jakes walked up to him.

"Friend of yourn?" Ben Jakes asked. There wasn't any pleasantness in his voice, so I knew right away that Ben Jakes had bitten off a mouthful of trouble.

"I know him."

"You might have to kill him," Ben Jakes said. "Afore long. You think about that, Munro, when you're fightin' for the Yankees. You might kill him, your pard, a good Georgia patriot, or he might kill you!"

Whirling, cursing, Julian swung and rocked Ben Jakes with a hammer-like fist under the chin. It's a miracle he didn't break that no-account's jaw. One punch was all Julian needed. The thing is—Julian didn't stop with that one punch.

Ben Jakes staggered back, somehow kept his feet, but he never lifted his arms—guess he had been stunned—and Julian pounced on him, hit him again and again and again, in the head, chest, stomach, knocking him backward until Ben Jakes fell against the stone building.

"I . . . quit. . . ." That's all Ben Jakes managed to say, but Julian didn't listen. I don't think he even heard. Acted like a hydrophoby wolf, just crazy. Crazy and mean. He landed a right that smashed Jakes's nose into a bloody pulp, forcing Jakes's head hard against the stone wall, so hard I thought my brother had knocked the fool's skull apart.

Wheezing, Julian stepped back, and I thought he'd let it go, but he didn't. When Ben Jakes started to sink to the ground, Julian grabbed him by his shirt front, lifted him up, and leaned him against the wall, then hit him. Again. And again. Ben Jakes couldn't say anything by then. In the light, I saw his face, or what had been his face. His eyes had already swollen shut, his lips and nose just mangled flesh, but Julian kept pounding him.

"No mas," Bartolomé added. *"No mas, por favor."*

Julian's reply came with a left that crushed Jakes's ear and felled him to the ground. The blowhard didn't move, but Julian did.

He kicked him, kicked him hard in the chest, and the snapping of ribs almost made me lose my supper.

"Julian!" I yelled. Mr. Fletcher and Bartolomé wouldn't move. Later, I heard Mr. Fletcher explain to Pa that it wasn't his fight, and that he had been raised better and knew better than to stick his nose in something that wasn't his affair.

It was my affair, though. If I didn't stop Julian, he might beat Ben Jakes to death, and I sure didn't want to see my brother hang for murder.

"Stop it!" I leaped behind him, tried to grab his arms, but Julian tossed me off, easy, like I was a feather, and I landed in the dirt with a thud.

"Stop, Jules! You'll kill him!" I clambered back to my feet, deciding to tackle Julian, wrapping my arms around his legs before he could kick the unconscious man again. He went down, crashing violently for I had surprised him, but quickly pulled out of my grip, and started up, moving back for Ben Jakes.

I rolled over, scrambling to get up, then saw Julian tumbling back toward the wall, away from Ben Jakes, and it took a while before I realized that Ben Jakes hadn't knocked my brother. Not hardly, Ben Jakes wasn't moving. I thought he might not even be breathing.

Pa done it.

Julian put out his arms to stop himself from smashing into those heavy stones, pushed himself away, and turned back.

"Leave it go, Son! He's finished!"

Pa, who had been in the stables, stood there, a mountain, and maybe Julian finally heard. He slowed, stopped, just stood, trying to catch his breath, letting everything that had just happened register. After the longest while, he brought his skinned knuckles to his mouth.

"Help your brother up," Pa told Julian.

"I don't need no help!" I fired back, forgetting all about those grammar lessons Julian had been teaching me, and climbed to my feet.

"You hurt?" Pa asked.

"I'm all right, but. . . ." I glanced at Ben Jakes, and sighed with relief when I detected his stomach rising and falling.

"Get him inside," Pa ordered Bartolomé and Mr. Fletcher. "What started all this?"

He was looking at Julian when he asked that, but Julian didn't attempt an answer, so I cleared my throat and told Pa what all had happened. It didn't seem much excuse for a fight, at least not something as savagesome as I had just witnessed, but when I had finished my account, Pa's head bobbed ever so slightly.

"I'm going for a ride," Julian announced. He headed toward the stables.

"It's after midnight!" I called out. "There's Apaches and. . . ."

"Let him go," Pa told me quietly, staring after Julian. "Let him ride it out. He'll be all right."

Then we went to check on Ben Jakes.

February 3, 1861

Julian didn't come back till this evening—and I ain't ashamed to write that I have been scared, fearing he might have run into Red Sleeves or some other contrary Apache—but he rode up right before the Westbound arrived. Good thing, because we needed him to lend a hand as Ben Jakes is off his feet with five or six busted ribs, broken nose, split lips. He swallowed two, three teeth Julian knocked out, too.

Pa expects him to be laid up for a couple of weeks. Knowing Ben Jakes the way I do, I figure he'll stay in his bunk three or four weeks, and it'll be me waiting on him, bringing him his meals, even having to empty his chamber pot. Thought of tending him like that just makes my gut spin.

Nobody said a thing about the ruction, at least not when I was around, but I'm certain sure Pa and Julian had a discussion in the stables after the Westbound went on its way. Don't know what they said, though, and I'm not in the mood to ask Julian about it and know better than to question Pa.

February 4, 1861

Julian rode off on Sweet Ainsley to see Alyvia and the Velásquez family this morning, and when he got back early this evening, he helped me through the *Reader* and we practiced writing and such.

Things getting back to normal.

February 5, 1861

Don't miss Ben Jakes at all around here, not with Julian helping. The Eastbound come, 10 minutes early, and got off without a hitch. Bartolomé told Julian that if he wanted to resign his commission, he was right certain Wells, Fargo, & Company would have a place for him on the Overland.

I laughed, but Julian acted like he hadn't heard, and walked off to the stables, and trotted off on Sweet Ainsley without another word. About three, four hours later, he rode back, climbing into the bed—I'm still sleeping on the floor now—and whispered something to himself. Maybe he was praying.

Something's bothering him, and I know what it is, least ways think I do. He's worrying about what he done to Ben Jakes, ashamed that I had seen that side of him. If he had stopped, if he had just knocked some sense into Ben Jakes, that would have been one thing, but the way he tore into Ben Jakes, that wasn't an officer and a gentleman and West Point graduate. He acted more like some monster. But things are better now. I'm glad.

February 6, 1861

We hear of trouble among the Indians around Apache Pass, and even more bad news come on tonight's Westbound. Texas has joined South Carolina, Mississippi, and all the other states that have left the Union. More later.

February 7, 1861

On February 1, the folks down in Austin voted to join the Confederacy. That's the word we got last night. That means seven states have already dissolved the Union: South Carolina, Mississippi, Florida, Alabama, Georgia, Louisiana, and Texas. The passengers on the stage last night all agreed that Arkansas, Tennessee, and North Carolina would also leave, but Virginia sparked debate. So did Kentucky, and Missouri, but most of the talk concerned Virginia, although I had more interest in Missouri, it being the place of my birth and where I'd grown up before leaving for the territory.

Today, however, everyone wanted to talk about Texas. That's why Pa saddled up the big old Percheron and rode off to Barney's Station with Freeman Thomas from Cooke's Spring, and Bill Dawson from Ojo de la Vaca. Mr. Barney had called a big meeting to talk about what Texas's secession will mean for the Overland, similar, I guess, to the meeting Pa held here a while back.

Julian, though, he didn't have much to say on the matter, even when Mr. Fletcher pried him on it. Instead, he just set me down at the table so we could practice reading and writing.

Same day, 9:30 p.m.

Pa got back, and Julian asked how the meeting went, and Pa just shrugged. "We wait," he answered, fetching a new jug.

"Seems like the whole country's doing that," Julian offered.

"Seems like," Pa agreed. He held up the clay jug. "Thirsty?"

Julian shook his head, and motioned me to follow him. So we retired to our room, me on the floor, Julian in my bed, and Pa at the table, alone.

February 9, 1861

I've just got to write about the newcomer, a raw-boned tall *hombre* who got off the Eastbound last night. He's come to help us, and we sure need an extra hand what with Ben Jakes all stove up from that pounding Julian given him.

"Soldier's Farewell!" Marco Max called out to his passengers as the stagecoach pulled in about 15 minutes late. "We'll be changing teams, so hold your horses. You can stretch your legs and visit the privy at Cooke's down the pike if we make up some lost time!"

Yet almost before he had finished his speech and set the brake, this gent hops down from inside. "Reckon I'll stay here, driver."

Hearing those words, I pulled away from the rigging I had

been working on, helping Bartolomé unhitch the team, and warned the stranger, who I couldn't see too well in midnight black. "You might not be able to catch another stage, Mr., for a spell. Coaches have been jammed full of folks of late."

"Reason I'm gettin' off," he said, brushing dust off his clothes with a wide-brimmed sombrero. "I'm a man who needs air to breathe."

"This ain't a hotel!" Pa, bringing out the harnessed fresh team with Julian and Mr. Fletcher, barked out those words, and the tall stranger straightened and stared into the darkness toward the shadow that was Pa.

"I expect to earn my keep." The man settled the hat back on his head, then just jumped right in and helped me with the mules. Well, we got the teams changed, put the tuckered-out span in the stables, and long before we had finished our chores, Marco Max had pulled out, so the stranger was stranded here, unless he wanted to take the "ankle express" to wherever he was bound, and with Apaches acting ornery, that wasn't exactly a healthy choice.

Bartolomé went to his bunk, and I walked alongside the stranger back to our house, where I knew Pa would be waiting. Had to walk mighty fast to keep up with the long-legged fellow. Only then did I realize the man lacked a valise or even a bedroll, so I hoped aloud that he didn't leave his possibles on the Celerity wagon.

"Travel light," he said with ease. "Got all I need."

"I'm Smith Munro." I remembered we'd been too busy for introductions. We kept walking.

"Folks call me Pinto."

"Pinto? Like the horse?"

"Or bean."

"Lots of folks around here ain't partial to that breed of horses," I said.

"I don't care much for that breed of bean," he said, opening the door and letting me go first.

Pa stood waiting, cup of coffee in his hand, Julian right behind him.

Mr. Pinto swept off his hat, and gave Pa and my brother a friendly nod. He introduced himself, and Julian asked if he wanted some coffee, maybe leftover stew.

"Nothing to eat, but coffee sounds invitin'," the stranger said. Maybe he thought our stew had beans in it.

He stood a hat crown's height over Pa and Julian, and I'd guess he still would have towered over them even without those high-heeled boots he wore. Brown corduroy trousers were stuck inside those boots, with a saddle-colored rig around his waist, brass buckle holding up a flapped holster on his right hip, pouch for shot, caps, and powder next to that, and on his left hip, a big Arkansas toothpick in fancy tooled sheath that didn't match the rest of his leather. A Mexican-style jacket of green wool hung unbuttoned on his lanky frame, with a red flannel shirt, and calico bandanna. Hanging from a rawhide thong around his neck, a heavy silver Cross of Lorraine completed his outfit.

His sandy hair looked dirty, greasy, long, and unkempt, but the man had been traveling on Marco Max's Celerity wagon for I didn't know how long, and he sported maybe a week's growth of beard on a pockmarked face highlighted by the coldest green eyes I've ever seen. Now that I could see him in the light, I didn't know quite what to make of him, though calluses covered his hands, and his knuckles were scarred, so he wasn't no stranger to hard work.

"I won't turn a man out," Pa told him. "I won't let any man go hungry from here, but this isn't a hotel. You're 1,051 miles from Fort Smith, 460 1/2 from Fort Yuma, and 6 inches to Perdition. Everyone here's an employee of the Overland Mail Company."

"Even the soldier boy?" Pinto stuck his jaw out toward Julian, in his dragoon britches and shirt.

"My son." Pa made the introductions. "Julian will be leaving for his next posting. He's on furlough."

"I see." He took the steaming cup of coffee from Julian, and sipped it. "You seemed short-handed tonight," he said after a moment.

"That why you got off the stage?" Pa asked.

Pinto laughed a little, shaking his head. "Like I told your boy here, I prefer good air in my lungs, and wide open spaces. Wasn't getting that in your mud wagon."

"Where you bound?" That wasn't a real polite question, but Pa didn't appear to be in a friendly mood.

"Texas," he said, not offended. "Home. Rusk County. Been at Vallecito for the past three, four years. But war's coming. Home's the place to be in a time of war."

"Texas pulled out of the Union," I sang out.

"So I heard."

A moment, a long one, too, stretched out as Pinto sipped his coffee, and Pa sized him up. Finally the stranger set the empty cup on the table and hooked his thumbs in his belt on either side of the brass buckle. "Mr. Munro," he said. "I ain't forcin' myself on you. You need a hand . . . like I said, I'm willin' to earn my keep. More'n willin', actually. I'd demand it. Not a man who cares for charity. If you don't want me here, just give the word and I'll light out. Walk to the next station or Franklin if I have to. Walk to Rusk County if need be."

"You'd walk?" Pa said. "After you paid, what, $150 in gold to ride?"

Shrugging, Pinto answered: "Not quite that much, for passage from Vallecito to Gainesville. Like you said, you didn't invite me. Wouldn't be the first bet I've made and lost."

"Giles Hawley is the superintendent," Pa told him. "He hangs his hat in Tucson. He does all the hiring. That means I can't pay you." He wet his lips, and quickly added: "If I let you stay."

"Didn't ask for pay. Coffee's fine. I'll work for found." He turned around and looked down at me, smiling. "Long as it ain't pinto beans."

"You know horses?"

"Worked in a livery in Vallecito. Rode herd for one of them big Mexican *haciendas* before that. Yeah, I know horses. And I know mules."

"He knowed better. . . ."

"He knew better," Julian corrected me. Now, I didn't like that, not one bit, not getting a school lesson in front of a stranger.

"Well," I said, "he didn't let the mules drink whilst they was . . . while they were hot." I had to stop myself from sticking my tongue out at Julian. I looked at Pa. "And you know how temperamental that big sorrel jack you call Hampton can be."

It's a wonder Hampton ain't died of colic.

"Never cared much for mules." When Pinto said that, I figured Pa would send him packing, but the stranger kept right on talking, and I ~~knowed~~ knew he might stand a chance as Pa's withering gaze slowly faded into something more like amusement. "Till I come to California. Learned a horse is a whole lot more impatient putting a pack saddle on than is a mule. And under that California sun, well, a mule's skin seems to weather better. Ain't so sensitive, a mule's hide. Mind you, I'm Rusk County-born, a Texican, and I don't reckon you'll ever find me raisin' mules. But I've learnt to respect 'em."

That pretty much sold Pa, who told Pinto to bunk with Bartolomé, Fletcher, and Ben Jakes. He told me to show Pinto the way, but the stranger said he could find it all right, and bade us all good night.

"What do you think?" Pa asked Julian after Pinto had left.

87

My brother shrugged. "He'll do."

Pa refilled his coffee cup. *"Vamos a ver,"* he said in Spanish. We'll see.

February 10, 1861

We saw tonight with the arrival of the Westbound. Pinto proved himself a right good hand. Were I Ben Jakes, I might start fearing for my job. But, no, I guess Pinto—I called him Mr. Pinto this morning, because Pa gave me the look, but he shook his head and told me, and Pa: "There ain't no Mr. to it, Smith. Pinto is all."—wouldn't take a job even if Pa and Mr. Hawley offered it. I keep forgetting that Pinto's on his way to Texas.

It strikes me as I write this that Pinto and Julian might become enemies, might have to face each other in battle.

Anyway, Pinto's a good worker, and works real fast with the teams, and fast is something Pa likes to see when it comes to changing Overland teams.

This morning, after breakfast, I found Pinto leaning against the stable wall, just looking at the hills and the yucca. The sky had turned the prettiest blue you'll ever see, no dust blowing, just a gentle morning breeze, and the cold spell has snapped. February in Boone County would have me as close to the fire as I could get. Missouri winters will just freeze the marrow in your bones, but this is the desert of New Mexico Territory, and the sun had already started warming everything.

"That's a view I like," Pinto said as, using a Barlow knife, not his big Arkansas toothpick, he cut off a piece of tobacco and stuck it in his mouth. "Put a man on that there butte, and ain't nobody going to come up on him by surprise. Not even an Apache."

"That's Soldier's Farewell Hill," I told him. "The one you're looking at. The other one, on the other side of the trail, is what they call Besse Rhodes. And that one, on the other side of

88

Soldier's Farewell, is named JPB."

"So one's named after some gent with the initials JPB, and the other's after some petticoat." He folded the blade, and slipped the knife into his coat pocket. "Had me an aunt named Bessie, but her last name was Denton."

"No one really knows the story there," I said, showing off my knowledge. "We found a rock up there with the names Besse and Rhodes scratched into it, and underneath them names they'd scratched out USA, so Jules suspects some dragoons named Besse and Rhodes done that, not a. . . ." I grinned despite myself at getting to say the word "petticoat."

"Uhn-huh. Could be. And JPB could be another Yankee handle. How did Soldier's Farewell get its name?"

"All sorts of stories about that." I smiled again, looking for Pa, hoping he might add another tale, but Pa remained inside, talking to Julian and Mr. Fletcher while Bartolomé brought Ben Jakes his breakfast.

"I'd be plumb tickled to hear one." He shifted his tobacco to the other cheek, and spit in the sand.

"Well, one time Pa said this troop of soldiers from Fort Bliss got ambushed by Apaches, and they got whupped on real good, the soldiers did, so they all skedaddled back for Texas, and the Apaches, they laughed and started waving to the soldiers as they run. So it was the Apaches who give this place the name. Soldier's Farewell."

He wiped tobacco juice off his lips. "Well, then," he said, "we might have to name this little knoll by my daddy's farm Soldier's Farewell. If the Yankees try and invade Rusk County."

My smile vanished. I didn't like that image, didn't like picturing such a fight, one that might involve Julian, and hated myself for thinking of that story among the ten or twelve lies, or maybe one was the truth, that Pa had told me in the past three years or so about the naming of this place. That's because I know Julian

89

wouldn't never have run from a fight like that one. They'd have to kill him. I felt mighty glad when Pinto changed the subject.

"Where's the trail run from here?"

"Right over yonder." I pointed. "It has to cross this draw just before it gets to our station."

"See it. That's why you'd need a sentry up on the hill. That draw's a good place for Apaches to sneak up in. Surprise you. Lot of good hidin' spots in there, 'specially if you're an Injun."

"Apaches have pestered us some," I admitted.

"And beyond the draw?"

"Well, the line runs west to Barney's, about 19. . . ."

"I mean east of here."

"It swings between Soldier's Farewell Hill and Besse Rhodes. You can't make it out from right here, but beyond that is what they call Burro Cienaga. You know what a *cienaga* is?"

"I lived in California," he said. "I savvy quite a bit of that lingo." He snorted. "Wouldn't quite call that a swamp, though, at least it ain't nothing like the swamps we got in East Texas."

"We have some swamps in Missouri, too, but that's what they call it, Burro Cienaga, and it'll hold some water, especially during the monsoons in late summer or when we get all the snow melt in spring. We get our water from the spring back yonder." He knew about that spring, because he had fetched water, but I wanted him to know my part in it, so I told him proudly. "I built the dam."

Ah, fiddlesticks. He acted like he hadn't even heard.

"How far to the *cienaga?*"

"Three miles."

Nodding, he looked again at the little hills, saying absently: "Soldier's Farewell appears taller."

"Yes, sir. But it ain't easy to climb. It's all rocky and steep. I know. I've clumb all three hills."

That sparked his interest. "You're a regular mountain goat,

eh?" He tousled my hair the way Pa and Julian sometimes did. "Pretty good view, once you get to the top, I allow?"

"I reckon. But if you're talking about a place for a sentry, I'd choose Besse Rhodes. For one thing, it's easier to climb, and it ain't but maybe 300, 400, no more than 500 feet lower. The thing is, you got hardly a thing blocking your view from up there. A body can look all the way to the Chiricahuas, even past the Organs. You got a clear view of the Overland Trail, too. You can see Cow Springs from up there, all the way to Cooke's Range. Emmett Mills, he's a good friend of Jules's, he works at Cooke's Station. We climbed up Besse Rhodes one time when he was visiting, and he pointed out all the mountain ranges to me."

"And how far's Ojo de la Vaca from here? Julian told me it was 14 miles."

"That's about right," I said. "Once you get out of China Draw, it's a pretty straight trail to here. Marco Max, he can get a team of mules to eat up a lot of countryside in those 14 miles. A 'land-eating gallop,' he calls it."

Pinto spit again. "I rode with him, remember? He'll have his mules at a land-eatin' gallop all the time. Quite the jehu."

"He's my favorite," I admitted.

"Talks like a Yankee," Pinto said, but I didn't say anything to that.

Pa and Julian filed out of the house, and Pinto thanked me for filling him in on the countryside.

I was glad to help.

"Come on, Smith," Pinto said. "Let's go feed some horse-flesh."

Again, I felt glad to help.

February 11, 1861

Pinto and Julian rode off this morning to visit the Velásquez family. Well, Julian went to call on Alyvia, and Pinto said he would admire to see some more of this country. Says he might want to settle down here after the Yankee threat in Texas is ended.

I'd wanted to go along, too, but Pa reminded me of chores to be done, piling more stones on the dam, and helping Bartolomé clean the stalls.

They didn't get back from their visit until late tonight.

February 12, 1861
After breakfast, I asked Pinto what he thought about the land he had seen, and he nodded with approval, said it would work mighty fine.

"Work?" I asked. "For what?"

"Hades," he answered, and I laughed.

That Pinto is quite a character.

Same night, or rather morning, after midnight
Eastbound came and went, on time. Stagecoach was chock-full again. Also have news of an uprising among the Apaches at Apache Pass, where that lieutenant named Bascom, who my brother went to the Academy with, has provoked Cochise into war. As if fighting Red Sleeves wasn't bad enough. Upon hearing the news, Julian shook his head and said that sounded just like something Union soldiers would do. Don't know what he meant by that. He's a Union soldier his himself.

February 13, 1861
Wednesday. Westbound come tonight, loaded with folks, a bunch of them Texicans, and they all got to jawing with Ben Jakes, who managed to drag his worthless hide out of his bunk for supper, and Pinto, who was helping me feed the horde while

the rest, excepting Ben Jakes, of course, changed the teams. Well, the passengers jawed and jawed with us, poured down coffee and ate the slumgullion without complaint. Everything sounded real sociable till one of the travelers said he'd be mighty glad to get to Sacramento before the war started.

"Where you from?" Pinto asked.

"Dallas," the man answered. He wore a plaid sack suit and big silk hat. I'd guess he had to be in his forties, and he wore a single eyepiece, what Julian just told me they call a monocle. I'd never seen one of those before he pulled it out, cleaned it with a handkerchief, set it over his right eye and studied the slumgullion, as if he didn't know what he might find in Pa's concoction.

"They must have run you out of town." Pinto poured a lady a cup of coffee.

Although he never looked back at the man from Dallas and smiled politely at the lady, Pinto didn't try to hide his bitterness. The room turned quiet, but Pinto kept walking around the table, topping off coffee cups, but the man in the silk hat stood up, returning the monocle to his vest pocket.

"What do you mean, sir, by that remark?"

Pinto looked up. "Dallas ain't known to cotton to cowards." He spoke in a matter-of-fact voice. "Nowhere in Texas tolerates cowards."

Puffing out his chest, his face turning redder than Pinto's flannel shirt, the man pushed back his coat and rested his right hand on the butt of a single-shot Derringer. "Are you calling me a coward?"

"You called yourself one," said the Texican, sitting right beside him, a burly man in a tan hat with a brown patch over his left eye and a scar stretching from one cheek across the bridge of his nose to the other.

The insulted man looked away from Pinto, who took that opportunity to place his hand on that big knife on his hip, the flap on his holster preventing him from getting to his pistol in a timely fashion.

" 'Twas you who said you wanted to get out of Texas before shootin' commenced." Slurping up a mouthful of slumgullion, the big Texican didn't even bother to look up.

"I . . . you . . . I. . . ." The Dallas man just got redder and redder. "Well." Then he found his nerve. "I don't see either of you bound for Texas to defend her sovereign soil."

Immediately he regretted those words, for the man with the eye patch pushed away his bowl, and stood. He carried a big old Walker Colt belted around his belly, and that took some doing, because a Walker's a horse pistol, meant to be carried on the saddle pommel, and a giant Bowie sheathed on his left hip. The fellow from Dallas had practically called Pinto, and the man with the eye patch, cowards.

The lady gasped, and the Dallas gent didn't look so red any more. He kept getting paler and paler, especially when Mr. Eye Patch said: "You best apologize or I'll blow a hole in your brisket."

Yet it was Pinto who spoke. "It's me who needs to apologize," he said, taking his hand off the hilt of his knife and lifting the coffee pot again. "Should have known better than provoke somethin'." He bowed at the lady. "I'm sorry, ma'am." Turning to Mr. Dallas, he spoke softly but firmly. "I withdraw my statement, sir. It's no business of mine what takes you to California."

"War's comin'," Mr. Eye Patch told Pinto. "Mighty soon."

"We'll be ready," Pinto said.

That's when Pa come in, and he frowned mightily at two passengers standing, one of them looking sick, and nobody talking. His eyes landed on Pinto, who wet his lips and went back to pouring coffee.

"Drink up," Pa said. "Coach leaves in less than 5 minutes."

Afterward, I had to explain to Pa and Julian what all had happened. I feared Pa would send Pinto on his way, so I came to his defense, saying how he had stopped bloodshed, had apologized. Don't think Pa liked it none, but he didn't say more on the subject.

Same night, 11 o'clock
About to turn in.

Julian just told me: "You seem to like this Pinto."

"He's all right," I said.

"I wouldn't get close to him, Smith," he said.

"Ain't like I'm replacing you, Jules," I said, with a grin. "You're blood. He ain't. He's just. . . ."

Julian cut me off, repeating what he'd said, but this time it came out more like an order. "Don't get close to him, Brother. He's a killer."

Killer?

February 14, 1861
All day, I've been thinking about what Julian told me last night. Pinto, Bartolomé, and Fletcher are shoeing horses. Pa's scratching out a report to send off to Superintendent Hawley. Ben Jakes is up and about, but not really lending a hand, and I've washed all the dishes. Don't know where Julian took off to, but he saddled up Sweet Ainsley and rode out, probably to court Alyvia. I haven't seen the Velásquezes in a coon's age, seems like.

Killer, Julian called Pinto. Don't know where he came to that conclusion, but it's got me wondering, maybe worrying.

Killer.

Well, it strikes me that Pinto stopped a killing last night. It was Pinto who apologized, who prevented Mr. Eye Patch from likely killing that guy from Dallas, who probably is a coward. Acted like one, if you ask me.

Pinto's all right. I guess what I like about him is he's different. And he's here. Somebody new. I mean, the one good thing about working at Soldier's Farewell is that you get to meet a lot of interesting folks. Schoolteachers and miners and drummers and soldiers and adventurers, people who have lived in the East, people who have seen the Pacific Ocean. You meet them, and they've come from all over the United States, mostly Missouri and California, sure, but all over. However, you don't get to know them. You just meet them, talk to them over their food if it's the Westbound, and if they're going East, you hardly even see them.

Pinto stayed. I don't know how long he'll be here, but he's different, and he's here.

It's coming on three years now that I've been living at Soldier's Farewell. People would come to Boone County, Missouri, and they'd place roots. You'd get to know them. Unless you count the men who work at this station, I haven't gotten to know hardly anyone, excepting the Velásquezes, since we got here, and maybe folks like Emmett Mills and Mr. Barney, but they are not really neighbors, just other employees of the Overland.

So . . . Pinto . . . he's here, he's new, he's different, and he listens to me. Seemed real interested and impressed when I told him all about the draws and such, and the difference between the hills around the station.

That's all. Not like he's my brother or nothing. He's just somebody new and interesting. I don't think he's a killer, though. Not unless you gave him cause.

★ ★ ★ ★ ★

February 15, 1861

"Killed him?" Pa looked incredulous. "Killed him?"

It's after midnight, the Eastbound is gone, and I'm sitting in the corner, scratching out these words, lessen I forget. Not that I think I could ever forget.

It happened like this.

The Eastbound pulled in right on time, with Marco Max driving, and, while Little Terry jumped down to help us with the team, Marco Max set the brake and climbed down off the stage, too, which he has never done while driving the Eastbound.

"Munro!" he yelled, and Pa, who was fetching the fresh team with Julian and Fletcher, pulled away and headed to him, while Pinto run from the team we were unhitching to give Julian and Fletcher a hand.

"What in blazes is going on?" Pa yelled, and Marco Max just kept walking to him, till he got real close, and they started jawing. Couldn't hear a word they said until Pa bellowed: "Killed him? Killed him?"

Well, that got all our attention. Bartolomé and me looked up, just stopped what we was doing, until Little Terry reminded us of the work to be done. We got back to the harness, but our ears stayed trained on Pa and Marco Max.

Bartolomé asked Little Terry something in Spanish, but the messenger just shrugged, spit out tobacco juice. "Mr. Munro'll tell you about it. Let's get a move on."

So we pulled the team away, and Bartolomé and I led the mules to the stable. I had time to glance over my shoulder, to see Pa and Marco Max still talking as the jehu headed back to the stagecoach and climbed back into the box.

The stage pulled out, and I felt certain sure I wouldn't. . . .

Pa's demanding I quit writing and go to bed. Will have to finish this tomorrow.

February 16, 1861

Back to what all happened last night. I thought Pa wouldn't tell me a thing about who had gotten killed, where, or why, figured he'd just tell me to go to bed, treat me like I was a kid, and then he and Julian and maybe Mr. Fletcher would talk about things. So it struck me like an axe when I walked into the room and Pa fired out hot words:

"What went on the other night on the Westbound, Smith? Between those two passengers? And Pinto?"

I looked around. Pinto wasn't there. Probably had turned in with the rest of the hands. Even Fletcher wasn't inside.

"I. . . ."

"What happened?" Pa roared.

I hadn't done a thing, so I felt scared and a bit angry. I hadn't tried hiding anything from Pa. He hadn't asked about the fight that never come about. Well, I told Pa, and Julian, the truth, how Pinto had called the man in the silk hat a coward, how the guy with the eye patch had done the same, but then how Pinto had done all the apologizing, and things settled down and all.

"Pinto stopped them from killing one another," I said, coming to Pinto's defense.

Pa spit. "Not hardly."

"But he did," I said. "You can ask him."

"I plan to. The guy with the eye patch shot the other one dead when they got to Barney's."

"Killed him?" I couldn't believe it. Sounded just like Pa had when Marco Max spilled the news.

"Killed him." Sagging, Pa sank into his chair and shook his head. "They exchanged some more words after leaving here. The man with the scar and patch kicked him off the stage, right out the door, when they pulled in to Barney's Station, jumped out, drawing his revolver, and shot him twice in the chest."

"Must have been some conversation between those two," Julian said.

With a snarl, Pa slammed his fist on the table. "This ain't funny."

"No, sir," Julian said.

"No, sir," I added, even though I hadn't laughed or cracked a grin.

"The company doesn't like paying customers getting killed," Pa said.

"It happened at Barney's," Julian said. "Not here. It isn't your fault. And it's not Smith's."

It's not Pinto's, either, I started to add, but instead reminded them: "That man, the one from Dallas, he had a Derringer in his waistband. I saw it. He started to pull it on Pinto. So maybe he tried for it, tried to shoot the man with the patch, and that's how come he got killed."

Pa kept quiet, but I don't think he considered anything I said. To him, Mr. Eye Patch had committed murder in cold blood.

"What happened after the shooting?" I asked.

"Took off, the man did, ran south. Other one was dead. Both bullets hit his heart. It was dark. Barney and two others went looking for him come first light, but they couldn't find the trail."

"You should get *Señor* Vee," I said. "He could track down that fellow."

Shaking his head, Pa slowly stood. "Trail's cold by now. Barney can't spare any manhunters, either."

"You can," Julian said, and that stopped Pa and me.

"Put Jakes back to work," my brother said. "He's fine, just lazy. Pinto and I'll scout for that *hombre*."

"Cochise or some other Apache probably has killed him by

99

now," Pa said.

"Did Marco know the man's name? Where he was bound?"

Pa shook his head.

"He went south." Julian considered this. "But I don't think he'd run or walk all the way to the border. Probably swing back north. To Burchville and the Pinos Altos mines. That's a good place for anybody to disappear."

"If he knows the territory," Pa said. "Coming from Texas, he might not."

"Maybe the man with the monocle drew his Derringer," I suggested again. "Could be it was self-defense."

"That's for the courts to decide," Pa said. "There's such a thing as the law, even in New Mexico Territory." He gave my brother a look I can't quite describe, like he was trying to figure something out. "What's your interest? Why should you risk your hide going after him? Like you just said, it happened at Barney's, not here. Not our concern."

"I'm a soldier."

Pa's head shook. "Not a military matter."

Julian suddenly grinned. "Then how about this, Pa? It'll give me something different to do. Something interesting."

Silence. Outside, the wind picked up.

"I'll ask Pinto," Julian said, deciding for himself. "We'll ride out at dawn. See if we can track down the man-killer. Bring him back here. Put him on the stage to Mesilla, or take him there ourselves. Let a grand jury sort it out."

Said Pa: "If you find him."

Julian grinned like he'd just been challenged.

"You could ride over to *Señor* Vee's," I said. "He's the best tracker in the territory."

My brother shook his head. "Wouldn't want to inconvenience him," Julian said. "Besides, I learned a few things about tracking while chasing Paiutes."

That's what Julian and Pinto done. Before breakfast, they lit out on two good mules, pulling an extra one, saddled and all, in case they found Mr. Eye Patch, behind them.

Pa just stood there, the wind blowing, just stood and watched as they rode out, till you couldn't see them any more, and then he walked away. He made a beeline for Besse Rhodes, started climbing the hill. When he reached the top, he'd watch the dust trail Julian and Pinto made.

It's noon now, and, though Pinto and Julian must be long out of sight, Pa ain't yet come down.

February 17, 1861
A Sunday. Julian and Pinto ~~ain't~~ haven't come back yet. This morning over breakfast, Pa told me not to worry about them, that Pinto and Julian could take care of themselves, then made me recite a Bible passage before I could eat. "And don't say 'Jesus wept,' " he instructed me. I thought about telling him that I wasn't hungry, and I wasn't, and therefore would not quote the Good Book this morning, but that would have just provoked a whipping. So I spoke from Deuteronomy, mainly because a lady passenger had said this a few days back when I dished her a bowl of slumgullion and wormy hardtack.

" 'Thou shalt not eat any abominable thing.' "

"You commenting on my cooking?" Pa tried to smile, to make me think he wasn't worried, either, but I could see through that plain as day.

Same day, half past 8
Julian still not home. Waiting on the Westbound.

February 18, 1861
No word from Julian, but *Señor* Vee showed up this morning,

and rode out after a private talk with Pa. I imagine Pa asked him to go looking for Julian. *Señor* Vee says we can expect a visit from the rest of his family.

I should take time to write some of the news we heard from the passengers last night.

No news about Fort Sumter, but the states that have dissolved the Union—South Carolina, Mississippi, Florida, Alabama, Georgia, Louisiana, and Texas—were meeting in Montgomery, Alabama, to elect a President and write a constitution for the new nation, the Confederate States of America. There were two men from Mississippi on the stage, and there was much talk about who would become President.

Another person, who was from Chambersburg, Virginia, I think, kept quoting from this newspaper called the *Valley Spirit*.

" 'Is the country to be subjected to the horrors of civil war? We hardly see how that calamity can be averted as things are going.' " He kept on, had most of this story memorized, or at least that's what he said, and the article had been written and published back in December. He kept on talking, until another passenger, and this one sounded like he just arrived from Ireland, he broke out laughing.

"Civil war," he says. "Trust me, lads, there will be nothing civil about the coming war."

One of the men from Mississippi snorted, protesting that the war would be over in six weeks, but the Irishman just looked up, and his face turned sad, and he didn't say a thing, just looked with his cold blue eyes, and the man from Mississippi stared at his coffee cup, and nobody else spoke until Pa come inside and announced the stage was fixing to leave.

February 19, 1861
Before the arrival of the stage, we had a fandango yesterday

afternoon. Julian and Pinto rode back, along with *Señor* Vee, just an hour or so after *Señora* Dolores arrived with Tori and Alyvia. We ate *chiles rellenos, frijoles, tortillas,* and *empanadas* stuffed with mincemeat, enough good food that would certainly make Pa's slumgullion, especially as watered down as it has been the past three, four days, seem like something abominable. It was like *Señora* Dolores knew Julian would be coming home, although she couldn't have.

The man with the Eye Patch wasn't with them.

"Any sign of him?" Pa asked while the womenfolk cleared off the table and washed the dishes, which made me mighty happy as I wouldn't have that chore to do later, or then.

"Apaches got him," Pinto answered, and Julian shot him an odd look. Reckon on account of how loud Pinto said it, might have frightened *la señora* and her girls. "We buried him." He sipped his coffee, swallowed, and shook his head. "What was left of him."

Señor Vee crossed himself.

"Well. . . ." Pa smoothed his mustache. "You cut any sign, Alejondro?"

Pa's Mexican friend shook his head, and Julian spoke up.

"We'd buried the *hombre* and were coming back home when we found Mr. Velásquez." A wide grin spread across my brother's face. "Or, I guess I should say, when he found us."

"Where'd you find the Texican?"

Julian and Pinto looked at each other. "South," Julian said uncomfortably. "Past Black Mountain."

"He covered a lot of ground, being afoot," Pa said.

"Yes, sir," Julian and Pinto agreed.

"I thought he'd turn toward the mines," Julian said. "Didn't know the country, I guess."

"Yeah." Pa nodded, but it looked like he hadn't even heard. He just sat, thinking, stroking that big mustache. "Didn't look like some greenhorn, though. Looked like a man who knew how to handle himself." He thought about this some more. "If not striking north for the mines, he should have made his way closer to the Overland Trail, where he'd know he could find some water."

"Good way to get caught," Pinto said.

"Sneak in at night. Draw water from the springs. Hide in the daytime." Pa shook his head. "How'd y'all cut his trail?"

"We didn't," Julian said quickly. "All we saw was the buzzards. Then we found him."

Again, *Señor* Vee crossed himself, and Pa sighed.

"Pa," Julian said. "I'm not sure he walked all the way to Black Mountain. I think the Apaches caught him quickly, maybe the night he killed the fool from Dallas. The Indians were riding for Mexico, and they brought him along, then tortured him, left him for dead. If you want, and if Mr. Velásquez will accompany me, we'll ride back in the morning, see what signs he can find. Maybe we'll learn a better account of what must have happened." He swallowed, and we all waited.

Pa started to speak, but Tori came over and asked if anyone wanted coffee, but we all shook our heads, and she left, disappointed.

"Well?" Julian asked.

"No," Pa said. "No point in that. I'll write a note to Barney and Giles, tell them what you discovered, and I thank you, thank you both, for going after him, giving him a Christian burial." He nodded at *Señor* Vee. "Much obliged, Alejondro. *Mil gracias.*"

"*De nada.*"

"Apaches." Looking off at the hills, Pa went back to fingering his mustache. "Could be more trouble. We'll double the guards."

"They were headin' for Mexico," Pinto said. "I don't think they'll trouble us."

"Maybe. Maybe not." Pa rose. "Still, just to be safe, we'll double the guards. Alejondro, you might want to spend the night here, with your family. In case Apaches are here. The women can sleep inside. The boys and me can bed down elsewhere."

"Your hospitality is much appreciated, *mi amigo*," *Señor* Vee began, and the way he looked over his shoulder, I knew he would decline Pa's offer. "But I want to go to my own home. This place. . . ." He stopped. Alyvia, Tori, and his wife had returned, smiling, and we all painted on our faces the most awful-looking smiles anyone has ever seen.

They left—they never wanted to be here of nights—and, true to his word, Pa doubled the guards. Not that he'd let me lend a hand.

February 20, 1861
Pa sent his report on the finding and burial of Mr. Eye Patch on the Westbound tonight, and he warned us not to mention the Apaches to any of the passengers. Guards are still doubled.

Spent this morning with Julian, like I was in school, going over the *Reader* and writing and talking in good English. He says my spelling's really good, and my construction and grammar keep getting better but still need some work.

February 21, 1861
More schooling from Julian. I'm starting to wish he'd leave for his new posting.

February 22, 1861
This morning, Julian saddled Sweet Ainsley and said he was going to ride over to the Velásquez place, just to make sure they were all right.

"Take Smith with you," Pa said.

That shocked me almost as much as it did Julian.

"I don't know," Julian said. "With the Apaches. . . ."

"Take him. Should be all right. Like Pinto said, those Indians are most likely in Mexico by now. And your brother has been cooped up here too long. Do him some good to see the country." I detected a twinkle in Pa's eyes. "And maybe a chaperone for you and Miss Alyvia."

"Pa!" Julian protested, and I started laughing real hard until Pa added something.

"Maybe your brother would like to court Victoria."

"Pa!" I shouted, and Julian got a turn at laughing.

Will have to finish this in the morning. Anyway, I'm back home, but tuckered out. Covered a lot of ground in one day.

February 23, 1861

Need to write about what happened. Julian told me not to mention a word to Pa, and that's fine, but I guess I can write about it. That's what this diary is for.

It struck me as mighty peculiar. Well, let me write just the way it happened.

Julian and I were riding, side-by-side, through this grove of yuccas, when, from out of nowhere, this man appeared. One second there was nothing but a bunch of desert, and in the time I blinked, I found myself staring at a cruel-looking individual blocking our trail.

"Apache!" I screamed, and started to tear out of this country, but Julian reached over and grabbed my reins.

"Smith!" he yelled. "It's all right. He's a friend."

I didn't hear him, not at first, must have gone a little crazy with fear, but Julian remained calm.

"Friend?" I looked at my brother, my chest heaving, my heart pounding like it might explode, and then looked again at the silent figure between the tall yuccas.

106

He wore Apache moccasins and duck trousers, a Mexican serape over a muslin shirt, straw hat, and a big .45 belted in a yellow sash. What I noticed most, however, were the long hair, flowing past his shoulders, and eyes, blacker that a raven's.

"He's a. . . ."

"He's a half-breed," Julian said. I couldn't see how he could talk so calm. "Scout for the Army. Trust me, Smith, he helped us when I was in the dragoons, scouted for us when we went after the Paiutes."

My lips still trembling, I made myself calm down, and the mean-looking *hombre* smiled.

"Thought . . . he . . . soil . . . britches." He spoke in a guttural voice, deep, broken, mean. He might have thought he was funny, but I found nothing comical, although I had to check myself, make sure I hadn't wet my pants or done something worse.

"What's his name?" I asked Julian.

"Nicanor," the half-breed said, no longer smiling. "But you call me Breed. Most do. I'm not insulted by the name."

"What's he doing here?" I blurted out at Julian. I didn't understand anything.

"I'm here," Breed said with some irritation. "Ask me."

I made myself look at him, swallowed down the fear in my throat, waited for my stomach to settle. Slowly Julian released the reins, and rested his hands on the horn of his saddle.

"What . . . ?" I swallowed again. "What . . . ?" I made myself sound friendly, casual. "What brings you here, Breed?"

The smile returned, revealing a couple of gold front teeth, and Breed turned, pointing down the road. "Horses," he answered.

"¿*Caballos?*" *Señor* Vee scratched his head, staring at the horses Breed had in a string, behind the paint horse he rode.

"That's right," Julian answered. "We just want to keep our horses here. For two, maybe three days."

"*Yo no entiendo.*" He looked past my brother, past me, and his face locked on the hard figure of Breed.

"It's like this, Mr. Velásquez," Julian said. "I rode with Breed with the 1ˢᵗ Dragoons. He's a good man, and he knows horses, *caballos. Muy bien.* We want to raise horses. Sell them to the Army."

Looking at the horses, I frowned. So did *Señor* Vee. Julian glanced over his shoulder, realized what bothered us, and grinned. "Yes, they're geldings. But that's what the dragoons want. The Army doesn't care to mix stallions with mares. Hard to form regular lines in battle. We'll raise horses, or buy geldings, break them, sell them to the dragoons. It's a business. Uh . . . *negocios.*"

"*Sí.*" *Señor* Vee stepped back.

"Sir," Julian said, "you know my father. He's a jackman. Mules are his life. *Mulas.* Now, do you think he'd let me keep a bunch of rangy geldings with his jennies and jacks, his horses and donkeys? Do you know what . . . how much Cain he'd raise if he found out his oldest son wanted to raise horses, *caballos,* in Texas, and sell them to the Army?"

I think Julian was talking to me, as much as he was to *Señor* Vee, when he said that. He removed his hat, and brushed bangs out of his eyes. He was almost sweating, so I could picture how nervous he would be if he had to explain all this to Pa.

"Two or three days," Julian said. "Then I'll be leaving for my next posting. . . ."

The rest of his words faded. Julian had said nothing about leaving. In two or three days. Hardly any time at all. My heart sank.

"*Días. Dos o tres,*" Julian said. "Then they'll be gone. *Deja.*"

Breed spoke up, in Spanish, doing a better job of it than my

108

brother had done, and at last *Señor* Vee understood, because he grinned a great big one, and said something, his head bobbing. He knew exactly what my father would say about Julian's choice in horseflesh.

"And I have to ask you," Julian said, but, again, he directed his words at both me and Pa's Mexican *amigo*. "Please, *por favor*, say nothing of these horses to my father."

Señor Vee nodded. "Your secret is safe with me. They can stay here two or three days."

"Breed can stay," Julian said. "I mean, with your permission. Uh, *con . . . su . . . permiso.* He'll tend the horses." Julian gestured at Breed.

"Durante dos o tres días," *Señor* Vee repeated, but he didn't sound like he'd enjoy having Breed around. I don't blame him.

I didn't speak much on the way home.

"You won't mention the horses to Pa, will you, Smith?" he asked.

I shook my head.

"Sorry Breed scared you, Smith. He looks mean, but. . . ."

The hoofs of the mules clopped along the rocks. In the distance, I could see the small peaks. Soldier's Farewell. Julian was leaving.

"Hey." Julian pointed to a cloud. "What does that one remind you of?"

"You're leaving," I blurted out. Petulant. Couldn't help it.

He reined in Sweet Ainsley, let out a heavy sigh, and, when I didn't stop, he barked out an order. I pulled Ivanhoe to a halt, looked back at my brother.

"You knew I wouldn't be here forever, Smith." He pointed east. "I'm on furlough. You know that. The war's coming. Pa can deny it all he wants, but that won't stop it. I'm obliged to fight. I have to fight. It's called duty."

Well, now, I couldn't stop the tears once Julian said all that, as much as I tried, as much as I wanted to act like a man in front of my brother, a second lieutenant with the 1st United States Dragoons. Criminy, the dam up and busted wide open, and suddenly I found myself bawling, gripping the saddle horn till my knuckles turned white. Ashamed, I felt, and more that a bit scared, not about the half-breed we had left at the Velásquez place, but for my brother, and the approaching war.

"I don't want you to get killed, Jules!" I choked out when he rode up to me, put his arm around my shoulder, hugging me close, almost pulling me off my mule.

"Mark my words, Innis Smith Munro," he whispered. "I won't get killed. I promise you that."

He waited until I regained some composure, and then, dabbing the tears and wiping the dirt off my streaked face with his bandanna, he warmed me with his smile. "There," he said at last. "You feeling better?"

Best answer I could manage was a feeble nod.

"Let's get back home." He retied the bandanna around his neck. "And, please, little Brother, don't mention those horses to Pa. He'd want to see them, then spend the next three days telling me what a poor lot they are. That's one fight I'm not ready for. That's one fight I'd never win."

February 24, 1861

Plenty to write about. Eastbound brings news of Jefferson Davis, who Pa knew back in Mississippi, a report about President Lincoln, and another—if you can believe this—gentleman traveler, who got off after buying a ticket from Tucson to Soldier's Farewell. Never heard of anyone buying a ticket for here, but he says he plans on joining some friends from Mesilla and heading to Burchville to try his hand at mining. They know to meet him here in a few days and continue the journey north.

His name is J.T. Cassady, and he speaks in a soft accent, although Pa says he sounds like his mouth is filled with cornbread and molasses. He has agreed to pay his way and sleep in the stable, and if he has enough gold to pay what Pa charges for meals, he doesn't need to be going to the Pinos Altos mines because he must already be rich.

He is a middle-aged fellow, bald on the top of his head, the rest of his hair dark and flecked with gray, but I ain't got no idea how old he is. Could be 40. Could be 60. A bit on the heavy side, dressed in a plaid sack suit, and wearing a gray bell-crown hat. Light brown eyes, which I heard Pa call rheumy, and lugging around a battered old carpetbag.

Anyway, he's here. Don't know for how long. Tends to keep out of our way and just walk around the yard, although Pa has told him not to wander too far from the buildings unless he wants to wind up in the hands of the Apaches. We haven't seen sign of Indians of late, but it pays to be careful at Soldier's Farewell.

Now, I should write about Lincoln and Davis. News seems to be spreading a lot faster these days. I reckon more folks are interested in what's happening, how close we're getting to the war back East.

Well, the Union President will be inaugurated next month, in just a few days. I reckon Mr. Lincoln is in Washington City already, as he left Springfield, Illinois, on February 11, but the big news comes from Montgomery, Alabama, where Jefferson Davis has been selected as President of the new Confederate States of America. That comes as a surprise to most, at least according to the jehu, Big Terry, and that J.T. Cassady gent, who says he has family in Mobile, which he tells me is on the Gulf of Mexico in Alabama.

What I noticed, reading the paper, is that North Carolina sent representatives to Montgomery with the rest of the states of the new nation, but North Carolina hasn't dissolved the Union yet. I pointed that out to Julian, but it was Mr. Cassady who spoke on the subject. "A matter of time," he said in that slow drawl. "A matter of time. Those Tarheels will soon join our just and righteous cause."

I guess it's all over. The Union, I mean. When I told Pa that, he didn't answer me, just sighed and walked outside, where I saw him standing at the stable, looking at our battered old flag, fluttering in the wind.

Over. Really over. At least, that's what the Mesilla *Times* is reporting. The headline in the latest paper declared:

IT IS FINISHED

Big Terry and Donnie Oh, the conductor, brought the paper on the stage, and gave it to Pa, and Julian suggested this morning after breakfast that I copy some of the story into my diary. Good to practice writing, he said. So this is from the *Times*, which, as I've written a while back, Emmett Mills doesn't think highly of, but it is news, important news, so here it is:

The deed has been done. We breathe deeper and freer for it. The Union is dead. It was a great, a glorious fabric; but its timbers had rotted at the heart.

I was rereading that passage aloud when Pa come in from the stables, and he frowned, spit, and suggested I take that newspaper to the privy, where it belongs.

"Smith's just practicing reading and writing," Julian told him.

"He'd do better practicing on something other than that trash," Pa fired back, turned, and walked outside. I guess he doesn't think much of the newspaper, same as Emmett Mills.

Same day, 5 o'clock

I just came in from the stables, and found Pa sitting at the

112

table, reading the *Times*. I didn't say anything to him, just came to my bunk to write this down. He looked mighty interested in the writing, especially seeing how he told Julian it was trash earlier today.

February 25, 1861

Waiting for Julian to tell Pa that he's leaving. It must be tomorrow. I wonder why he ain't mentioned it. Today, he rode off after breakfast on Sweet Ainsley to see Alyvia, but I know he also went to check on his geldings, and Breed. Pinto asked if he could ride out, too, but not with my brother. He wanted to ride along the trail for a bit, and Pa let him. Ain't seen much of Mr. Cassady today. No sign of those men who he's supposed to meet here. Hope the Apaches haven't gotten them.

Same day, half past 9 o'clock

Julian rode back around suppertime, said he wasn't hungry, and after I went out to fetch a bucket of water from the spring, I come back inside and found him reading this diary.

That riled me some, and Julian slammed the cover shut.

"I'm examining your grammar, Smith," he said. "You're getting the hang of it, but you need to remember that there is no such word as ain't."

"Well, you ain't supposed to read another person's diaries. That's what Ma told Pa long ago." I felt madder than a scorpion. " 'A diary is for the person writing in it.' That's what Ma said. So I don't think you need to be reading about my thoughts, wishes." I had to think about what all Pa had told me when I first got this book. "Hopes," I added. "Dreams."

Julian's face revealed how angry he was when I first started snapping at him, but it softened when I mentioned Ma, and he gently handed me the book. "You're right, little Brother," he said. "I apologize."

I snatched it from his hand, sat down in my corner. "When you telling Pa you're leaving?" I asked. That's really what kept festering, not the fact that he had read my innermost thoughts.

"Tomorrow," he replied softly. "Maybe the day after. Thanks for not telling him about that, Smith. Or about the horses at Mr. Velásquez's place."

"You tell Alyvia that you're going?"

His head shook, and he stared at his stocking feet. "Haven't told anyone. Only you. And Alyvia's father, of course."

I handed him back the diary. "You can read it," I told him. "I don't really mind. I don't have many hopes and dreams."

He shook his head. "You should. A boy your age should be filled with hopes and dreams." He let out a little laugh. "Why, I remember when I was your age. I had big plans and dreams. I was. . . . Well, it doesn't matter about me and those long ago dreams."

"You got any dreams now?" Prying, I was, trying to see if he planned on marrying Alyvia, but Julian didn't answer. Just rolled into his bed—my bed that he had been borrowing all this time—and said he was tuckered out.

He's snoring now. Almost as loud as Pa.

February 26, 1861

Big excitement when the Eastbound arrived this morning right on time.

Excitement at first, I mean. Then trouble. Bad trouble.

It all started when three passengers got off as soon as the stagecoach pulled to a stop, one from inside the Celerity and the other two climbing down from the top.

Before Pa could yell at them, the jehu said this was their destination, and Pa shouted that Soldier's Farewell was no boarding house.

"Ve vill not inconvenience you very long, *Herr* Munro," said the one who had been inside the coach. "Uh . . . ve vill not be here long." He clicked his boot heels and bowed slightly. "Captain Ulf Beckenbauer, 6th United States Infantry. At your service!"

He pointed a redwood staff, which he had carried under his left armpit, at the two other men, who, just from how they stood, I had already determined to be soldiers.

"Lieutenant Day *und* Sergeant Scott, of the dragoons."

It was one of those associates who grabbed my attention when he asked Pa: "Is Julian here, sir?"

Lieutenant Richardson Day must have been the tallest man I'd ever met, with light blue eyes and wavy blond hair, and dressed in the uniform of the 1st U.S. Dragoons, so I figured he had fought with Julian against the Paiutes. The other fellow, Sergeant Lucas Scott, resembled a bear, with a thick black beard and a chest shaped like a water barrel, and about as solid as one, too. The strip of black fur on the headband of his forage cap made me think even more of a bear when I looked at him.

Captain Beckenbauer was a big man, too, silver hair and mustache painted with brown streaks, and a left hand that I tried not to stare at . . . only couldn't help myself. It looked like a vine that had withered and turned black after a killing frost, but I wouldn't say that bad hand made the captain weak. Nothing like that at all. He appeared as tough as Lieutenant Day looked tall.

"What brings you out this way?" Pa asked as we poured them coffee in our little abode after the stagecoach left.

Silently Julian stood back in the corner. I figured he would be glad to see some pals of his from Fort Tejon, but he looked to be off his feed. Oh, he had shaken their hands and all, outside, after hearing Lieutenant Day ask about him, and again, inside, when we came in out of the chill, but he wasn't treating these soldiers as friends. To me, he seemed to study our visitors with a bit of anxiety.

The big German made a face as he tested Pa's coffee, and nodded at Richardson Day, so the tall lieutenant did the answering.

"Captain Beckenbauer has been ordered to intercept known Southern sympathizers. Sergeant Scott and I are on detached service with him."

"You expect to find sympathizers at Soldier's Farewell?" Pa asked.

Almost immediately I thought about Ben Jakes shooting off his mouth about Texas and fighting Union soldiers, and silently I cursed him, thinking his wild talk had been reported by some of the Overland passengers, and now they had sent the Army to arrest all of us.

Lieutenant Day looked uncomfortable.

"It's. . . ." He stared past Pa and at Julian. "I figured you would have joined the Rebels back in Carolina by now, Jules." Hearing this, Pa and I both whirled, barely catching Day's following words. "Hoped that's where you'd be, anyhow. Not here."

"Rebels!" Pa roared. He started for Julian, stopped, spun back to stare at the soldiers.

Day dropped his head, muttered something underneath his breath, and then looked back up, his face pale, frustrated, confused. "I'm sorry, Jules," he said hoarsely. "I thought your father knew."

"Knew what?" Pa asked, but he knew already. So did I. We didn't need the big German to answer.

"*Herr* Munro is . . . a traitor."

"Captain." Lieutenant Day straightened. "There's no cause for that. Jules is doing what he thinks is right. So have a lot of other officers."

"*Ja, ja, ja.* Und you threw a party in his honor ven he resigned. Bid fond farewell. Shake hands, pour champagne. Till ve meet on the battlefield. I, however, would not toast this man, nor any of his ilk."

The captain spit coffee onto the floor, flung the tin cup rudely on the table, and stared at my brother with hatred filling his eyes. "A traitor," he said again.

"I'm no traitor," Julian said. "I'm doing my duty. To my home." He stood tall now, my brother, and he walked up to Pa. "I resigned my commission, Pa. I guess I should have told you. I'm bound for South Carolina. Home. To defend my home, my people."

"Your home's here," Pa told him. "Or Missouri."

"No, sir. I was born in South Carolina."

"Your. . . ."

"Pa, I'm Carolina-born. I grew up in Mississippi. That makes me Southern. Even Missouri's likely to pull out of the Union."

"Southron, as they say." The captain spoke with a quiet bitterness. "Traitor. Coward."

For a moment there, I figured Pa would knock down Julian, but when the German kept saying that, calling my brother a traitor, then a coward, Pa practically tore the captain's head off. He spun, rammed a fist into the soldier's nose, slammed the officer back against the wall. The redwood stick dropped from underneath the captain's arm and rattled on the floor. "Shut up, Mr.," Pa said tightly, and, when the sergeant's hand dropped for his holstered pistol, Pa warned him. "Touch that pistol, Sergeant, and I'll kill you."

I stood there, frozen. Couldn't move. Couldn't say a thing. Not even sure I could breathe.

"Leave it be, Sergeant Scott." Lieutenant Day remained the only calm person inside.

"This is my home," Pa told the soldiers. "And this is a private

117

matter between me and my oldest son. You'll leave us alone for a few minutes."

"*Nein.* Not possible." The captain pressed a handkerchief to his nose.

I'll say one thing for that German. Angry as he was, embarrassed, bleeding, he kept himself from losing control, from starting a fight that would lead to a whole lot more bloodshed, and I thought he would do just that for a while there.

"I could have you arrested, *Herr* Munro." He spoke tightly. "Put you in irons." Trembling with rage, the captain started to say something, maybe issue an order to that effect, but he reined himself in, examined his handkerchief, and nodded at the sergeant to pick up his redwood staff.

"I vill forget this," Beckenbauer said when he had the big stick back under his arm, and the handkerchief under his nose. "But if you touch me again, ve vill meet on the field of honor."

"Captain," Lieutenant Day pleaded.

"Lieutenant Day," the German said. "Remember *your* duty."

The tall lieutenant let out a long sigh. "A Southern sympathizer named J.T. Cassady left Tucson. He bought a ticket on the Overland to Soldier's Farewell."

"He's here." Suddenly Pa looked troubled. Concern filled his soft voice, and Pa, when riled, usually didn't speak quiet at all.

"Our orders are to detain him," Day said. "Stop him."

"And protect the payroll," the German said, anger rising again. He thrust the bloody piece of cotton at Julian. "That he plans to rob!"

I should point out that as I write these words, I'm sitting against the wall with Pa and the others. Prisoners. It's like one of those dreams I've written about before, where you wake up and aren't sure if what happened is real or not, but I know. This is no dream. I'm awake. Sitting here, a prisoner in my own home. Writing . . . and waiting. Starting to hate my brother.

That German captain, he's dead. They're making Bartolomé and Mr. Fletcher bury him now that it's daylight.

This is what happened.

"Payroll?" Pa glanced over his shoulder at Julian, then turned back to the soldiers. "What are you talking about? What payroll?"

"Army payroll," Lieutenant Day said. "For Fort Tejon. It's coming on the Overland stage."

Pa shook his head. "You're loco. The Overland carries passengers and regular mail only. We don't ship payrolls. It's not allowed. Never has been since Mr. Butterfield started this enterprise."

"That's true." Beckenbauer examined his handkerchief, realized his nose had stopped bleeding, and tossed it beside the coffee cup. He nodded at Lieutenant Day, who sighed and started talking, never taking his eyes off my brother.

"Colonel Dawson, our commanding officer at Fort Tejon, received reports from Tucson of a plan to rob the next payroll shipment. Through communication with Jefferson Barracks, it was decided that the next payroll wagon would be armed, not with money, but guards, so if the bandits tried to hit us, they would be in for a surprise. In the meantime, three couriers, in civilian clothing, would carry the payroll on the Overland, in money belts and in their grips. No one at Wells, Fargo, and Company would know of this."

"*Und* no one did," the German said in a harsh whisper. "But him." He pointed the staff at Julian.

"Well," Lieutenant Day said, "Colonel Dawson knew, as did his adjutant, a couple of others at Fort Tejon, and those involved at Jefferson Barracks. But, yes, Julian knew, because of his duties as commissary of subsistence. The problem is, Colonel Dawson and the others have not resigned, are not joining the Confederacy."

"Traitor," the German said again, and I started for him,

started to tell him to quit calling my brother that, but Julian pulled me back, and he went after the captain himself, jerking the staff from the big fellow's hand and flinging it across the room.

"Traitor!" He pointed a finger in the captain's face. "You're the traitor, Beckenbauer! You and those other high-and-mighty, holier-than-thou fools blinded by the North's treachery and deceit. You've broken your promises, your vows. The Army in California is no longer protecting the citizens. What right have you to stop men from leaving California and the territories simply because they feel the South's cause is just?" Julian swung his outstretched arm at Day. "And you, Rich? Are you going to arrest your own brother? You told me yourself how Kenny said he would resign his commission, no matter what Kentucky did, and join the Confederate army. You want to ride up to Canton-ment Burgwin, stop him, maybe put him in manacles? Or kill him?"

For a moment, no one spoke, but then Pa asked Julian: "You'd fire on the flag of the United States?" Laughing, without humor, Pa shook his head. "That's like spitting in my face, Ju-lian. I always figured a man could trust his sons, could depend on them. I. . . ."

"Don't start on that, Pa." Julian now stood face to face with my father, and I feared they might come to blows. "I remember you saying umpteen times, how a Scot from Boone County by way of South Carolina and Mississippi could depend on his sons. Southern states, Pa. Southern! What do you want me to do? Fight the friends and family we had back in Camden and Port Gibson? Fight Ma's relations?" He thrust his arm at the captain. "Fight for him? *Him?* They're arresting men just for what they believe in. They're forgetting what they taught me at the Academy, about *habeas corpus,* about the principles our na-tion was founded on. It's like the editor wrote in the *Times.*

'The Union is dead . . . its timbers had rotted at the heart.' "

"Your duty. . . ."

"Duty?" Julian shook his head. His eyes were wild, tears welling but blocked from falling by my brother's iron will. "You told me before I left for the Academy about duty, about honor, but I think I left all that at Fort Tejon. We went after those Paiutes, Pa, because Captain Carleton said they had killed some settlers. But those Indians had nothing to do with those killings, Pa. Carleton knew that. Colonel Dawson knew it. We all knew it, but we still pursued the Paiutes. We killed a lot of them. For what? Nothing. Nothing but glory for Dawson and Carleton. Because nobody cares if an Indian is innocent. You want me to fight for that? Or maybe do what George Bascom has done at Apache Pass? Cochise was at peace with us before Bascom started a war. For nothing! That's Union duty for you. Yankee duty. I believe in the Confederacy, Pa. I won't fire on the neighbors we had in Camden and Port Gibson. Or Boone County. That's where my duty belongs. I'm going to South Carolina. I'm going to join Wade Hampton. I'm. . . ."

"Wade Hampton?" Pa fired back. "Son, the last I heard, my dear friend was a senator for the United States."

"He'll resign," Julian argued. "Same as your other dear friend, Jeff Davis. President Davis! Wade Hampton will fight for Carolina. You know that better than anyone. His loyalty is to South Carolina. Same as mine!"

"All right!" Pa's roar sounded like a cannon, so loud, so violent, Julian had to take a couple of fearful steps back. "If that's what you believe in, fight. Get yourself killed for all I care. But there is no war. Not yet. God willing, it won't come to that, and it won't come here. No shots have been fired. Certainly not at Soldier's Farewell. So you tell me, Julian, and you look me in the eye. You tell me that this German and your lieutenant pal are wrong. Dead wrong. You tell me that you know nothing about robbing an Army payroll. Because unless there's war, that ain't a military action. That's a bunch of bandits stealing. That won't get you any medals. It'll get you hung."

We waited.

"Tell me!" Pa trembled with rage. No, I guess he was fearful, too, just like Julian. Just like me.

Julian swallowed, and stepped away. He couldn't even look at Pa. "Mr. Cassady says the South needs that money."

I barely heard him.

Now, I've always thought of Pa as . . . I don't know, a mountain, bigger than Besse Rhodes or Soldier's Farewell, bigger than anything, but when Julian said that, just above a whisper, and his words registered, well, I thought Pa would charge him, spin Julian around, knock teeth down his throat, but, instead, Pa's shoulders sagged something awful, and when he turned, I could see just how pale his face had turned. He walked to the corner of the room, away from the rest of us, and he just stood there, finally holding out his right hand and leaning against that wall for support.

"Vell," Captain Beckenbauer said. "It is done. If you vill direct us to *Herr* Cassady, ve shall arrest him *und* your son. Vere is the other conspirator?"

The door swung open, and I heard that Southern voice say— "Here I am, boys."—and saw the muzzle flash in the darkness, the belching white smoke, heard the deafening report of the pistol, heard the German grunt, and, turning, I saw him just crumple, letting out a short groan.

Sergeant Scott tried to catch him, but couldn't reach him in time, and then he reacted to the gunshot, tried to draw his pistol, but two men had walked inside, and that J.T. Cassady fellow, who wasn't even holding a gun, warned the sergeant not to be foolish. I almost threw up when I realized who the second man was, the one who had pulled the trigger, for that pistol was in his hand.

"Shuck the sidearms, boys," Pinto said, thumbing back the

hammer. "Or join your Yankee captain."

Beckenbauer died directly. After Lieutenant Day and Sergeant Scott unbuckled their belts, they knelt beside the big German, rolled him over onto his back, and lifted his head. "I am killed," he whispered, and, just like that, he died.

I'd never seen a dead man before. Well, not dead like that. I think Pa and Julian had taken me to wakes and funerals back in Missouri, but I can't really remember those, and, sure, Apaches had killed folks all across New Mexico Territory, and white men had done their share of killing, but I hadn't witnessed those, just heard the stories from Pa, *Señor* Vee, and others. Beckenbauer, though, he was shot, shot without warning. I didn't like the German at all, but I sure didn't want to see him murdered.

"You didn't have to kill him," Julian snapped, and Pinto shrugged.

Julian had warned me about Pinto, told me he was a killer. I hadn't believed him.

Noise came from behind them, and Pinto and Cassady stepped aside, and Fletcher, Ben Jakes, and Bartolomé walked inside, followed by another gent that took me a little while to recognize. Then it hit me. He was the man from the stagecoach, the big Texican who had killed the dude from Dallas over at Barney's Station. Apaches hadn't killed him at all. Julian had lied. Lied to me. Lied to Pa.

"You boys grab a seat against the wall there," Cassady said. "You, too, Munro," he told Pa. "I want you-all sittin'. You Yankees do the same. There's nothing you can do for your captain." He looked at the big Texican. "Howell, you and Pinto watch 'em. If they move, let 'em join the captain." Smiling, he ran his hand over his bald head. "Gentleman, please, do not try anything stupid. We'll be together for a little while, waitin' for the Westbound stage, then we shall take our leave. This is for the Confederate States of America."

"I knowed it!" yelled Ben Jakes, wincing from the pain in his ribs. "I'm a Texican myself, by grab. You need any help, just let me know. Always willin' to join a fit for Texas, yes, sir!"

Cassady shot a glance at Pinto. "He's all right," Pinto said. "Full of wind, but he'll do."

"We could use another hand," said the murdering Texican, Howell.

Cassady's head bobbed just slightly. "Very well. Mr.?"

"Jakes. Ben Jakes." He climbed to his feet.

"Very well, Mr. Jakes. Fetch the sergeant's pistol yonder, and welcome to the Southern cause. You stand guard here with Howell. Pinto, come with me. We'll wait outside, consider our options."

"What about him?" Julian pointed at the dead captain.

"We'll bury him come dawn," Cassady said. "In the meantime, have your brother fix us some coffee and food. Something, I dare say, better than that awful slumgullion your father subjects his guests to."

It's dawn now. I'm writing in this book, which has provoked the man named Howell.

"What's he doin', writin' words all this time?" the ugly, one-eyed Texican said a moment ago.

"Leave him be," Julian said. My brother wouldn't look at Pa, wouldn't look at me. He won't even look at Lieutenant Day or Sergeant Scott.

I wonder if they'll kill us after it's all done. Wonder if I'm writing these words for nothing. If they kill us, if they don't burn this book, then whoever finds this diary should know that my father, me, and the Overland hands were shot down in cold blood by the following men:

Ben Jakes.

Pinto.

Howell.

J.T. Cassady.

Julian Munro. That captain was right. He is a traitor.

I have described these men in earlier pages in my diary. Pretty accurate descriptions. We also have an ambrotype of Julian, before he grew his mustache. I hope *Señor* Vee doesn't find this. He doesn't read or write English and. . . .

The Velásquez family. Oh, Lord, Breed. The half-breed named Nicanor. He's part of the gang of robbers and murderers, too. Let me add him to the list of men you should go looking for. Find my description of him.

I hope, I pray they do not harm Tori, or her sister, her parents. I'm such a fool.

I should have known. Maybe I did know, just didn't want to believe it. Julian wouldn't let Breed kill Alyvia. Would he? But Julian's here, just sitting there, sipping his coffee, and he didn't stop Pinto from killing Captain Beckenbauer.

Pinto and Ben Jakes are outside, making Bartolomé and Mr. Fletcher dig a grave and bury the German soldier. The rest of us remain inside.

Bartolomé and Mr. Fletcher are back. They didn't say anything, just came in and sat down. Nobody talks much. Not sure what time it is.

A few minutes ago, I heard a horse whinny, followed by talking just outside the door. My heart sank when the door opened and in walked Breed, followed by Pinto.

Is Tori still alive? She's always tormenting me, but I guess, deep down, I really like her, and you won't find better people in all New Mexico Territory than her folks. Her sister's real nice, too.

Cassady came storming through the door a short while later while Breed helped himself to coffee.

"You were supposed to wait for us!" Cassady yelled, but Breed merely shrugged.

"I got tired of waiting, *amigo*," Breed said.

"I don't care how boring you think it is."

"The horses are safe. They'll be there."

"They had better be!"

"*Mi amigo*, don't you trust me?" Breed's grin showed his gold teeth.

"I think it's you who don't trust us," Cassady said angrily.

Breed shrugged. "I want to be certain."

"Then finish your coffee, Breed, and keep an eye on things from the top of the hill outside. Climb up the tallest one."

Pinto shook his head. "No, head up the other one, Breed, the one they call Besse Rhodes. You got a clear view of the whole country from up there, ain't that right, Smith?"

I didn't say anything, but Pinto's laughter as he walked out the door with Breed made me angry, real angry.

"The family?" Julian asked before they got through the door. "Mr. Vel- . . . where you were staying?"

I noticed how he stopped himself from mentioning *Señor* Vee's name, so he doesn't want the rest of us to know where those horses are. That should bring me some relief. That means my brother doesn't plan on killing us after they rob the stage.

Breed grinned. "Today he went hunting. He promised to be back by tomorrow. He trust you, *amigo*." He laughed wickedly then. "No one has harmed his adorable daughters, or his wife." He shook his head, and said: "Her health is good. *Muy bien.* They all fine."

"You better be telling the truth," Julian said, but he was talking to a closed door.

Must be around noon now, maybe after. My fingers are getting cramped from writing all this down. That's all I can do at the moment.

Writing and waiting.

And hating my brother. Hating myself, too, for being so blind, so stupid, so trusting.

Same day, middle part of the afternoon

They made me fix them all some dinner, more coffee and what's left of the stew. They haven't fed us a thing, not even offered us water, not that I'm hungry. Not even thirsty. The door's open, and Ben Jakes is leaning against the wall just outside, slurping his coffee, watching us, then looking out toward the trail. Wish I had poisoned the coffee, but I wouldn't know how.

Pinto, Howell, and Cassady are sitting where we typically feed the Westbound passengers. I guess Breed remains up on top of Besse Rhodes. Julian's at the table with his 1847 musketoon and a bowl of stew, but he's not eating. He seems distant. Must be his conscience eating at his gut.

No, I reckon not. My brother has no conscience. No soul. Certainly no honor.

The stage isn't due till tomorrow evening. Maybe we can get out of here before then. But how?

I want to ask Pa, but he's just sitting there. He doesn't bring to mind a great mountain of granite any more. He looks, well, I don't know . . . broken? Whipped?

It's all Julian's doing!

When those brigands finished eating, they started for the door, J.T. Cassady picking his teeth with a sliver he'd carved off the table—our table—with a folding knife. When a big gust of wind come along, he heard the flag popping, and he shook his head and spit through the doorway.

"That flag sickens me to my soul," he said. "Old Glory. There's nothin' glorious about that flag any more. Take it down, Pinto. Take it down. It's such a ragged thing anyway. Take it down, I say, and burn it."

"You'll do no such thing."

I don't think anybody had spoken a word, not among us prisoners, I mean, until Pa said that. He looked up from where he was sitting in the corner, his eyes blazing with hatred. "You'll not soil that flag with your grimy fingers. Not a man among you."

Laughing, Cassady flicked his toothpick at Pa's boots. "You'd try and stop us."

"You'll have to kill me before I let you soil that flag, you filth. And you sure won't burn it. Not while I'm alive."

The laugh died in Cassady's throat. He could see Pa meant it. Wasn't brag. My throat went dry as the dirt outside.

"It's a piece of cloth," Cassady said.

"To you. Not to me." Pa's head turned, and he looked straight at Julian, looked at him till Julian bowed his head. Pa started talking, not loud, not angry, just talking like he was telling a story, which he hardly ever did. Well, not this kind of story, I guess. Everyone listened, even those outlaws, and especially me. I hope I don't ruin his words. This is how he told it, best as I can remember.

"It was a beautiful morning. Not cold at all, not for February, but this was Mexico. Not a cloud in the sky, the sun just blazing. I remember that, see it clear as if it were yesterday. I can hear the bands playing 'Yankee Doodle' and 'Hail Columbia', and see old General Zachary Taylor riding Old Whitey, strutting like a peacock.

"Must have been an hour or so before noon when the

Mexicans sent in this surgeon, and he started reading . . . I dis-
remember his name . . . saying how we were surrounded by
20,000 men. The doc was a German, part Dutchy anyway. I
think his mother must have been a Mexican. That Army captain
you murdered last night reminded me of him, his accent and
all, the way he carried himself. Old Santa Anna, the surgeon
said, wanted 'to save you from catastrophe' . . . yes, sir, I recall
those words. Those were the last words the doc got out before
Old Zach cut him off, and I won't forget what he said.

" 'Tell Santa Anna to go to hell! Major Bliss' . . . Bliss was
the adjutant, you see, William Bliss, good man . . . 'put that in
Spanish for this damned Dutchman to deliver.'

"Well, that ended the talks, and three hours later, we were in
full battle. Fought all day. Savage. Those Mexicans had us
outnumbered, outgunned, but we fought like devils. Only darkness stopped the butchery. I remember being so tired. My face
black as midnight from powder. So tired, but I couldn't sleep.
Didn't even want to close my eyes. All night long, I could hear
Santa Anna's soldiers crying out . . . *'Viva* Santa Anna' . . .
those poor, misguided fools. *'Libertad o muerte.'* And hear
something else, too, in Spanish and English. Men, men I'd rode
with, men I'd been shooting at. Hearing their cries. Begging for
water. For their mothers, *madres.* For death. Not long after that,
Jeff Davis came, told us the general wanted to ride out and take
a look-see at our defensive positions at Saltillo, make sure Santa
Anna couldn't breach those, cut us off, strike us from behind.
After that ride, I reckon I could have slept, just went to sleep
forever, but then the Mexicans opened up with their eight-
pounders. All night long. Come daylight, there was nothing
beautiful about that dawn.

"They charged. The lines looked like they stretched all the
way to the far end of Mexico, bayonets glistening in the sun,
banners unfurling, lancers on horseback ready to strike,

uniforms spotless, as if they'd just come into battle. Brave boys, those soldiers Santa Anna had. Never saw men die so brave. Those Mexicans. Our boys . . . from Illinois, Kentucky, Arkansas, and my fellow Mississippians. Must have been 1,000s, and those Mexicans came like a bolt of lightning.

"The Arkansans broke. Couldn't blame them at all. They dropped their muskets, mounted their horses, ran. Ran for Buena Vista, but Santa Anna was ready for that, and on came the lancers. Slaughter. No other word for that. Lancers cut most of them down. I reckon the whole Army would have been destroyed, wiped out, cut to pieces. Probably would have ended there if it hadn't been for those boys with the Illinois infantry. They didn't run. No, sir. They stood their ground and just gave those Mexicans buck and ball. Put a big hurt on Santa Anna's boys, but I reckon Santa Anna would have still won the day, but here came Old Zach.

"They called him Old Rough and Ready . . . that he was. Virginia-born, if I remember right, but Kentucky-raised, or maybe it was Tennessee. Grew cotton. Owned a plantation in Mississippi, had another home in Baton Rouge, but he was Army. He was a fighter. Why, I reckon he had seen more fighting than any man alive at Buena Vista. He'd fought in the War of 1812, the Black Hawk War, led the Army against the Seminoles down in Florida. I voted for him for President, you know. Guess he would have been a mighty good one, had he lived longer. Didn't look like a general, not Old Zach. Wore a straw hat with a wide brim and clothes that hadn't seen brush, water, or soap in months." Pa gave out a short chuckle. "Looked like the rest of us, I guess. Warrant that's why we all admired him so.

"Well, like I was saying, the general rides back about this time, and this officer, don't know who he was, came loping up beside him, reined in, his face filled with fear. 'General Taylor,' he says, 'we are whipped!' And Old Zach, he answers . . . 'I know it, but the volunteers don't know it. Let them alone. We'll see what they do.'

"Just then I saw this man. Oh, he wasn't a man, just a boy from Arkansas, carrying the colors, that flag you think you're game enough to burn, and I watched them Mexicans cut him down. There was nothing anyone could do, cut off from the rest of us like he was, but seeing that, hearing him cry for help, but always waving that flag, wondering, if he had thrown the flag aside, if he might could have gotten free. Probably not. It didn't matter. Reckon I just went clear out of my head, spurred my horse, and charged. Crazy. I heard Jeff Davis yelling for me to come back, others screaming that I'd be killed, but I didn't listen. Didn't care. One of those eight-pounders hit right about the time I reached those Mexicans. Killed the Mexicans. Killed my horse. Should have killed me, but it didn't. God was with me. My ears were ringing. I stood up, dazed, and the first thing I saw was the flag, lying on the ground, staff busted. I grabbed for it, took it off the busted pole, tied it to my rifle, and staggered back. I don't know how far it was, 200 yards maybe. Waving it over my head. Daring those Mexicans to come charging me, try to kill me. Jeff Davis and my Mississippi pards were no longer yelling at me. They were cheering, yelling hurrahs and huzzahs, cussing Santa Anna.

" 'You're wounded, Munro!' Jeff Davis says, and that I was. But I wasn't about to leave my friends, and I wasn't about to hand that flag to somebody else. Jeff and Old Zach saw that in my face, and they never pressed me on the subject.

"So Jeff Davis give us the command. And off we went.

"Proud, we were. In red shirts and white paints, armed with Bowie knives and our prized Mississippi rifles. We cut down those poor Mexican infantrymen. Battle they called it. More like murder. Then it looked to be us getting murdered. Lancers came right at us, lowering those spears, but I could hear Old Zach giving us the command . . . 'Steady, boys! Steady for the honor of old Mississippi.'

"Jeff Davis had us close the ranks, and we waited. Waited, watching those lancers come galloping toward us, waited until they were 80 yards from us, and then they did the strangest thing. They stopped. Just reined their horses to a stop. Jeff Davis, he later said that he suspected that it had been a trick, that the lancers were trying to draw our fire, that they didn't know the range of our rifles, figured we couldn't hit them at 80 yards, but they were wrong. Boy howdy, were they wrong. 'Fire!' Jeff Davis yells, and we fired. And that was murder. We killed them by the scores, killed them with one volley, men and horses, and then we watched them run.

" 'Well done!' the general was yelling, waving his hat. "Hurrah for old Mississippi!'

"And Jeff Davis rides over to me, and he shakes my hand, and I start to hand him the flag, present it to him, him being our commander and me slowing, getting some sense back in my head, but he says . . . 'No, Conner Munro. You earned that flag. It's yours, Mr.'

"There was more fighting to be done, and I did my share, till I'd lost so much blood they carried me, me and that flag, to the surgeon. It rained that afternoon, blessed rain, and the Battle of Buena Vista was over. They say we killed or wounded 3,500 Mexicans there. We had less than 300 dead, maybe 400 wounded.

"Well, I've carried that flag with me for 14 years, and I've carried something else with me. What I remember is Mississippians, Arkansans, Kentuckians, Illinoisans . . . all of us fighting together. We were Americans. Not Northerners. Not Southerners. Americans. Fighting together."

He nodded, satisfied, finished.

"That was another time," J.T. Cassady said, and he didn't say this mean or anything like that. I even thought he spoke with some measure of respect. "And this is another war."

Pa gave him a slight nod. "That may be, but you ain't touching that flag."

You couldn't hear anything for a minute or two, just the wind, and that flag popping outside.

"He's right, Cassady," Julian said at last from his seat. "We don't want to do anything that'll make the jehu on the stage tomorrow night suspicious. Marco Max will be expecting to see that flag."

"In the dark?"

"Moon will be up," my brother said.

"It ain't worth it, J.T.," Pinto told Cassady. He pointed the barrel of his revolver at Pa. "Look at that old bull. You'd have to kill him. And we might have need of him before this deal is done."

Cassady chewed on his lip, trying to stare down Pa, but he couldn't do that, so he gave a little shrug, and walked outside without another word. The flag had won. Pa had won.

I can hear the flag right now. Pa hasn't said anything since Cassady left. He's a prideful man, and, right now, I'm proud of him. Prouder than I've ever been.

February 27, 1861

This is the day. Time's running out. We have to figure out a way to stop them from robbing the stage. Stop Julian. But how?

At breakfast this morning, which was crackers and coffee, J.T. Cassady talked like he was a general, that this was the first strike for the Confederacy.

"After our victory, Arizona Territory will be open to all Southerners. This southern strip will give the Confederacy an avenue from Texas, all the way to California, with her vast riches and a port in the Pacific Ocean. I can then see a Confederate army striking northward from here, into New Mexico, all the way to the gold fields in Colorado."

I think Pa's right. These aren't soldiers. They're bandits.

The moon had gone full two days ago, and, with no clouds, it will be light out from the time the moon rose till it set, so those outlaws will have a good view from wherever they set up. Come 8:30, when the Westbound's due, it won't be dark at all.

Cassady pulled a big old watch from his pocket and checked the time, smiling, and I realized that it was Pa's watch, the solid gold watch he had bought when he had first taken the job with Mr. Butterfield, and I got hopping mad.

"You stole that!" I leaped to my feet. "That's my pa's watch, you low-down thief." I went straight for him, but Julian grabbed my arms and pinned them behind my back. Oh, I fought as hard as I could, trying to kick Julian's shins, fought even harder when J.T. Cassady, that miserable thief, laughed at me.

"It's all right, Smith," Pa said quietly, but it wasn't all right at all. Not to me.

"We're robbing the Army," Julian said firmly, still holding me, but looking straight at J.T. Cassady. "Not civilians. That's what you told me when you first approached me about this. Remember?"

They looked at each other long and hard, and I stopped kicking at my brother when J.T. Cassady pulled out the watch again and held it in his open palm. Julian let me go, and I walked over to Cassady, expecting him to drop the watch on the floor and crush it with the heel of his boot, but he didn't. He let me take it out of his hand, and I hurried back to Pa and handed the watch to him.

"Thanks, Son," he said, sliding the watch into his pocket.

Cassady laughed. "Twelve hours. Then the war begins."

Pa chuckled. "Maybe. What happens if the stagecoach can't

134

get through?"

There hadn't been much conversation since those vermin took us prisoner, but Pa was in the mood to talk, and I listened, wondering what he was trying to do. Me? I had no interest in conversing with pigs.

"I've watched the Overland in Tucson, sir," Cassady said. "And here. You can keep time by the stagecoaches almost as well as you can with your fancy watch."

"Sometimes. Not always." He pointed at the newspaper. "Take a gander at the *Times* . . . if you can read."

Cassady's face flushed, and he just stared at Pa, while Julian picked up the Mesilla paper.

"The Rio Grande's rising," Pa said. "Next page. Rising rapidly."

Julian must have found the item, because he nodded. "I see that."

"If the jehu can't ford the river at the crossing, he's stuck at Fort Fillmore till the river goes down."

"You think I don't know about the ferry?" Cassady said.

"If the ferry's operating," Pa said. "But if the river's rising as high as it probably is from the snow melt and the rains up north, I'm not sure they'd be able to get a Celerity on the ferry. At least, I doubt if it will be here on time. They can make up time once they get to Yucca Flats. But the Overland Mail Company knows to be safe. We don't like our passengers drowning." He gave Howell a stern look. "Or getting shot."

"Reckon we'll just have to wait and see." Cassady tried to sound confident.

"Uhn-huh. But then there's that other wagon. The payroll wagon, or what is supposed to be carrying the payroll. The wagon full of soldiers. It must be heading for Fort Tejon now, too." He pointed out the door. "Those Army boys travel the same road as the Overland. Likely to stop here for water. The dragoons have been camping here long before the Overland started running. The six of you plan on fighting off a squadron or two of dragoons?"

"If we have to, Munro. We are soldiers of the South."

Cassady walked outside, but he didn't strut so much.

Same day, noon

Well, I did it. Tried to escape. But they caught me.

It came to me, the idea, a little while after Cassady went outside. I figured Pa had been lying, trying to play with their nerves, figured that nothing, certainly not some high water between Fort Fillmore and La Mesilla, could stop good Overland men from getting a stage to a timetable stop on the Overland on time, or close to it. The more I thought on it, the more it struck me that somebody had to get out of here, get to the nearest station, warn them about what was happening here at Soldier's Farewell.

Pinto and J.T. Cassady were somewhere outside, and I figured Breed remained stationed up on the hill. Julian had gone somewhere, too. I think to talk to Pinto and Cassady, so that left us being guarded by Ben Jakes and the man with the eye patch, Howell. So without telling anyone what I aimed to do, I just stood up and walked over to the door. I could feel Pa's eyes staring at my back, could feel the rest of us prisoners watching me, wondering, worrying, and then Ben Jakes turned around and aimed that big pistol at my belly.

"What you think you're doin', boy?"

Howell put his hand on the hilt of his big Bowie knife, but he didn't say a thing.

"I have to go to the privy." I hoped my voice wouldn't quake with fear, but it did, and maybe that was for the better, make them think I was scared. Well, I was scared.

"Hold it," Ben Jakes snapped.

"I can't. I got to go," I said, almost whining. "Real bad."

That worthless Ben Jakes lowered the revolver he had stolen from Sergeant Scott and cackled. "Go in your pants," he said.

Well, a tear rolled down my cheek, and I quickly brushed it away, and I feared my plan wouldn't work at all, but then the Texican with the eye patch came to my defense. "Let him go," he said. I guess he thought I was nigh crying because of my bowels. Maybe he didn't want me to stink up the house.

Frowning, Ben Jakes shoved his pistol in his waistband and turned to Howell. "I ain't wet-nursin' this kid. Thinks he's better than me or anyone else. You take him!"

That would kill my plan right away. I didn't stand a chance of getting away with Howell guarding me, wasn't even sure I would have enough gumption to try it, remembering how he had shot down the man from Dallas.

Well, that big Bowie came out if its sheath in an instant, and Howell had the massive blade pressed against Ben Jakes's throat, had Jakes pushed against the door frame, and it was Ben Jakes, the sorry cur, who wound up wetting his britches.

"You don't give orders," Howell told him. "You don't never tell me what to do."

"What's going on here?" J.T. Cassady had walked up with Julian.

"It's a private matter," Howell said tightly, pressing the knife's point deeper into Ben Jakes's throat until a trickle of blood ran into the braggart's banded collar.

"Howell," Cassady said, "put that pig-sticker away. You almost ruined our plan when you killed that man down the road at the next station. Think, Howell, for once, just think! You would have had half the territory chasing you for murder if Munro here hadn't tracked you down, let everyone think the Apaches had killed you. We might have need of Mr. Jakes."

The knife vanished, and Howell turned away and glared at Cassady. He wasn't the type of man who liked to be told to do something by anyone, even his boss. He started to say something, choked it back, and tilted his head sharply at me.

"Boy here needs to do his business in the outhouse."

Cassady peered inside. "Take him," Cassady ordered Ben Jakes. "And clean yourself up, too."

I let out a big sigh, hadn't realized I'd been holding my breath all this time, filled my lungs with air, and passed Cassady through the door. I heard him tell Pa . . . "Were the soldiers at Buena Vista as insubordinate, as beetle-headed, as what I have under my command?"

The privy lies behind the big stone stables, just off the northwest corner. It's a two-seater, but I hoped Ben Jakes wouldn't come in with me, and he didn't, just held the door open for me and told me to hurry up, that he hadn't all day. Then he fingered the little nick in his neck, and held it there, looking like Howell had sliced his jugular.

Now, I hadn't really planned on what I'd do if I got this far. Wouldn't have time to grab Ivanhoe, or any mule, the gate being on the opposite end, and I had no idea where Pinto was all this time. Breed, from up on the hill, would have a good aim at me, but I wasn't certain he'd be able to hit me at that distance, although he would see me, could direct the rest to where I was. But just beyond the big wall of the stable ran the draw, and Breed couldn't see me through all the rocks and brush. I could hurry past the spring, just keep footing it, follow the draw, north maybe, follow it as far as I could, then cut out, dash behind Soldier's Farewell Hill. They wouldn't think of me doing that, I hoped. Make a beeline across the desert, keeping low, using yucca for cover, run those three miles across the open ground till I hit Burro Cienaga. Run for my life to Ojo de la

Vaca. Get help.

I used the bathroom, surprised I had to after all that, buttoned my trousers, and just charged out the door. Ben Jakes cried out when the wooden door smashed his head, started cursing, and I started running.

"You lousy little . . . !" I couldn't hear the rest of Ben Jakes's words because the pistol shot drowned them out. Man, was I scared then, didn't think Ben Jakes would recover in time to shoot at me, but he did. The first shot went way wide, but the second one buzzed past my ear and whined off the rock wall. That got the mules on the other side of those rocks braying and squealing. Pa's prize stallion took off running and neighing, and one of his brood mares almost kicked down the wall in her stall. Sounded like that anyway.

The high stone wall ran 40 feet. 40 feet to the draw. Felt like 40 miles.

I heard others shouting then, but I just crashed through the brush, dropped into the draw, and ran. Another bullet smashed off a rock a few rods behind me. I knew this part of the station, it being right near the spring. Knew it well from all the time I'd spent out this way building the dam, then fixing it, fetching water. Another shot, then Cassady cursed Ben Jakes for being a fool. "Don't waste lead!" he yelled.

Somebody fired again, but this sounded farther off, from the station, maybe. I couldn't tell for sure.

I ran.

All of them couldn't come after me. They had to keep watch on Pa and the soldiers, Fletcher and Bartolomé. I figured Ben Jakes and Cassady were chasing me, but that might be enough. I had a good jump on Ben Jakes, who couldn't run fast after the pounding he had gotten, and, like I said, I knew this country better than they did.

I ran.

Three or four times, I stumbled. Rocks and cactus cut through my pants, left my knees bloody, but I didn't stay down long. I'd jump up, keep footing it, winding along the draw, my brogans pushing hard into the sand. Sweating. My throat parched. Knowing my feet would be bad blistered before long.

I ran.

Along about then, it struck me how they'd probably expect me to go this way, east I mean. Ojo de la Vaca was the closest station to us, five miles nearer than Barney's, and the stage that they planned on robbing would be coming from the east, so it made sense for me to light out that way. At that instant, I decided to change course, cut out the other way, run west. I knew a lot of those boys who worked at Barney's Station, knew how much Pa respected Mr. Barney.

It was 19 miles to Barney's Station, 19 open miles once I left the draw, 19 miles of cactus, rocks, and, maybe, Apaches.

19 miles. Criminy, I don't think I made it a mile.

The ringing of metal hoofs on the rocks sang out behind me, thundering, and I screamed like a little girl, knowing somebody horseback came after me, knowing I could never outrun horse or mule. I saw this grove of yucca, weaved in and out of it, hoping that would slow down my pursuer, and I reckon it did, but then I was back out in the open, running down a little hill, hearing the pounding hoofs draw closer, could hear the horse snorting, the rider cursing, and then felt the horse and rider right beside me, and I yelled out again, expecting a bullet in my spine, tried to duck, but a hand gripped my shirt, lifted me up, and I was tossed, smashed into the rocks, and figured I was dead.

When I came to, I saw Julian, his face drenched with sweat, felt him pressing a silk bandanna against my throbbing head, blood gushing from my forehead.

"You want to get killed?" Julian cried out at me.

Julian! He had ridden me down, not Howell or Breed, not any of those ruffians, but someone worse than them. My own brother.

I pushed the bandanna away, pushed him away, and shot to my feet, then fell right back down, the whole world spinning, blood pouring into my eyes.

"That was a fool thing to do!"

I didn't know what he meant. Standing up just then? Well, yeah, it probably had been stupid. Running away? Maybe I would have made it had my treacherous brother not outsmarted me. He'd almost killed me himself.

"Come on!" He jerked me up, threw me onto the horse— Pa's fastest stallion, a big blood bay—and swung up in the saddle behind me.

"All you have to do is wait, Smith," he told me as we rode back to the station, me lying like a sack in front of him, his left hand pressing me down, blood dripping into my hair, onto the ground for the ants. "Wait a few more hours and this will all be over. I won't let them hurt you, but don't try anything like that again."

I laughed a little. "You didn't want that German captain killed, either," I told him. "That didn't stop them."

He pushed me down harder.

"Nice friends you got, Jules."

"Shut up! I'll fix your head when we get back to the station."

"You ain't touching me."

"Ain't is not a word. Remember?"

"Shut up. Some teacher you are. That captain was right. You are a traitor. To the Army. To your country. To me. To Pa. I hate your guts."

By then we'd reached the station, and Julian reined in, pulled me up roughly, then dumped me onto the dirt, pitched the bloody bandanna beside me, spurred the stallion, and loped off for the stable.

It was Pinto who helped me up, his hands gentle, and he brushed the dirt off the bandanna, and pressed it against my head, lifted my right hand, knuckles skinned, bruised, palm bleeding, and let me hold the rag against the wicked cut.

"You're game, kid," Pinto said. "I like that, respect that. But try that again and you'll wind up dead."

Walking inside, knowing I had failed Pa and the others, I wished I were dead.

Same day, half past 3 o'clock
Bleeding has stopped, but my head keeps pounding.

After Julian hauled me back to the station and Pinto helped me inside, I learned how I hadn't been the only body thinking of escape. Pa, Bartolomé, and the lieutenant were all hunched over the body of Sergeant Stone, and Mr. Fletcher lay, spread-eagle, a short distance away. Gasping, I wondered if I had gotten those two good men killed, but then I noticed Fletcher's chest rising and falling, and spotted a big knot forming on the side of his head.

"Smith!" Pa jumped up and ran, and Pinto backed up a couple of steps and put his hand on his revolver, but Pa didn't notice, and he wasn't going after no one, just me. He pulled me close, grabbed the bandanna, started working on the cut on my head.

"I'm all right," I said.

"Who did this?" Pa demanded.

As I write this, it strikes me funny. Reckon it struck me something similar then. Must have. I didn't answer at first, just watched Pa snatch a rag from his trousers pocket, and use it to wrap around my noggin, his hands gentle, trying not to hurt me, wiping the blood out of my eyes with Julian's silk rag.

"Who did it?" he asked again.

"I fell," I said. "The half-breed was chasing me." I just left Julian out of it. Did Pa know I was lying? I can't tell. He finished tightening the bandage, then leaned back, put both hands on my shoulders and gave a little nod as he examined me. I thought he was grading his doctoring skills, but that wasn't it at all.

"I'm proud of you," he said. "Though I don't want you to try anything like that again. Ever. Promise me!"

My head bobbed just slightly, though I reckon I was lying to my father again.

I asked him: "What happened here?"

Sergeant Stone groaned. At least he was alive, too.

Pa shot a glance at the sergeant, then over at Fletcher, who had lifted his left hand gently, moaning softly, and gently felt that growing lump, the skin tight and purplish.

The sergeant let out an oath, prompting a chuckle from Lieutenant Day, who said: "He'll be fine."

"Let's see to Mr. Fletcher," Pa said, and steered me to our hired man.

"How you feel?" Pa asked.

Fletcher blinked twice, and slowly shook his head. "Well. . . ." Sounded like he was considering some options.

"Pour some water on this." Pa handed me Julian's bandanna, and I went to the bucket, wet the rag, then brought it back to Pa, who started gently bathing Fletcher's wound.

"When we heard the shooting, the shouts," Pa said, "the sergeant and Fletcher here jumped up, made a rush for the door. Like they were expecting you to try something." Pa gave me a curious look. "I hadn't figured on it. Bartolomé and me, we tried to help out, but it was over in a heartbeat. That big man with the eye patch. . . ." Shaking his head, Pa pulled the wet cloth away from Mr. Fletcher.

"That hurt?"

"The barrel hurt a whole lot more," Fletcher said.

Pa placed the rag on the big bruised lump again. "Hold it here, Fletcher." He did as he was told. "You want some water? To drink?"

"No, sir. I'll be fine."

"Think you can sit up?"

"If it's all the same to you, sir, I'll just lie here for a spell. How's the Army fellow?"

Pa looked over at Sergeant Stone, Lieutenant Day, and Bartolomé. I did the same. They had pulled off the sergeant's tunic, ripped open his shirt, and were patching up a little hole in his left shoulder. I reckon the lieutenant had dug out the bullet, because Sergeant Stone was fingering it in his right hand.

"Looks like he'll live," Pa said.

Fletcher nodded ever so slightly.

"The big man." Pa returned to his story. "Howell, that's his name. He's a fast one. Thought we could jump him, his attention at the privy, but he heard us coming, shot the sergeant, then laid out Fletcher, here, with the barrel of his revolver. Bartolomé instinctively caught Stone as he was falling, and I, like a fool, just tripped over Fletcher when he dropped at my feet." Pa rubbed his own forehead, and I saw the scratch where he had skinned himself.

"Sorry about that," Fletcher said.

"Wasn't your fault."

"Well," Fletcher said, "reckon that Texican could have shot us all down."

Pa's head shook thoughtfully. "No," he said in a whisper. "They need us alive. That's why he didn't kill us. Need us for when the stage arrives."

A short while later, Cassady walked in, surveyed the scene, and clucked his tongue. "I trust, gentlemen, that we'll have no more displays of stupidity."

Nobody answered him. Other than me, no one even looked at him, and he shook his head, turned quickly, and marched outside, barking orders to Ben Jakes, Pinto, and Howell.

"All that scratchin' makes me nervous," Howell just told me. "You best give that pencil a rest."

I kept right on writing.

"Boy! Stop writin'. . . ."

"Leave him alone." Julian keeps pretending he's my defender.

They're back inside, most of them. Haven't seen the half-breed, still atop the hill, I reckon, and Ben Jakes is outside. I can hear him whistling and shuffling his boots.

"What's he writin'?"

Julian tossed the dregs of his coffee in the spittoon. "His innermost thoughts. His hopes and dreams. Leave him be."

Howell spit on the floor. "If he writes down our names and descriptions, the law can. . . ."

"Union law," Julian said. "It won't hold in the Confederate States of America. Once we're in Texas, we're free. So let him write."

With a grunt, Howell turned and left, and I could feel Julian staring at me, wanting me to know how he had protected me, wanted me to write all I wanted to write. So I'm putting down this pencil, and shutting the journal, and I'm going to just stare at him, and let him know what I think of him, my wicked big brother.

Same day, 6 o'clock

Somehow, I had fallen asleep, but a shot rang out, and I jumped, wide awake.

Had it been a dream? No, because a tenseness filled the station. We prisoners were back against the wall, looking, wondering, but Ben Jakes and Howell, guarding the doorway, started talking, pointing, and I heard Cassady yell out: "Where did that come from?"

No one could answer him.

Cassady cursed. A mule brayed. The leader of those ruffians cursed again, louder, nervous. "Someone's comin'!" I think Pinto must have shouted that. Cassady barked at Howell and that no-good Ben Jakes to get inside, and they did.

From inside the doorway, Ben Jakes pointed, and Howell grunted.

"By jingo, what if it's that wagon full of dragoons?" Ben Jakes kept shaking, sweating, his Adam's apple bobbing as he tried to swallow down his fear. "What if . . . ?"

"It ain't the Army, you yellow. . . ." Howell choked back his curse. "Just a speck of dust. One rider."

But who?

I wet my lips, longing to know that answer, wanting to get up, see the dust for myself, but knew I couldn't.

"Watch 'em!" Keeping his eyes trained outside, Howell motioned toward us, and Ben Jakes, trying to look brave, kept that stolen pistol in both hands, staring at us, but never for long. Always, he'd look back at Howell, try to see over the big man's shoulder, find out who was coming.

I wondered if we should try to rush them again. No, not with Howell quick as a cat. Wounded as they were, Mr. Fletcher and Sergeant Stone wouldn't be of much help. All we could do was sit and wait. And worry.

Lifting his revolver, thumbing back the hammer, Howell stepped back slightly.

Slow hoof beats sounded, and Ben Jakes squeaked out, "What . . . who?"

"Quiet!" Howell said in a harsh whisper. A moment later, he snorted, lowered the hammer, and stepped outside. "It's Breed," he announced.

Ben Jakes let out a little giggle of relief, and quickly found a chair, waving the pistol in our direction and warning us not to make any sudden moves. I thought about asking him if he had wet his britches again, but decided against provoking him. Besides, the men outside had started talking to Breed.

"What happened?" Pinto asked, but then someone said: "Who's the *hombre?*"

I looked at Pa, but he didn't say anything, just tried harder to listen.

"Breed," Cassady began. "I told you . . . who is it? What happened?"

"He's a quiet *hombre*. I respect this *hombre*."

"You shoot him?"

"Who else?"

Well, after that, Cassady and Breed continued talking, but too muffled for me to make out much of anything.

Right then, it struck me, and I knew who they were talking about, knew it with my heart, dreading it, and when they dragged in the dark-skinned man, Pa swore and Bartolomé practically cried.

"You should have stayed with the horses, Nicanor," Cassady snapped at the half-breed. "You put us all at risk."

Breed shrugged, and grinned.

Pa and I were up, running to *Señor* Vee, rolling him over, terrified at the ghastly hole in his side. Lieutenant Day and Bartolomé came over, and we lifted Tori's dad, brought him to the corner. Fletcher was up, weak as he was, but he fetched the bucket of water.

"He came sneaking up," Cassady said. "Suspicious. Nicanor says he was pretty good." The Southron laughed slightly. "Just not as good as my man here." He patted the half-breed on the back, the same man he had just criticized for not staying at the

Velásquez place with the horses.

Pa had pulled up the blood-soaked homespun shirt. He looked at Cassady. "We need whiskey. Clean the wound."

"Why? In an hour he'll be with his ancestors."

Ignoring Breed, Pa looked hard at Cassady. "Whiskey!" he demanded, but those men just sauntered out the door, with Cassady calling back with a laugh: "We ain't wastin' good whiskey on a Mexican, Munro!"

Now, I stare at my hands, stained with blood. My own blood, and *Señor* Vee's. He's in the corner, sleeping, covered with blankets. We've done all we can for him. It's hard to think about it all.

When Cassady and the others left, leaving Ben Jakes and Pinto to guard us, Pa told me to put on some water to boil, then he hurried to the kitchen and pulled out a knife.

"You best put that down." Ben Jakes thumbed back the hammer of his revolver.

Pa ignored him. He stuck the blade in the coals.

"Put it down!"

"He ain't gonna stick you, Jakes," Pinto said lazily. "Let them work on the greaser. He's a good man, I warrant. Better than you."

That's what we did. About 10 minutes later, Julian walked in. The bullet had gone clear through *Señor* Vee, and we had cleaned it up as best we could. Julian knelt over the unconscious man, the man I'd always figured would wind up being his father-in-law, and he was shaking, Julian was, tears welling in his eyes.

"I didn't. . . ." He shook his head, reached inside his hunting shirt, and pulled out a flask. "Here."

Pa snatched it from him without looking, without thanking him. He unscrewed the cap and poured the whiskey into the bullet hole.

Unconscious, Alyvia's daddy screamed, then dropped into a deeper sleep.

"Fetch the knife," Pa told me.

Julian had backed away, unable to watch, and he was gone by the time I brought the knife back. The others knew what was coming, because they took hold of *Señor* Vee's arms and legs, holding him down. The knife blade looked hotter than the desert wind in August. "Lay the flat side over the hole," Pa told me. "Quickly."

Can't get the smell out of my nostrils. Can't forget the noise. The muted groans of agony. The terror. I burned that bullet hole, like, well, like nothing I know. Then, like a silly girl, I just sank down on the floor. My eyes rolled back in my head, and I was out like *Señor* Vee.

I woke to Bartolomé pressing a wet rag on my cheeks. Those cheeks turned red quickly when I realized what I had done. Passed out. Just plumb sat down and fainted. Pa, or somebody, had heated the blade again and sealed the exit wound in *Señor* Vee's back. Cauterized it, Lieutenant Day said. I reckon they hadn't had to burn Sergeant Stone's shoulder like that. He hadn't been bleeding as badly as *Señor* Vee, though.

"How . . . will he . . . is he going to . . . ?" I couldn't talk straight, couldn't summon up the words.

Pa was beside me again. "You all right?"

"Yes, sir. I'm sorry I. . . ."

"I shouldn't have had you do it. That was my fault." He pressed his hand on my shoulder and squeezed it. "You did fine, Smith."

Same evening, must be right around 8:30
Well, it's full dark now. Moon's rising. A short while ago, Cas-

sady came inside with the others and laid down his rules—what was expected of us, what was going to happen.

"When the stagecoach comes in, you'll act just like always. We've even done some of your work for you. The team's hitched and ready. Nicanor will be watchin' from somewhere close, and. . . ." Grinning, he nodded at the still-sleeping *Señor* Vee, and continued: "You all know what fine work that half-breed does. Moonlight'll give him a clear shot at anyone outside. Howell and Pinto will have y'all covered. Move and you're dead. Shout a warnin' and you're dead. Try anything. Julian will be with y'all, workin' just like always. Only Julian'll have a gun, and he's a mighty fine shot, too." He had walked over to me, and put his hand on my head, messing up my hair. "Try one thing stupid, and I'll put a bullet in the boy's brain. Remember that.

"You usher the passengers inside, where Mr. Jakes and I'll be waitin'. We get the money from the soldiers, and we be on our way. Nobody gets hurt. We relieve the Union tyrants of some money, which we deliver to the Confederacy for honor and glory. You can spend the rest of your days enjoyin' this . . . paradise."

No one said anything. We waited.

Stage is coming. Just heard the shout. Don't know what'll happen. God willing, we'll stop them. Stop Julian. If not. . . .

March 24, 1861

Back home at Soldier's Farewell. I burned the *McGuffey's New Fourth Eclectic Reader* that Julian gave me, and came close to tossing this diary in the flames, as well, but. . . .

Been ages since I wrote in this. Plenty of news.

We carried *Señor* Vee, still unconscious, to my bunk, and left Sergeant Scott with him, along with Ben Jakes as their guard.

Pa went out with the rest of them, even Fletcher, who remained groggy from the wallop Howell gave him earlier.

Inside, I waited, fear gnawing the insides of my stomach something terrible.

Outside, came the pounding of the hoofs, the jingling of traces, growing steadily, and soon I heard commotion and curses, just like always whenever a stage arrived. I sat alone in the station with Cassady, a Pocket Colt aimed in my direction though his attention remained outside as he listened, just as I did, nervous with anticipation, or just plain nervous.

Waiting for a shot, I braced myself. Not a shot at me, but somewhere outside. It never happened, though. The door swung open, and folks started filing inside, weary and grouchy like normal, unaware of what was happening, and Cassady backed himself into the corner, hiding his little revolver inside a coat pocket, warning me with his eyes not to say a word.

I'm not sure how I felt about all this. Disappointment? Anger? Hard to say. Deep down, I had hoped Pa and the others would try something, warn those soldiers carrying the payroll disguised as civilians, jump Pinto and Breed, disarm them. Something like that. On the other hand, I didn't want them to try anything because it would be fruitless. I didn't want Pa to get killed.

"Where's the grub and coffee?" a bald gent in a dust-covered broadcloth suit shouted. Another asked about the privy, and then Howell slipped inside, quietly drawing his pistol.

I said nothing. I counted 9 passengers, kind of a low number considering how many folks had been traveling on the Overland in recent weeks, seven men and two women, one of the latter silver-haired and dressed in black like she must have been a widow, the other middle-aged, hanging on the arm of a younger man with a thick brown mustache.

"The privy?" the gent in plaid britches and a striped shirt repeated, embarrassed.

"You'll have to wait." Howell thumbed back the hammer.

"What's the meaning of this?" exclaimed the bald man, indignant.

Cassady showed his pistol, aiming it at the three men he figured were the couriers, and he sure had that figured right.

"Shuck your hardware," Cassady said, his voice surprisingly high-pitched. Nerves, I reckon. "All of you. Do something quick, and you're dead. We've got 40 men outside!"

Ben Jakes showed himself, along with the revolver he had stolen, keeping the two wounded men in the corner of his eye, making himself look big and brave.

"Now!" Cassady stretched his arm, putting the barrel close to a passenger's face.

"I said . . . ," began the uppity gent, but he never got to finish.

"Shut up!" Howell barked. "One more word from you, Mr., and you'll never say another."

The silver-haired woman gasped, and I thought the man in need of the privy would wet himself.

Then Pa filed in, followed by Bartolomé, Lieutenant Day, Mr. Fletcher, Marco Max, and Little Terry, all holding their hands high, and they walked to the wall near me, and sat down, clasping their hands behind their heads, just as they had been instructed. Pinto and Breed followed them, guns out.

"Your weapons, gentlemen," Cassady instructed again. "Drop them at your feet, then kick them toward my associate." His head tilted toward Pinto.

At last, the sidearms fell to the floor, and Breed picked them up and stuck them in his waistband. Outside, a mule hee-hawed, then sounded like it just screamed. I wondered what Julian was doing all this time.

"Now, I'll relieve you three gentlemen of your money belts, while our associates are finding the money you've hidden in your grips on the stagecoach." Cassady watched, smiling, enjoying this moment, his voice dropping to its normal pitch. When the young fellow with the brown mustache, traveling with one of the ladies, started for his own belt, Cassady told him to stop.

"We don't rob civilians, sir." Cassady smiled with pride. "This is a strike for the Confederate States of America, the first battle in Arizona Territory, the first fight for liberty." I think he had practiced that statement.

The man who thought he was being robbed let out a sigh of relief, but then Howell spoke up. "Wait a minute, Capt'n." He walked over to the couple, addressing the man. "Where you from?"

The man wet his lips. The lady, clinging to his arm, squeezed tighter.

"Oh- . . . Ohio."

"Yankee!" Howell spit. "I reckon we'll take that belt, after all. And your fancy watch. And your sweetheart's broach."

Pursing his lips, Cassady started to object, but he didn't want to quarrel with Howell, ruthless as that big man could be.

"Vermin!" the older lady said.

Howell eyed her. "And where are you from, ma'am?"

"Trash!" She spit on his boots. "Swine. Filth!"

"I asked you where you was from." Howell showed no emotion as he tapped the pistol's barrel on a dainty watch dangling from the woman's neck on a silver chain. "You ain't Southern, that's certain sure. Right pretty," he said, resting the revolver's barrel on the face of the watch. "Reckon I'll take it."

"Leave her be." It was Pinto who spoke. "Take the man's money and watch if you want," he said when the one-eyed man turned toward him, glaring. "But leave the woman alone. And you're not taking the other lady's broach."

The two gunmen eyed each other, and I hoped they'd start shooting each other, but I guess Howell desired no quarrel with

Pinto, so he picked up the money belt the man had dropped, snatched his gold watch, and left the two women alone, the younger one trembling, the older one defiant as blazes.

"That's right," Cassady said. "As Southern men, we are brought up to respect the fairer sex. My apologies, ladies. Mr. Howell sometimes forgets his place, his manners."

Yeah, I thought, eying Cassady with growing contempt. You didn't say one thing till Pinto spoke up. You're as big a coward as Ben Jakes.

Howell leaned against the wall, his face a chunk of granite.

All this time, the three couriers had reluctantly dropped their money belts, which Cassady and Ben Jakes now picked up. As Cassady hefted one, his grin widened. "Heavy," he said. "The boys at Fort Tejon will be sorely disappointed. Now, everyone, join the Overland hands at the wall. Hands locked behind your heads, and all of you sitting on the floor. Ladies, you may stand where you are, but please don't move, and I'm afraid I must also ask you to keep your hands held high. Munro!"

A moment later, Julian stuck his head in the door.

"Horses and mules ready?"

"Yes, sir," my brother answered.

"The stage?"

"Crippled. They'll have to replace two wheels."

So that's what my treacherous brother had been doing.

"Good." He nodded at Pinto and Breed, who stepped outside and past my brother. When Julian started to go with them, Cassady told him to wait, but first he had to warn the rest of us. "We'll be taking our leave," he said. "The first battle of the war has been bloodless, and I'd like to leave here without having to kill anyone."

I held my tongue. Bloodless? What about the German captain they had murdered? What about Sergeant Scott and *Señor* Vee wounded? What about Fletcher getting buffaloed, and me getting my head busted open?

"We'll be outside," Cassady went on, "riding off to glory, but I'm leaving the half-breed behind with instructions to kill any man foolish enough to stick his head outside. He has Mr. Munro's Mississippi Rifle and plenty of other weapons. Two hours. That's all you have to wait. Then Nicanor will be gone to join us, and you can return to your travels."

He waited. No one spoke.

With a signal from Cassady, Ben Jakes and Howell walked outside, with Howell relieving Jakes of the two money belts he had draped over his shoulders.

"Munro!" Cassady called to my brother.

"Sir?"

I tried not to show any emotion as Cassady walked to me, knelt, and, keeping the revolver pointed at my head with his right hand, reached over with his left and snatched the diary, the pencil falling out by his feet. Quick, he was. I'll say that for him. I started to protest, realized the hopelessness of that, and determined not to give him any satisfaction. He was up, away from us, reading silently as he'd flip over a few pages, read some, flip over some more, stop and read again. Reading my thoughts. Reading stuff not meant for him. I hated that bandit. I cursed him silently, and I cursed Julian as the cause of all this.

Cassady managed fairly well, using that one hand, keeping the Pocket Colt trained on us, but not looking at us, just reading bits here and there. At last, he tossed the diary to my brother, who tried to catch it, but missed, and it fell on the floor. As Julian picked it up, Cassady looked at me. "Your writing skills have improved, my friend," he said. "At least your understanding of grammar. Some. You learn fast. And your descriptions of us might prove handy for the authorities. So we'll take this with us. Your brother will carry it with him. Give him something to read over the next few weeks until we whip the Yankees and preserve the rights of the South."

Tucking my diary underneath his arm, Julian said softly: "Like I've said, Federal law can't touch us in the South. Let Smith keep his diary."

Cassady clucked his tongue. "We're not in Texas yet."

"It's not far."

"Far enough. You can mail it back to him when we're in Austin. Or even Janos, perhaps."

"But. . . ."

"Can you follow an order, Munro?" Cassady barked with rage.

Looking down, Julian started to join the others outside.

"One more thing, soldier!" Cassady called to my brother. "After we ride out, go to the stable. Kill the mules."

I started to jump up, but Pa grabbed my shoulder, pulled me down. So I yelled: "You can't do it!"

They didn't listen to me.

"They can't take the stagecoach anywhere," Julian protested. "And Breed will give us time. . . ."

"They can ride the mules, Munro," Cassady fired back. "Ride to the next station, ride to Fort Fillmore for all I know, ride to the dragoons."

"But Breed. . . ."

"Kill the mules! All of them! This is war, Mr., and it's a long ride to freedom, to victory. Kill them!" He was shouting those orders as he stormed outside, pushing Julian aside, disappearing. Silence.

Then Cassady's voice again: "Victory! Long live Jefferson Davis! Long live the South!"

More hoofs, followed by nothing but the wind, nothing but Julian staring at us, till Pa stared him down. My brother swallowed. "Remember Breed's outside," Julian warned. "Don't try anything."

The door closed.

Quickly the three couriers reached behind them, drawing pistols they had secreted in shoulder holsters, boots, or behind their backs.

"How'd they know?" one of the soldiers asked Lieutenant Richardson.

"They knew," he answered flatly, standing, joining his fellow soldiers.

"Traitors!" one of the soldiers said.

"Filth!" the old lady repeated.

"You civilians," the oldest soldier said, "I want you to go inside that room there. Stay low. Keep quiet." He looked at Pa. "Sir, do you have any weapons?"

Pa, still sitting, still holding me, shook his head slowly. "They took what we have after they captured us. Colt revolvers, couple of shotguns, revolving rifles, and my old Mississippi Rifle."

"They killed Captain Beckenbauer," Richardson Day said. "Murdered him. Didn't give him a chance. Wounded my sergeant." He pointed at Sergeant Scott, who had stepped into the main room.

"Shot another good man who lives nearby," added Fletcher, nodding toward my bunk.

One of the soldiers stood by the closed door. "You think he was bluffing?" he asked with hesitation. "About leaving a man behind?"

Sergeant Scott came up to the door. "I'll help," he said.

That's when the gunshots started from the stable.

I fell back, crying, because you could hear more than just shots, and Pa pulled me close, and I wanted to just stay there, crying, but it was like all I could hear were those screams. My brother stood in the stable, killing our mules, our breeding stock, Pa's love. Butchery!

"No!" I cried, and started for the door, pulling away from

157

Pa's grasp, wanting to go outside, not caring about Breed, ignoring the warning, the threat. Someone stopped me. I thought it was Pa, but turned to see Bartolomé, saying something in Spanish, while Pa just sat there, listening, rigid, tears welling in his eyes.

"Let's go!" Lucas Scott jerked open the door. Ducking, the sergeant, unarmed, bolted outside, and the other soldier started to follow him, but a rifle spoke, and he dropped in the doorway. Musketry continued. A bullet spanged off the top of the doorway. Another splintered the leg of Pa's chair.

The younger lady screamed.

"Stay down!" someone yelled.

A rifle roared. Breed was well-armed.

Another soldier got to the door, firing into the night. Then the third man, the oldest soldier, crouched beside him, shooting. "Go after the sergeant!" He pulled the trigger, and the other one leaped out the door. I lost count of the shots. A bullet whined off the rock.

Mules screamed.

Bartolomé released his grip. Smoke burned my eyes, but that's not why I was crying. Another ricochet.

"Somebody!" the soldier said from the door as he fired, ducked, aimed again. "Get Benson out of here!"

Fletcher and Marco Max ran over, without caution, grabbed the downed soldier's arms, dragged him from the opening, rolled him over. Little Terry busied himself rifling through the room, looking for something to shoot with, but that was no use.

"He's dead!" Fletcher said.

The younger woman gasped, and Marco Max closed Benson's eyes, whipped off his own jacket, covered the dead man.

Mules screamed. I wonder if I really heard them, with all the gunfire, the shouts, ricochets, curses. Wonder if I heard those mules being shot down, or if it were only in my mind.

"What can I do?" Marco Max yelled.

The sound of slaughter continued, grew louder, deafening.

Another gun spoke, and I realized Lieutenant Day had picked up the dead soldier's revolver.

"What can I do?" Marco Max yelled again.

"Nothing!" the shooting soldier said. "Not unless you have a gun!"

I looked at Pa. He just sat there, tears streaming down his face.

Mules screamed.

And I ran outside.

The oldest soldier focused on reloading his pistol, and a shot from Breed had kicked dirt into Lieutenant Day's eyes. Those are the only reasons I made it out the door.

"Smith!" Pa screamed, but I was gone.

Immediately a gun barked, a bullet buzzed over my left shoulder, and I stumbled toward the side of the house, falling face down in the dirt. Another shot, but this one must not have been aimed at me. Suddenly, savagely rough hands grabbed my shirt, dragged me to the side of the house. A bullet whined off the rock wall.

I heard heavy breathing.

"You . . . fool . . . kid!"

I looked up at Sergeant Lucas Scott.

"Smith!" Yet another shot answered Pa's yell. My bravery, or tomfoolery, had broken whatever grip it was that had weakened Pa.

"He's all right!" Scott yelled. "I've got him."

More gunfire sang out somewhere in the darkness. The sergeant and I pressed as hard as we could against the wall, made as poor a target as we could for Breed, wherever he was hiding and shooting, but I kept contemplating my next move. The side door to the stables lay just a few yards away, the door

closed, but I ought to chance it. I had to. That close to all of
Pa's animals. I could make it. I knew I could. I just had to make
it. To stop Julian. To save Pa's stock.

Sergeant Scott must have read my mind, because he pressed
down hard on my shoulder and said: "That door's barred shut,
boy. I tried it. Like to have gotten killed."

"The front then!" I barked at him.

I'd go around to the gate, get inside that way.

"You'd never make it. That half-breed would cut you to pieces
before you got to the wall. Or your brother inside. That breed
came mighty close to killing me. And he. . . ."

"We could. . . ."

"Forget it. This fight's all but over. Those boys have won, for
now. Thing we got to do is stay alive."

I couldn't hear the mules any more.

Hoofs sounded, and a horse and rider thundered out of the
gate, heading away from the house. He must have turned around
the corner and loped around the back of the stable, avoiding
getting shot by the soldiers in the house. Riding around the
back, he cut around the rear and galloped not 20 yards from us.

Julian!

Unarmed, the sergeant and I could only watch hopelessly as
he disappeared. I don't know what Sergeant Scott thought he
could do, running outside without a weapon. That had been as
stupid as my bolt out of the house. Looking around for the
other soldier who had followed the sergeant outside, I finally
spotted him propped up against the right rear wheel of Marco
Max's Celerity. At first I thought he was just hugging the
stagecoach tight for cover, but then I knew. He was dead.

I saw something else, too—the team of mules, still in their
traces, in front of the coach. Julian had done more than just
busted up two wheels. He, or someone else, but one of his *com-
padres*, had killed every one of those mules, slitting their throats

while they stood there in harness, worn out, trusting, helpless.

"Maybe the Apaches'll butcher ever' last one of them," Sergeant Scott said dryly as the hoof beats from Julian's mount faded away.

"Yeah," I heard myself telling Sergeant Scott. "I hope the Apaches kill them all."

For the next half hour, an eerie silence filled the night. No more shots were fired. I looked at the stable, its high stone walls looking haunted in that moonlight, with a sickening in my gut. Deeper than that, I think. I had wanted to run to the stable, stop my brother, end the slaughter, but I couldn't do anything.

We waited.

Maybe 10 more minutes passed, then Sergeant Scott said something to me that I didn't really hear, and he stood up, hesitant at first, braced his back against the wall, and peered around the corner. For what seemed an eternity he stood there, then his Adam's apple bobbed, his fingers tightened into fists, and he stepped out into the open.

Swallowing down fear, I told him to get down, that Breed would shoot him dead, reminded him that Cassady said the Breed would wait two hours, and not an hour had passed.

"He's gone," the sergeant said, but he didn't sound like he believed it much.

He walked to his dead companion by the wagon, swore softly, picked up the revolver, and stepped into the open. "They're all gone!" he shouted, and Lieutenant Day and Pa stepped outside, equally uncertain, followed by the other soldier. I shut my eyes tight, knowing with all my heart that Breed sat out there somewhere, waiting patiently for all the men in the station to step outside, lulling them into a false security, waiting to kill every last one of us, shoot us down in the open.

Pa knelt beside me. "You all right?" he asked.

161

Eyes shut tight, I could barely nod.

"Marco!" I heard Pa yelling. He was standing, moving with the others, taking command. "We got to get the wheels fixed. I got spares in the stable. You menfolk! We'll need your help. Ladies, get some coffee boiling. How's the soldier yonder?"

"Dead," Sergeant Scott said.

Pa muttered an oath.

When I forced my eyes open, I found myself looking into Pa's stern stare. He was back beside me, waiting, maybe thinking of something to say, but remaining quiet. In the moonlight, I could see the paths tears had traced down his dirty face, but he wasn't crying any more.

"Come on, Smith." He held out his hand. "There's work to do."

I let him lift me to my feet, then followed him, my heart sinking as we approached the stable gate.

"Buck up," he quietly told me. "We got to work through this. You and me, both. There's men to be buried. The coach to fix. Maybe. . . ."

We went inside.

I don't think I'll ever get free of that smell, ever forget the sight of those mules, donkeys, and horses. Gunsmoke, blood, and manure. The smell of death. The sight of savagery.

The outlaws had stolen our best stock, the stallions, the fastest horses and mules. On the wall of the room that served as quarters for our crew, Pa fetched a whale-oil lantern, turned up the flame, told me to go inside and fetch a hammer and wrench, which I did. When I came outside with the tools, Pa stood where I had left him, holding the lantern up, looking, not wanting to believe, not wanting to see.

He hoped—I guess we both had prayed—Julian would have surprised us, done something decent for once in his life, disobeyed Cassady's cruel order. Yet all we saw at first were dead animals.

My heart sank at the thought of my brother's mule, Sweet Ainsley, and I feared finding that beautiful Tobiano amid the carnage.

Above our heads, the ragged flag Pa had fetched at Buena Vista popped in the cool wind, and I thought of Pa telling us how a man could depend on his sons, and I thought of how wrong he was.

Because of Julian.

Then I saw one of the dead animals, and I couldn't help it, couldn't fight back the tears, and I dropped to my knees, just bawling.

"He . . . Ju- . . . he . . . killed. . . ."

No, it wasn't Sweet Ainsley. It was a sorrel mule, long ears, rather silly looking, a bit temperamental who'd eat more than a jackstock man could really afford.

"He killed . . . Ivanhoe!"

Pa sat beside me, pressed a hand on my shoulder. He glanced at my mule—my mule!—head shot, lying as if had wanted to roll in the dust. Pa took a deep breath, slowly exhaled. "Yes, he did, Son. But we have to press on. Smith, there's work to do." He helped me up, and we continued.

We didn't find Sweet Ainsley. Now that I could think back on it, I realized Julian had ridden off on that great Tobiano. Two mules were still alive, but, shot up as they were, I knew Pa'd have to come back with a gun and put those poor beasts out of their misery. Some lay against the slab walls. Others sprawled in the center, but near the flagpole, we found three donkeys alive. Not even shot. Scared, but alive. Maybe Julian had run out of powder and lead. Maybe he'd run out of time. Or lacked the grit to finish the job. Maybe there had been some decency in him.

It didn't matter. Three jennies out of two dozen horses,

mules, and donkeys. If that's decency. . . .

We got the jennies out of the stable, along with the spare wheels and some tools. Usually Pa would breed a male donkey with a mare, but sometimes he'd have one of his stallions couple with one of these jennies to breed what most mule men called a hinny. 'Course, it took longer to get a jenny in the family way, but Pa was patient about these kinds of things. The donkeys struggled, fighting over the smell of blood, but calmed down once we cleared the gate and hobbled them on the far side of the stable, away from the dead mules still hitched to the West-bound stage.

"We'll take those mules," the oldest soldier said. "I am Lieutenant James B. Trenton, sir. We'll go after those bandits."

Ignoring him, Pa told Marco Max: "How long to fix the wheels?"

"We'll get her done, Mr. Munro."

"The mules . . . ," Lieutenant Trenton said.

"They're donkeys, bub."

"Be that as it may, we need them now. It's our duty, and your duty to. . . ."

"I don't care what you need, Trenton." Pa stood straighter, and the lieutenant backed away. Guess he thought Pa would be weak, but Pa's old self had returned. Certainly he wasn't the same man who had been so hurt and weak back in the station house.

"My duty's to the Overland Mail Company, a company that you, sir"—Pa jabbed a finger in Trenton's chest—"and the Army put at risk. We don't carry payrolls. Not on the Overland. You disregarded that." His hand swept out toward some of the passengers who had ventured outside. "You could have gotten these people killed. I have a schedule to keep, sir, and I'm keeping it as best as I can." He turned back to the jehu. "Marco, I'm giving you two mules. You'll have to nurse them to Barney's."

"Will do it."

"Tell him what happened here. Take these fool soldiers with you. Maybe Barney can spare some stock for them. Bartolomé!"

"*Sí, señor.*"

"You need to ride to Ojo de la Vaca. Ride fast. Tell them what happened here, that those butchers have stolen or killed most of our stock. We need a team here for when the Eastbound comes through. Need some firearms, too. And any men he can spare. *¿Comprende?*"

"*Sí, Señor* Conner."

"Good. Light out. Watch for Apaches. And those bandits might be headed that way, too, might have doubled back to the east. *Vaya con Dios.*"

The soldier started to protest again, thought better of it, and sighed in defeat. Pa glared at him. "Moon's still up," he said. "You want to bury your two men?"

"I guess."

"Fletcher, show him where the graveyard is. Couple of you soldier boys can dig the graves, the rest of y'all can drag these dead mules out yonder. You men!" he yelled at the gentlemen passengers. "Lend a hand." Then looked at me. "Smith, you and me'll help Marco and Little Terry." Back to the soldiers. "Get moving. Time's a-wasting. Quicker we get that coach fixed, quicker you get to Barney's and can go after those. . . ." He spit.

Before Pa could squat down to assist with the wheel, however, the older woman from the stagecoach stepped into the doorway. "Mr. Munro?" she called out tentatively.

"Yeah?"

"The Spanish gentleman. The one in the bed who has been dreadfully wounded. He's awake, sir, asking to speak to you."

It must have been midnight, probably later, by the time the two wheels were fixed, the two jennies hitched to the Celerity, and the passengers loaded.

"Can you make it with two donkeys?" Pa asked Marco Max as he climbed into the driver's box.

"I'll make it. Have to go easy. Make some of those gents walk a time or two."

"You know what's best."

"Good luck."

"Luck to you, Marco." Pa handed him a note. "Send that on to Giles Hawley in Tucson. We'll need mules to replace those Julian killed or stole."

The jehu shoved the letter into his pocket. "Will do."

Lieutenant Trenton helped the ladies into the coach, then looked at Pa. "Mr. Day says one of those bandits was your son."

"He was. Was a dragoon, too. That's how he knew your plans."

"Does he know this area?"

"Some. I warrant those other *hombres* know it better. I warrant Smith here knows this country better than Julian."

Maybe the lieutenant decided he couldn't trust Pa, though I don't know why, and he looked at me. "Do you know where your brother's going?"

I shot Pa a look, but his face remained a rock, and the lieutenant was telling me, ordering me, to answer him, not to look at my father.

"I. . . ."

"Son." Trenton decided to try sympathy. "I don't want to hurt your brother."

A bitter thought swept through my mind: I do!

"I don't think he meant for this to happen. Not all of it. But that money . . . well . . . where would you go?"

I fought the urge to look again at Pa, shuffled my feet, then said. "I . . . well. . . ."

Earlier, Lieutenant Day and Trenton had discussed the same

subject. The robbers had ridden out west, but Day suggested they'd double-back, make a beeline for Texas and the Confederacy, but Trenton thought they might head to Tucson, it being full of Southern sympathizers and secessionists, and avoid pursuit from patrols out of Fort Fillmore. That didn't make much sense to me—there were forts out west, too—but Trenton remained adamant about it. So the officers agreed that Lieutenant Day and the other soldier, a corporal named McLaughlin, would walk to Ojo de la Vaca, procure horses or mules there, and proceed to Fort Fillmore to alert the commander of the robbery. Lieutenant Trenton and the wounded Sergeant Scott would travel on to Barney's, where Trenton would form a posse, and Scott would travel on to alert the dragoons at Fort Aravaipa on the other side of Doubtful Cañon. Of course, by that time, Julian, Cassady, and that lot of thieves would be long gone.

"Son, I'm the only chance we have of stopping them," Trenton was telling me now. "I need your help. Which way? Did your brother tell you, give you any indication . . . ?"

"Trenton!" Marco Max yelled. "With or without you, I'm pulling out."

Cursing, the lieutenant turned away from me and climbed into the coach.

"The Janos Road!" I shouted at him, and he turned. "They'll take the Janos Road into Mexico."

The stagecoach pulled away.

"They'll head to Mexico," I told him, "then swing through Sonora into Texas."

"Thank you!"

We watched the Celerity leave, slowly. It took forever for the stagecoach to disappear. When it was out of sight, I turned, feeling Pa's stare, and looked up.

His backhand flattened me.

I don't think he meant to hit me as hard as he did, for I tasted blood in my mouth. Tears welled in my eyes, and I looked up to see Pa standing over me, fists clenched so hard his knuckles now whitened.

"Thought I taught you better. . . ." He took a deep breath, trying to regain control. Behind him, Fletcher took a step away, wetting his lips, looking worried. "The Janos Road?" Pa asked mockingly.

"I. . . ." I didn't know what to say.

"You lied to those soldiers." He pointed to our home. I didn't know what he meant by the gesture, not right away. "You know they're not taking that road. You know exactly where they're going. Why'd you lie, Smith? How long have you known what Julian was up to? Why didn't you go with him?"

"I. . . ."

"Answer me! Answer me, and, by thunder, you'd better tell me the truth. Tell me everything. Or so help me I'll leave welts on your back and backside that'll take months to heal."

In all my years, I'd never seen Pa like this, not this angry, acting like the devil himself had taken hold of him.

"The horses," Pa said. "The horses at Alejondro's place!"

Señor Vee, lying on my bed, wounded by that barbarian half-breed. He had told Pa about the geldings left at his place.

"You put Alejondro Velásquez at risk, boy," Pa continued. "Those butchers might have murdered Alyvia, Victoria, and Dolores. You think about that, boy? Now tell me!"

"I didn't know what was going on." My confession came out more as a wail. "Jules said he and Breed were going to raise horses, sell remounts like those geldings to the Army, said that's why he wanted to leave them at *Señor* Vee's place, said you'd never let him hear the end of it if you saw that stock."

True enough, although I wonder, deep down, if I really believed that, if I knew my brother held some other motive, although I never would have guessed anything as dark as what had come about.

"I didn't know he meant to do this!"

Pa's fists unclenched, then balled again. He turned away, stopped, looked back at me, staring with cold, cruel eyes.

"I promise," I squeaked. "It's the God's honest truth."

"The Janos Road?" He took another deep breath, releasing it like some fire-breathing dragon I'd read about in old storybooks. "You sent that fool Trenton in the opposite direction."

I couldn't look into those eyes. "Yes, sir," I mumbled.

"They left the horses at Alejondro's to change mounts. Run the stock they stole here, get fresh horses up there. Keep riding."

"Yes, sir. I guess that's what they planned."

"Good tracker would figure that. . . ." He shook his head. It didn't matter. "Why'd you lie to that soldier?"

I wiped my busted lip, and, sniffling, made myself look into Pa's eyes. "Jules," I said, "is my brother."

My emotions must have been like riding a bucking mule, jarring, unpredictable. Some times I hated Julian for all he had done. Often I wanted to fight him, maybe even kill him, for all the pain he had caused, the grief, the senseless slaughter of our livestock, our livelihood. But then . . . well . . . he was blood. My only brother, a man I had admired, loved, worshipped. I didn't want him dead.

Not yet.

That has changed as I write this, but I can't regret my decision to send Lieutenant Trenton south toward Mexico, away from Julian, Cassady, and those other murdering bandits. I still don't want the dragoons to kill Julian.

I want to do it myself. And I make this vow: I will kill him.

Pa spit and shook his head when I gave my reason. "You have no brother," he said with a bitterness I'll never forget, a bitterness I would inherit. "Get up. On your feet. You're coming with me."

He had turned to Fletcher when I slowly picked myself up, ignoring my dumb question of where we were going, speaking to the hired hand. "Fletcher, I hate to leave you like this, alone and all. Need you to tend to Alejondro. Bartolomé or Barney will be back at some point, with help. Least, I hope so. I'll also send Dolores and her girls here. They can help out."

"I'll take care of things, Mr. Munro."

"I know you will, Fletcher. You're a good hand. If the Army comes here, tell them where we're going, where Julian and the others rode. North to Alejondro's place, not south to Janos."

"Yes, sir. Where you think they'll go after they get fresh horses?"

"They ain't getting fresh horses," Pa said, and Fletcher raised his eyebrows. "But I don't know. Wouldn't make sense to ride down to Janos, and I don't think they'd ride along the Overland Trail."

"Tucson?"

"No. That Trenton's a fool if he thinks they'd go to Tucson."

Fletcher agreed, thinking aloud. "Has to be Texas, but how they'd get there . . . through the Jornado del Muerto." He shook his head. "I don't know. Reckon that gold-toothed half-breed knows some Apache trails."

"Likely," Pa said. "We'll follow them, though. As long as it takes."

Pa had shoved a revolver, belonging to one of the soldiers who had been killed, I guessed, in his waistband, and two canteens over his shoulder. He tugged his hat down low, and glanced back at me. "Let's go," he said, and I followed him, walking away from Soldier's Farewell, making our way through the night toward the Velásquez place.

★ ★ ★ ★ ★

We didn't speak during the first hour or so, just walked, although I wondered about the hopelessness of our pursuit. They were mounted; we were afoot. Finally I mentioned it to Pa.

"They'll be long gone," I said. "And they'll have fresh horses."

"No," he said softly. "They won't."

At that moment he stopped, unslung one of the canteens, and handed it to me. I drank greedily, hadn't realized just how thirsty I was.

"One thing you ought to learn, Smith," he said, gentler now, the rage gone as he focused on the task of steady pursuit. "Outlaws aren't smart at all. They're stupid. They're lazy." I started to return the canteen to him, then realized I should help out, carry my own. No point in Pa laboring like that, carrying everything. He took a quick sip from the other canteen, then continued talking, although now we had resumed our march.

"They think they'll find fresh mounts, but they won't. Alejondro hid them in a cañon behind his house. Hid his wife and two girls there, too. He knew Julian was up to no good, and he sure wasn't going to leave his family with a man like that half-breed killer. He waited and watched, and when the half-breed took out for Soldier's Farewell, he got the horses and his family hidden, then came to help us. So they'll run my mules and horses full out. They'll be blowing mighty hard. By now, they've already found out they've been played for the fools they are, and are having to nurse those winded animals wherever they're bound. They're cussing each other."

"They might find the horses," I suggested.

"Wouldn't have enough time. Couldn't chance it. We'll get those horses, though. How many did you say there were?"

I had to think. "Five."

"Five." He considered that a moment. "Good stock?"

"Geldings," I said. "Kind of rangy-looking. More like mustangs than the horses we got. Not as big, not as powerful as our mules or your stallions."

"Likely stolen. Any tack?"

I shook my head. "I didn't see any saddles or bridles, only halters and rope."

"Five," he said again. "We might have to ride bareback. I don't know if Alejondro has any saddles. But one of us might get a saddle. Yeah, I expect one of us will."

We kept walking.

Over the rolling hills, through arroyos, past the small forests of yucca, we kept moving, the occasional scattering of horse apples telling us we had chosen the right direction, not that any doubt had ever entered either Pa's or my mind. Dawn had broken long before we ever came to the Velásquez place, the sight of turkey buzzards circling causing my stomach to knot with fear, although Pa never stopped his stride until we crested the hill overlooking the small *jacal*, corral, and outbuildings.

Carefully he drew the revolver, and eased back the hammer. Crouching behind a twisted yucca, we must have waited a good ten, 15 minutes before he felt satisfied, then told me to follow him, and we started down the hill, revolver still cocked, water sloshing inside our canteens.

A coyote bolted out of the open door to *Señor* Vee's house. Above us, the buzzards waited patiently. Pa didn't seem concerned, and he walked straight into the house. He was kneeling over the body by the time I caught up with him, holding something in his left hand that I didn't recognize at first, the Colt revolver now back inside his waistband.

Those ruffians had ransacked the house, and I could just picture their frustrations, finding, as Pa had said, no fresh horses waiting for them. I hadn't expected them to kill anyone, though.

Pa had said they'd be cussing each other, but they'd done a sight more than that. They'd started killing each other.

Ben Jakes sat propped up against the wall beside the fireplace, mouth open but eyes closed, hands still resting against his stomach where one of the bullets had entered. Another had pierced his heart.

Now, I've never tried to hide my contempt for that no-account. He had betrayed us, joining Cassady's lot, a Judas, but I can't say I wanted to see him dead, not really.

"Why'd they kill him?" I asked Pa.

"Five horses," Pa said. "They never planned on keeping him around."

Five horses. For Julian, Breed, Pinto, Howell, and Cassady. Pa had it figured all this time.

"But there were no remounts here."

Pa rose. "No," was all he said. He held the book, which had been in his left hand, out toward me, and I blinked, not believing, then snatched the diary. My diary!

"Must have dropped it," Pa said, "accidentally."

My head bobbed in agreement, but I'll never be sure it had been an accident. I think Julian left it behind for me, on purpose. For forgiveness? Well, if that were his reason, he'll be disappointed, for I can never forgive him. Not even for Ben Jakes. I looked at the body again.

"There was no reason to shoot him," I said.

"No," he said again. "There wasn't. But they didn't need him any more." He sighed. "Took his mule, though. I'd hoped they would have left it behind. Come on. Let's get him out of Dolores's *casa*. No need for her and the girls to see this."

It wasn't fitting, the burial we gave Ben Jakes, but I didn't have much to work with, and Pa ordered me not to spend too much time and muscle on the likes of him. The only tools I had were a garden hoe and my own hands, but I went to work on the side of the hill, away from the house, while Pa walked to the cañon to fetch Tori, her sister, and her ma, and the horses. I carved out a shallow hole for Ben Jakes, rolled him into it, and managed to get some of that hill to slide over him, then piled what rocks I could find atop the shallow grave. By the time I'd finished, Pa had returned, and I have to admit relief swept over my whole body when I saw Tori and the others. Coming over the hill, I dropped my hoe, and ran out to greet them, hugged Tori something tight, then Alyvia, then, crying now, I hugged *Señora* Dolores.

"I'm sorry," I told her. "I'm sorry about everything."

"Is all right," she said tightly, struggling with the English. "We fine, Smith. *Muy bien.* God has taken care of us."

Somehow, I managed to nod, and stepped away, damming the tears, wetting my lips, but then I looked at Alyvia, saw the tears flowing down her cheeks, and I wanted to say something, wanted to apologize for Julian, wanted to say I know how she felt, her heart breaking, feeling betrayed, but our reunion had to be short. We had to go on, after Julian and his friends, and Tori and Alyvia were needed with their father lying wounded at Soldier's Farewell.

Five horses. After filling our canteens in the well, we rode two piebalds, bareback and with hackamores, while Pa let *Señora* Dolores and her daughters take the other three geldings back to the stagecoach station. Tori carried my diary. I asked her to return it to Soldier's Farewell. It contained the descriptions of Cassady and the others, which might come in handy for the law, and I didn't really have a way to carry the book with me.

Besides, I told myself, I'd have no need of it, not where I was going.

Where were we going?

Texas lay east, a hot ride on worn-out mules, but the trail led

us northwest, eventually intersecting a well-used road and following it toward the mountains. Maybe they planned on leaving
the road at some point. After all, I had heard of a route through
the Mimbres Mountains, up toward Fort Craig on the Río
Grande, but, then, I couldn't see them going that way. Santa
Fé? Why would they go north? Yet if they kept traveling this
direction, they'd wind up among the Navajos. By jingo, already
we found ourselves deep in Apache country, with Red Sleeves
himself on the prod. Maybe they planned on turning back, going south, perhaps to Tucson after all, or finding Cooke's Wagon
Road or the Janos Road and making their way into Mexico.

But, no, they moved northwest, making no attempt to hide
their tracks.

"I don't understand this," I told Pa as we watered our horse
in a hidden pool. "There's no reason for them to go this way."

"No?"

"This road don't go nowhere," I said, before remembering
Julian's school lessons in spite of myself. "Anywhere, I mean.
Doesn't go anywhere, I mean."

"No?"

Tugging on the hackamore, he pulled his pinto gelding away,
and let the horse carry him back up the road.

"Then why'd they build a road?" he said once I caught up.
Pa was toying with me, testing me.

"Well, it goes to Burchville, I reckon." I'd never been there,
but had heard plenty of stories and met a few folks on there
way to or from the camps and mines in those mountains. "The
Pinos Altos mines."

"Uhn-huh."

I studied on this for 5 minutes. With a furrowed brow, I asked:
"You reckon there are . . . ?" I had to remember the term. "You
reckon there are Southern sympathizers at those mines? You
reckon they're going to turn over the money they stole to

Confederate officials there?"

Now Pa's brow knotted, and he reined in the pinto, looked me in the eye, and said: "That money was never meant for the South, Son."

"But. . . ." No, he couldn't be right. "But Julian . . . but Cassady. . . ."

"First of all, I know Jefferson Davis and I know Wade Hampton." He kicked the horse into a walk, and I followed. "Know both of them, I reckon, as well as I do any man, especially Wade. They would have no part in a robbery such as this. I will grant you that there are many Southern fire-eaters . . . what's that they call them, Southrons? Well, sure I'll bet my bottom dollar you'll find many of those praying for war. But not Jeff. Certainly not Wade. Not many of them, I warrant. They want to leave the Union peaceful. This was robbery, an act of greed, not an act of war. Wade would never back anything like this. No righteous man would."

"Cassady said he was a soldier."

Pa spit. "Smith, I've seen soldiers. Was a soldier once. Cassady ain't got the makings. Nor does that half-breed, and certainly not Howell, probably not Pinto. They ain't nothing but a pack of thieves."

"And . . . ?" I couldn't mention my brother's name.

"You ever heard the word hornswoggled?"

"Yes, sir."

"Know what it means?"

"Kind of like you got fooled."

"Right. I think Cassady hornswoggled Ju-. . . ." His lips tightened. He couldn't say the name, either.

I thought about this as we rode, trying to get everything worked out in my mind. Julian's a Union officer at Fort Tejon, but he's Southern-born, probably knows he must follow South Carolina and Mississippi, his home states as they were, or maybe

Missouri. I remember when he had been arguing with Pa, trying to explain why he had joined Cassady. What do you want me to do? Fight the friends and family we had back in Camden and Port Gibson? Fight Ma's relations?

So Cassady had gotten to know Julian, gotten close to him, learning of his work at Fort Tejon. Cassady had planned the robbery, and had hornswoggled my brother, preyed on his Southern ties. Julian thought this was a strike for the new Confederacy, when in reality it was a strike for Cassady's pockets. Maybe that's why they had really killed Ben Jakes. They just didn't want to split the money with him.

During the robbery, they had announced to everyone their plans, to raise money for the Confederacy, to let the Army think they would go to Texas, somehow, even if by way of Mexico, maybe to turn in the money to the treasury at Montgomery, Alabama. That way, the Army would look south for the robbers, concentrating on the Mexican and Texas borders. Even I had sent that fool Lieutenant Trenton toward the Janos Road. No one would think to look in Burchville. Or maybe they'd go on from the mines. To the mining camps in Colorado Territory, or even as far away as San Francisco.

Robbers! Not partisan soldiers.

Pa was right. They had hornswoggled Julian.

No, I thought, if Julian wanted no part of robbery, if he had thought this had been for the Southern cause, if he had not been fooled, then why were we following his tracks to Pinos Altos? Why hadn't he stopped them from killing Ben Jakes? Why hadn't they killed him, too? Something else troubled me, too, as I thought about Pa's theory.

"Why bother to change mounts?" I asked. "It ain't that far to the mines, is it?"

He considered this for maybe a quarter mile. Maybe he hadn't reasoned everything out, but at last he shook his head.

"Stolen mules would give them away in Burchville," he said. "Folks might recognize the brand. Maybe these geldings weren't stolen, after all. And changing horses would make the Army, the law, maybe even me, think they had planned on going far, taking a long way to Texas. Besides, by the time anyone thought to look in the mines, there would be no tracks to follow." I wasn't that sure Pa was following any tracks by now anyway, just going along the road, in no particular hurry. "But I warrant we'll find them in Burchville."

The weather turned cooler, downright cold, and the country changed, too, as the road climbed upward, leaving creosote and saltbush behind, the yucca making way for Gambel oak and mahogany. We had stopped talking now, both of us deep in thought, I'd guess, riding along in silence, hearing nothing but the clopping of hoofs. I let my gelding fall in behind Pa, wet my lips, and must have drifted off to sleep.

My head jerked up, and I realized we had stopped. Blinking away sleep, I started to say something, but Pa raised a hand, and I knew he wanted me to keep quiet. His revolver was out, thumb on the hammer, and he watched carefully.

Here the road forked, the branch to the left trailing alongside the beginning of the mountain range, crossing a sandy arroyo up ahead, shady, and it sure looked like a good place to take a nap and slake my thirst for I could hear a brook bubbling somewhere in that little wood. The road to the right would go into the mountains. I had to think about this. Left went on to Burchville and Pinos Altos, I determined, while right took travelers to Santa Rita, where I guess men have been digging for copper since before Pa was even born, with Mexicans hauling the stuff down to Chihuahua City and Indians finding the stuff long before that. Fact is, copper had been drawing men to these parts for what seemed like forever until they discovered gold at Pinos Altos back in '59. Then it struck me that maybe Pa hadn't

figured everything out just right, that maybe I had been correct.

Julian and the others could have turned right, taken the old road to Santa Rita, not Burchville, and then followed that trail through the Mimbres Mountains all the way to the Río Grande. Shoot, that made a whole lot more sense than hitting Burchville. Nobody would think to look for them going that way. Sure, it would prove risky, what with the Apaches acting up, but those same Indians would scare off much pursuit—and Julian had that half-breed with them. By grab, they might have even made a deal with the Apaches to let them pass through peaceable. Now, I didn't know a whole lot about the country northeast of here, but it struck me from what I did know that once they reached the Río Grande near Fort Craig, they could cut across the Jornado del Muerto all the way to the Pecos River, then just follow the Pecos south to Texas.

Mr. Fletcher had even suggested they might cross the Jornado, especially if Breed knew the trails, the water holes. Not many white men would venture pursuit through that rough country.

"They split up," Pa said at last.

"Which way do we go?" I asked him.

Sighing, Pa shoved the revolver into his waistband, clucked at his horse, and turned right. We started into the mountains toward the copper mines.

I've always wondered why we chose that path. Pa had seem jofired on going to Burchville, but, with little comment, he turned toward the copper mines. Maybe he figured Julian went this way, or maybe he thought Julian had gone to Burchville, and, deep down, he really didn't want to meet up with his oldest son.

I never got a chance to ask him about it. Not sure he would have answered me.

Pa reined up again, but this time slid off the horse, handing me the hackamore and telling me in a hoarse whisper to wait here. Crouching, he moved a few rods and braced himself against a large boulder, revolver cocked, studying what must have been an old camping place just up the road.

Well, I could see what vexed him so. A mule stood in the shade at the edge of that clearing, drinking water and grazing. One of our mules, old Hampton, still saddled, still bridled, the reins dragging on the ground at that old sorrel jack's feet.

Ben Jakes's mount! Or this mule had played out and one of the outlaw's had taken old Ben's. The jack just stood there, oblivious to us, and my pinto started getting ticklish, wanting to join the mule in that pasture, wanted to get his fill of water. He didn't have Pa's patience. A branch snapped, and I saw what else must have troubled Pa.

A saddled mare walked over from the forest, its reins also trailing, stopped, and drank. Well, I'd know that mare anywhere, for Pa had brung her with us when we left Missouri. He liked breeding that horse, who had been the dam of many of our best mules.

For what must have been 20 minutes, Pa just stood there, watching, studying, waiting, while I struggled to keep my gelding in place while holding onto Pa's. Finally he let out a heavy sigh, and looked at me.

"You see anything?"

I couldn't believe he was asking me, and I felt mighty proud—at least, right then—and shook my head. "Just Molly and Hampton," I answered. "You reckon they both gave out?"

"Could be," he said, whispering, still not convinced. "One of them might be riding double now."

A chill raced up my backbone. They had killed Ben Jakes because they didn't have enough horses. They might have killed

Julian for the same reason here. He could be lying in those woods.

"Could be they had more horses waiting for them here," Pa said. "Could be anything." He went back to scouting, listening, watching, but only for 5 more minutes, then he looked back at me and said: "Wait here." Slowly he stepped onto the road, and cautiously began making his way down the road to the clearing, his revolver sweeping across one way, then the other, toward the woods, up into the hills, down the road, even behind us.

He hadn't gone 15 yards before the first shot rang out.

His scream roared above the pounding echoes of the gunfire, and I caught a glimpse of him falling, dropping his revolver, unfired, but that's all I saw. I had my hands full trying to keep my seat as that pinto started pitching and snorting. I dropped the hackamore's to Pa's mount, and that horse took off for parts unknown, heading down the road to the fork. My teeth like to about broke in half, and I grabbed a fistful of mane, but I was bareback, and that mustang was scared and angry, so I didn't keep my seat for long. The gelding landed, then bucked high, lowering his head, and I went flying, losing my hold on the hackamore, yelling as that boulder rushed out to greet me.

It's a miracle I didn't break my neck, but all I came away with was a bloody nose. I bounced off the boulder and landed on my backside, crashing hard, but I pulled myself up in a hurry, as another gunshot drowned out the pounding of hoofs as our horses bolted away.

"Pa!"

He lay writhing. Another bullet hit him, rolling him over, and he groaned and cursed.

I started for him.

"Stay . . . back!" I don't know how he could even manage to speak, but I didn't listen. A bullet tugged at my shirt, and I grabbed his shoulders, tried to drag him back toward that boulder, but Pa's a mighty big man, and I didn't have the muscles even to budge him.

Something hard bashed the back of my head, and I went sprawling on the dirt, away from Pa, my head just swimming as I landed, stunned, but conscious, and recognizing that cruel voice.

"Mi amigo."

Breed!

Opening my eyes, I saw Breed press the foot of his moccasin under Pa's stomach, and roll him over. *"Adiós,"* he said, and aimed a double-action Kerr revolver in his right hand. In his left, he held a revolving rifle.

He had been waiting for us all that time. Waiting to kill us. I guess that was his plan, although I don't know how long he planned on waiting on the road. Maybe Cassady paid him extra for this duty as a rear guard.

He'd never collect.

I shot him in the thigh.

I'd landed beside the cocked pistol Pa had dropped. Perhaps Breed thought he had knocked me cold, when he split my head open with the barrel of his .45, but I reached out, grabbed the weapon, pointed, and pulled the trigger.

Pa and the others never had let me pull guard duty or anything like that, and I couldn't really blame them. I wasn't much of a hand with a pistol, and it had to be luck that my first shot struck Breed at all.

"Mother of God!" he said, staggering away from Pa, dropping the rifle but still holding the Kerr, seeing me sprawled out, smoke rising from the barrel. He spread his legs, raised his pistol, and I used my left hand to cock the revolver, then steady my aim. Breed pulled the trigger first, but, instead of a roar, I heard only a small pop, knew his gun had misfired.

Mine didn't.

But I missed.

He pulled the trigger again. Another misfire. No, he was empty, and he flung the revolver at me in rage, then whipped a knife from his sheath, and started limping toward me. I had cocked the gun again, closed my eyes, knew I was dead, and pulled the trigger.

I would have missed him that time, too, or maybe, with God's luck, I might have wounded him, but Pa reached out and tripped him, so, instead, the bullet smashed into the top of his head, and Breed fell in the dirt, dead before he hit the ground.

Pulling myself up, leaving the smoking revolver on the dirt, I raced to Pa, tried not to look at the man I had just killed. I fell at Pa's side, tears blinding both of us, tried to think of what I could do, how I could help him.

"Listen to me," he said.

My head bobbed. Blood dripped down my hair, into my shirt.

"You gotta get . . . me some . . . help."

He had been shot in the left arm, between the wrist and elbow, and again in his left side.

"We'll get out of here, Pa," I told him. I looked up, but Molly the mare and Hampton the mule had taken off during the shooting, too, loping up the road toward Santa Rita.

"Santa Rita . . . closer," Pa said. "Get . . . help."

"I ain't leaving you!"

"You got . . . to."

With his help, I managed to get him off the road and to the camping ground, propping him up against an oak tree near the little stream. I bathed his wounds, plugged the hole in his side, and started wrapping a bandanna over the bad hole in his arm. He screamed in pain, and I fought back tears, nausea. The bone was broken, broken bad, part of it sticking out of the skin.

"Best . . . hurry," he said. I'd never seen him so pale. I knew he was right. I had to leave him, had to get help, or he'd die.

Looking back on it, I think he knew he was dying then, and didn't want me to see him die like that, in such horrible pain.

"I'll get help!" I leaped up.

"Smith," he said. "I shouldn't . . . have hit . . . you. Back . . . at Soldier's . . . Farewell. Wasn't . . . your fault."

"Yes, it was," I told him, and, ignoring my pounding, bleeding head, sprinted toward the copper mines.

Pa didn't die.

Fooled the doctor, he did. Fooled *Señora* Dolores. Even fooled me.

Fearing I'd never see Pa alive again, I raced up the pike, but had gone scarcely three miles before I ran into a bunch of Mexican traders heading down from the copper mines. In broken Spanish, I pleaded for their help, and they understood the bulk of what I was trying to say, so they hurried on down, and we found Pa where I'd left him. The leader was an old man, and he said they had a *bruja* traveling with them, his sister, a wrinkled old crone who started making a poultice and chanting some song while the white-haired gentleman built a fire and spoke softly to my father, who by this time kept drifting in and out of consciousness. The old man said something to one of his men, and that *hombre* disappeared behind one of the carts, then came back with a hand saw.

"You ain't . . . ?" I started to cry again.

The old Mexican spoke sympathetically, his head firm, nodding as he told me what I guess I already knew. He was right. This had to be done.

I won't write down all that happened. Just don't want to relive it. They sawed off Pa's left arm at the elbow. Deep down, I expected the shock to kill him. So did the old man and his sister, but once they tied off the arteries, got that bleeding stopped, got the bullet out of his side and that hole patched up, they loaded Pa onto the back of an ox-drawn cart, and we started down the road. They were Christian folks, mighty good to us, and I can never thank them enough. Certainly can't repay them, and they deserved a whole lot more than Breed's revolving rifle that I forced on them as payment. Going to Janos, they said, but they went by the Velásquez home, though it was out of their way, and left Pa and me there. I didn't think Pa had enough strength to make it all the way to Soldier's Farewell.

For a couple of days, there was just Pa and me, for I couldn't find the courage to leave him alone, what with him half out of his head, speaking to Ma, sweating, likely dying. As if answering my prayers, though, *Señora* Dolores returned, and she took over the doctoring. Tori and Alyvia came home, too, with their father, weak but alive, and growing stronger. I can't write enough praise for Tori's mother, either—how she tended those two wounded men, can't applaud Tori and Alyvia for all their help. So Pa and *Señor* Vee kept improving, and *Señor* Vee said I'd become a man. After a week, I took Pa home.

Mr. Barney fetched a doctor from La Mesilla, and that pill-roller said Pa'd eventually die, but that was a week ago, and Pa's up and around, barking orders. One of the first things he did, and one of the last things for the Overland, was post a letter on the Eastbound. I don't know who he wrote, but he was up half the night composing it, alternating between writing a few words and taking a few sips of mescal.

He has taken more to drink. Don't know if that is brought on by pitying himself, hating Julian, numbing the pain from his wounds, or lamenting the loss of the Overland job.

The Overland has stopped. Moving north, but we really knew that would happen once Texas left the Union. The last coach came through right after the Mesilla doctor checked on Pa. So we've said good bye to Mr. Barney, Mr. Fletcher—hate to see him go. Bartolomé's staying, not with us, but working over at

185

the Velásquez place. Emmett Mills plans on sticking around at Cooke's Spring, too, with a handful of others, but most of the Overland crews are parting ways, either taking jobs with the Overland up north, on the Central Route, or going home, to get ready for the war that's coming. Marco Max said farewell, said he'd be going back to Vermont to preserve the Union, if need be.

Pa's not going with the Overland, though. We're staying put. Don't know what we're going to do.

Tori and her ma came by today, and while *Señora* Dolores looked after the stump of Pa's arm, Tori asked me why we'd stay here after all that had happened. Oh, she said, she'd enjoy it much if I were to stay here. It would fill her heart with much happiness, she said, and she took my hand into hers.

I didn't answer her. Couldn't. I didn't want to break her heart. I know why we're staying here. Pa's waiting on Julian to come home. So am I.

So I can kill him.

April 2, 1861

I don't write in this book the way I once did. Don't like the memories. Wind's blowing like a gale tonight, and Pa's drunk again. Seems that's all he does of late. Maybe Tori and her ma were right. This place is cursed.

Found the diary beside my bed while I was looking for a rag to clean my revolver after killing a rabbit for supper. When those Mexican traders were working on Pa, cutting off his arm, some others buried Breed in that camping spot where he had ambushed us, and they brought me his revolving rifle and the double-action revolver. I gave the old man, the leader, the rifle, insisted he take it as payment for all he had done, but I kept the Kerr .45. It's English-made, a five-shot, and I keep it well-oiled.

It's the gun I plan on using to kill Julian.

April 21, 1861

Well, the war has started. The fire-eaters in Charleston, South Carolina torched their cannons and started shelling Fort Sumter. We got news yesterday from some dragoons came through, bound for Fort Yuma. The bombardment on Sumter started on April 12, and the Union soldiers held out for as long as they could—brave lads, they were—but in less than two days, it was all over.

Wonder if Julian was there.

April 25, 1861

More visitors today, but I'd just as soon never have seen these. They were soldiers, too, with the grim task of digging up Captain Ulf Beckenbauer. His relations want to bury him back home in Chester County, Pennsylvania. Pa and I walked with the soldiers down the little trail to the burial ground.

"Which one is it?" a sunburned corporal asked, and pointed. "That one?"

"No," Pa said softly. I wonder if he knew for certain, in his cups as he was. "That one."

Four graves I saw, and did some ciphering in my head. The German captain had been killed, and two of the couriers. Yet there was another grave, older, and it struck me odd that I'd never noticed it before. As much exploring as I'd done around here, I hadn't realized someone had been buried here. Well, there was no marker, or at least there hadn't been one for ages, just a mound of rocks, and many of them scattered about over time.

"Pa?" I asked hesitantly. "Who else is buried here?"

He sighed. "You need us for anything else?" he called out to the corporal.

"No, sir."

We walked away, and when we got back to the old station

home, Pa uncorked a keg of mescal and shook his head. "That's how this place got its name, Smith. Dragoons were camped here years ago. Story goes one of the soldiers woke up one morning, just ran out, called out good bye to his friends, put a revolver against the side of his head, pulled the trigger."

I swallowed. "You mean . . . he killed himself?"

"Yeah. Must have gone insane. The wind . . . this country . . . it can drive a strong man mad."

"And that's why Tori and her ma . . . why they think this place is cursed, why they never will spend the night here?"

"I suppose." He lifted the jug and drank. "Soldier's Farewell. Some farewell, eh?"

May 15, 1861

"Pa!"

I stood out by the stable, had been there a while after I spotted the dust. I'd been feeding the mules. Our mules. Pa had bought two jacks and a jenny from the Overland before the company moved to the Central Route, and *Señor* Vee had tracked down Hampton and Molly the mare, tracked them all the way to the Pinos Altos mines once he got back on his feet, so we have five animals. Not that we ever go anywhere much, except when I'll go hunting us up something to eat.

He came out of the house, pulling the suspenders over his shoulders, and staggered out to see what the commotion was about. He squinted, his vision blurred from the mescal he had been drinking for breakfast.

"One rider," he said. "Ain't no Apache."

"No, sir."

Recognizing the animal, same as I did, Pa went straight as a flagpole. "Get inside, Smith," he told me, and I was mightily glad of the order. I left him waiting to greet our visitor, while I darted inside to fetch the Kerr .45.

It's hard to write how I really felt when the rider reined up on that wonderful Tobiano mule. I came outside ready to kill my brother, but stopped in my tracks, feeling foolish holding a heavy revolver while Pa patted Sweet Ainsley's neck and invited the bearded miner to light down and have a whiskey.

"Mighty neighborly of you," the stranger said. "Was hopin' you could spare some water, but John Barleycorn would taste even better."

"Smith!" Pa called to me. "Feed and water this man's mule."

The man called himself Jesse Holden, and, after a few drinks, said he had bought the mule in Burchville. He was giving up on striking it rich, wanted to go back home to his ma's place south of Fort Lancaster in Texas. New Mexico Territory, Arizona Territory, whatever you wanted to call it, just wasn't safe with Red Sleeves and Cochise riled up and butchering any white man or Mexican they could find.

"Burchville," Pa said.

Remembering how we had tracked Julian and his pards, I felt foolish. "They split up," I reminded Pa. "You said so, remember? Split up. Some went to Santa Rita, others to Burchville. We never went to Burchville."

Holden, ignoring us, helped himself to Pa's jug.

"One." Pa stroked his rough beard. "One man rode to Burchville. I'd forgotten."

"So did I. Just wanted to take care of you."

By the time Pa had beat away the devil or death, I figured Julian, Cassady, Howell, and Pinto were long gone. After all, the soldiers looking for them never cut any trail, and, after a month or so, they gave up that money as lost.

"He wouldn't still be up there," I said.

Pa studied on it. "Might find something about him, though," he said.

189

"About who?" Holden asked.

Pa ignored him, sober of a sudden, but I decided to answer the question. Maybe Holden knew something.

"The man who sold you that mule," I said.

He snorted. "Quinn Nation? Runs the livery."

"Nation?" My first thought, or hope, was that Julian had changed his name, had used his share of the money to buy a livery, but then I realized the truth of it all. Julian had sold Sweet Ainsley, had bought another mount, had ridden out of Burchville months ago.

"Maybe Mr. Nation knows where he went," Pa said. A long bet, for certain.

"Who?" Holden asked.

"The gent who sold that mule to your livery man," Pa said.

Holden blinked. "You got a right heavy interest in that old mule," he said.

"I do," Pa said. "Fact is, I'd like to buy her off you. Got a pretty good mare in the stable who'll get you across Texas a whole lot quicker than a pinto mule."

"Criminy." Holden smiled drunkenly. "If that hoss'll walk, you got yourself a deal. Ain't fittin' for a white man to be ridin' a pinto. And that mule is bad luck. That's how come I got her cheap from Quinn Nation."

"How'd Nation get her?" I asked impatiently.

Holden looked at me as if I were the dumbest man on earth, as if everyone had heard what had happened in February in Burchville.

"He killed the man who rode in on her," Holden said.

May 16, 1861

We're back from Burchville, a wasted trip in some ways—not that I expected to find Julian up there, or even his grave. Pa traded Holden for Sweet Ainsley, and, as soon as that drunken

Texican rode off on Molly, we saddled up and rode for the mine country.

Quinn Nation didn't have much to say about the man he had killed in a saloon, even after I tried my best to convince him we had no interest in avenging the man's death or demanding a coroner's inquest.

"He was cheatin' at cards," Nation finally sang out. "Would have killed me if his pistol hadn't misfired."

"Catch his name?" Pa asked.

"Never give one. Buried him in the cemetery." Bitterly he shook his head. "I had to pay for the funeral."

"Young man?" I asked. "Dark-haired? Had a mustache? Looked a bit like me?"

The livery man splattered tobacco juice against the wall. "Not hardly. Big man, right big, and ugly as sin. Had a patch over one of his eyes and a terrible scar." With a thick finger, Nation traced a line from one cheek, over the nose, and onto the other cheek.

Pa and I looked at each other. Howell. The cold-blooded Texas man-killer.

"He have any money on him?" Pa asked.

It took Nation a while to answer. "Just enough to buy in the game."

He wasn't much of a liar, but I didn't press him. Quinn Nation wore brand-new boots, a silk hat, brocade vest with a silver chain hooked onto a William Johnson watch. I remembered that watch, could picture Howell taking the timepiece, chain, and elk-tooth fob off the man from Ohio, along with his money belt, during the robbery at Soldier's Farewell. New duds? A solid gold London-made watch? Quinn Nation dressed too well for a Burchville livery man. I don't think he spent his own money to bury Howell, either, but it didn't matter.

Howell was six feet under, while Cassady, Pinto, and my

brother had ridden on to Santa Rita and, most likely, out of New Mexico Territory.

July 30, 1861

Sad news to report. Emmett Mills is dead. From what *Señor* Vee says, poor Emmett and six others were attacked by Apaches at Cooke's Spring, had tried to escape in an abandoned stagecoach, but the warriors cut all seven of them down. This was the work of Red Sleeves. Emmett was a good man, and *Señor* Vee suggests that it is no longer safe for us to remain at Soldier's Farewell. After killing Emmett and the others, the Indians burned the station, and that's too close to home for *Señor* Vee, who is bound for La Mesilla with his family and Bartolomé until the Apache troubles are over.

Pa refuses to retreat. He says Red Sleeves and Cochise will leave us alone.

We also have heard of a big battle in the East. Confederate soldiers have whipped the Union Army near Manassas, Virginia. Southern sympathizers are dancing in the streets of Mesilla, saying the war will be over in a week.

September 4, 1861

A letter came today. *Señor* Vee brought it from Mesilla. It's from Wade Hampton, now commanding a legion or something in the Confederate Army. Hampton was wounded at Manassas, but that's the only part of the letter Pa mentioned. I asked Pa if Senator Hampton wrote any news of Julian, but Pa never answered me. He merely thanked *Señor* Vee for bringing the letter, which he burned in the fireplace.

December 25, 1861

Christmas. Yet I feel Jesus has abandoned us.

January 2, 1862

A new year. No news from the war. No news from Tori Velásquez. No news from anywhere.

February 5, 1862

I remember Pa always telling me how the war would never touch us in New Mexico Territory, but the war has come here. Cassady even predicted it back when he was robbing the Fort Tejon payroll, and now a Confederate general named Sibley has invaded the territory. He has an army of 20,000 men, we are told, with plans to capture Santa Fé and go on up to the Colorado mines and take that gold for the Confederacy.

Heavy traffic on the road, much more than recently. Some Rebel soldiers rode through here on their way to Tucson, and we have learned that Union troops are marching from California to stop these invaders.

February 25, 1861

More news of a major battle on the Río Grande near Fort Craig. The Confederate Army has defeated Colonel Canby at Valverde. 1,000s of dead have turned the river red.

Pa took the report silently, and stayed awake all night. He woke me this morning—sober . . . he hasn't been drinking at all—and said we needed to saddle up. "We're riding out."

"Where?" I asked him.

"Valverde."

I let that sink in. "What for?"

"To see if Julian's there. Dead or alive."

Shaking the sleep out of my brain, I couldn't believe it. "Pa," I said. "That don't . . . that doesn't make a lick of sense. Those troops came from Texas. Julian's off fighting with Wade Hampton back East."

"No." He sounded more like the old Pa, determined, right, a

mountain. "He ain't with Hampton. Get up."

April 18, 1862

Back home. We never should have left. While we were gone, Apaches stole the stock we left behind, tore down the stable, wrecked our home, but they didn't burn us out.

A forlorn hope. That's what this trip was.

Well, we did learn a few things. First of all, Sibley's army didn't number any 20,000. It was more like 2,500, and 1,000s were not killed at Valverde. Doubt if they buried more than 200.

We didn't locate Julian. I never once thought we would, but Pa must have hoped we would have found him, dead or alive. A Union captain at Fort Craig took us to the post hospital, where we, to my shock, found Lieutenant Day—can't recall his first name, though it's probably written down in this book—badly wounded. He had lost both eyes from canister, and the captain said a stomach wound would prove mortal. For the life of me, I can never figure out how Pa recognized that dying mess that had once been a man, had once been a friend to my brother.

Pa sat by the bed, whispering, telling the dragoon he would be all right. I leaned against the wall, hating the smell of the place, staring silently, mouth open, unbelieving.

"Did you see my . . . son?" Pa asked at length.

"Julian wasn't here, sir," Day replied weakly. "You know he wasn't."

"Well. . . ."

"It wasn't his fault," Day said when Pa rose, and Pa just looked down on that blind, dying man, looked down on him with pity, or was it curiosity or contempt? "He followed his heart."

Having heard enough, I turned to leave.

"I've forgiven him," Day said. "You should, too."

Sibley's troops kept on going north, capturing Albuquerque, then Santa Fé, and went right on, marching, bound for victory at Fort Union, the Rebs figured, but they never got that far. From what we hear down south, the Confederates turned back another Union force at Glorieta Pass, but some Colorado volunteers under command of a major named Chivington struck the supply train, wiped out the whole train, so the Rebels are hightailing it back to Texas.

Seems like the war's over in New Mexico Territory.

August 4, 1862

The last of the California Column came through the other day, bound for old Fort Thorn on the Río Grande.

Union volunteers have been moving down the road for about a month, chasing those Texas Confederates who have been out of the territory since spring. I wouldn't write much about this, on account that I see this book is almost filled up, but the commander of the troops stopped by to talk to Pa.

He's General Carleton. I remember when Julian served under him at Fort Tejon, he was just a captain with the dragoons. Didn't like Carleton much. He said he wanted to personally thank Pa and me for all we had done trying to stop the payroll robbery last year, said had he known of Julian's treachery, he should have killed him back when they were chasing the Paiutes. He started to curse Julian, called him a yellow dog, and that's when Pa sobered up, and told him to withdraw those comments or they'd get shoved down his throat, said Julian was his son, following his heart, and, by thunder, no body ever called a Munro a coward.

That struck me as odd, and Carleton rode out of here madder than a bee-stung bear, but I reckon he wasn't half as riled as me. As Pa poured two fingers of mescal in his coffee mug, now that he was drinking again, I asked him: "Since when do you defend Jules?"

"He's a Munro. He's your brother."

With a snort, I cursed Julian and Pa.

That's only the second time I can recollect Pa hitting me, not spanking me or giving me a good whipping as a kid, but knocking me to the floor. Split my lip, but I've grown some, and haven't been living on mescal, so I jumped right back up, balled my fists, and almost struck back.

"You once told me I didn't have a brother!" I shouted. "And I don't." Turning, because I knew the tears would flow soon, I stormed outside, stopped, and pointed my finger at Pa. "And don't you ever hit me again."

August 15, 1862
Still not on speaking terms with Pa.

September 3, 1862
Things back to normal at Soldier's Farewell. I do the hunting and cooking, hire out for a couple of days, sometimes in Mowry City or Burchville, to earn enough for flour or beans, powder and lead. Pa gets drunk on mescal, which he trades for or begs from travelers, even Apaches. We're talking again. Just don't have much to say.

December 1, 1862
Just realized my birthday has passed again without notice. I'm 14. I probably would not have even remembered but a man on a jackass brought a letter today from La Mesilla, a letter from Tori Velásquez, who wished me much happiness, said she missed me, and shared some news. Alyvia is to marry Bartolomé Diego Chavez y Chavez—never knew his full name till this letter

came—at the San Albino Church on the plaza at La Mesilla on Christmas Eve, and she, her sister, and her parents would be honored if could pull ourselves away from business and come to the wedding.

Business. That made me laugh.

Yet it would be nice to see Tori, talk to *Señor* Vee, eat some of *Señora* Dolores's good grub, but I can never leave Soldier's Farewell. It's like the curse has anchored me here, and Pa, waiting for Julian's return.

February 10, 1863
Old Red Sleeves, Mangas Coloradas, is dead. A couple of soldiers stopped by today for water, said they were carrying a dispatch from Fort McLane to Fort Union, although I suspected they were deserters lighting out to Pinos Altos.

"Killed tryin' to escape," one of the bluecoats said, and laughed and laughed till tears ran down into his beard.

"Came in for a peace parley," the other soldier said, "that Apache butcher did, but we took him captive, then Gen'ral West, he says to us . . . 'Men, that ol' murderer has left a bloody trail stretchin' 500 miles. I want him dead come tomorrow morn.'

"So Harv and me heat up our bayonets, you see, put 'em under than old redskin's feet, and he's a tough ol' coot, but he finally sits up and shouts for us to quit tormentin' him so." Their laughter turned my stomach. "And that's when the boys shot him to pieces."

"Tryin' to escape," the other soldier said.

I was glad to see them go. Not because they were a couple of vermin, but because somehow I sort of understood Julian's feelings. I kept hearing those words he yelled at Pa all those months ago.

You told me before I left for the Academy about duty, about honor,

197

but I think I left all that at Fort Tejon. We went after those Paiutes, Pa, because Captain Carleton said they had killed some settlers. But those Indians had nothing to do with those killings, Pa. Carleton knew that. Colonel Dawson knew it. We all knew it, but we still pursued the Paiutes. We killed a lot of them. For what? Nothing. Nothing but glory for Dawson and Carleton. Because nobody cares if an Indian is innocent. You want me to fight for that?

It doesn't matter, though. I'll still kill Julian when he returns.

March 12, 1863
Julian's birthday today. Wonder where he is.

July 19, 1863
Word comes of great Union victories in Pennsylvania and at Vicksburg, Mississippi. Also, the Velásquez family has returned to their home, what with the ~~death~~ murder of Red Sleeves. Well, the newlyweds, Alyvia and Bartolomé, remain in La Mesilla, where Bartolomé is working at a livery stable. *Señora* Dolores commented on how much I have grown, while I just kept staring at Tori. She looks like an angel, and I forgot all those memories of her as a kid, pestering me to death.

Señor Vee, he looks much older, and needs a cane to get around good, and that's when I found myself staring at Pa, and realizing just how much he has aged. Hardly any meat on him. Part of that's from the liquor, but we've been living off varmints I can shoot, and beans. His beard is unruly, practically halfway down his chest, and although they'd never say anything rude, I know the stink of both Pa and me offended Tori and her folks. We invited them to spend the night, but, naturally, they refused.

Nighttime now. They're long gone. Wind's howling.

October 3, 1863
Pa's dying. Found him this morning slumped over the table, jug

overturned, mescal spilled all over the floor. I got him to bed, but it's like the whole left side of his body isn't working. Then I mounted Sweet Ainsley, the only mule we have left these days, and rode to fetch *Señora* Dolores and Tori, hoping they can tend to Pa while I ride to Mesilla and bring that lousy saw-bones.

Please, God, don't let Pa die before I get back.

October 30, 1863
The Velásquez family has been staying with me, even spending the night, forgetting the curse of this place. The doctor said Pa suffered what he called a cerebral apoplexy. He doesn't believe that Pa will live to see Thanksgiving, but this is the same pill-roller who told me Pa would die after that old Mexican sawed off his arm.

He can't talk, Pa, and Tori has to spoon breakfast and supper down his throat, clean him. Breaks my heart seeing him this way.

I. . . .

November 7, 1863
No change in Pa.

January 1, 1864
We've been trying to communicate with Pa some other way. His left side doesn't work, but that's the stump of his arm, so, yesterday morning, I put a pencil in his right hand and a scrap of paper on the Bible, asked him if he needed anything, and he blinked a few times—wasn't certain he understood—then scrawled out, NO.

Funny how glad that made Tori and I feel, and then Pa wrote something else. THANKS.

★ ★ ★ ★ ★

FORGIV

January 12, 1864
That's Pa's handwriting above here. He scribbled it today. I can't write about it just right now.

January 15, 1864
About Pa's one-word message: *Señora* Dolores had gone home to get some supplies, Tori was off somewhere, and I was oiling the Kerr revolver when Pa got all agitated, trying to talk, but only grunting, slobbering, and slapping his hand on the side of the bed.

"What is it?" I felt so useless, trying to understand him. Frustrated, he pointed, and I spotted the pencil. Urgently I put it in his hand, wrapped his fingers tightly around it, looked around for some paper, couldn't find anything, and at last I saw this diary. I turned to the blank page, and he went to work, moaning, desperate. Stepping away from him, I called out for Tori, wherever she was, frightened as I've never been frightened before, and, a moment later, the pencil fell on the floor, and Pa drifted off to sleep.

Tori ran in as I picked up the paper and my diary. She looked at the word, then at me, finally at Pa. A few hours ago, she talked me into letting her saddle up Sweet Ainsley and ride to La Mesilla.

To fetch the priest.

January 28, 1864
Father Miguel has come and gone, did the best he could with the last rites and all. I hope Pa don't mind, us never being raised Catholic. The Mesilla doctor came by, too, and left, said it's a matter of time now. Pa's asleep, has been since he wrote

that lone word.

February 11, 1864
It's over.

February 13, 1864
Sunday. Alone at breakfast, I poured coffee, looked at the bowl of stew *Señora* Dolores had left me, pushed it away, and told myself I must say a Bible verse before eating. I started talking, tears falling down my face.

" 'Man that is born of a woman is of few days and full of trouble. He cometh forth like a flower, and is cut down: he fleeth also as a shadow, and continueth not. And doth thou open thine eyes upon such an one, and bringest me into judgment with thee?' "

Two days ago, I found Pa in his bed, eyes open but not seeing, his flesh so cold, and cursed myself, blamed myself. He'd died while I slept. Well, *Señor* Vee calls it a blessing and—it really is—and a wonder Pa's heart hadn't given out months, or even years, ago. He looked older than Methuselah. Wasn't but 45.

I always thought Pa's funeral would bring in tons of mourners, but it was just me and Tori and her parents. We buried him in the little cemetery, away from that old dragoon who'd killed himself, away from those two soldiers shot down in the stagecoach robbery, away from where we'd first planted that old German captain. *Señor* Vee and his wife left me there for a while, to say good bye, and then Tori started pulling on my arm, begging me to come with her.

"The devil owns this place," she said. "Always, it cursed. It kill you, too, if you no leave. Get out, Smith. Get out. Please, for God's sake, you must go, for your own sake."

I just laughed, and she looked at me funny—no, scared—and

I told her I had to wait here, had to wait for Julian.

"Perhaps he dead," she said, but I shook my head.

"He promised." Oh, I could just picture my brother, see him as clear as if it were yesterday, on our way back to Soldier's Farewell from the Velásquez place, him whispering while I cried.

Mark my words, Innis Smith Munro. I won't get killed. I promise you that.

She's gone. Practically flew from the cemetery, said she'd pray for me, ran.

I don't think she'll ever come back.

April 29, 1865

My Lord, has it been this long since last I've written in these pages? The war is over, the Union preserved, the Rebels whipped. I wait for Julian.

July 24, 1865

The prodigal son is home. Walked up 10 minutes ago, and looks as if he has been on the ankle express forever. Savage. Thin as a rail. Bearded, dirty, one butternut sleeve pinned up at his left shoulder. Stepping out of what's left of the stable after feeding the one mule left, I almost didn't recognize him. Didn't recognize him, not really, until he asked: "Where's Pa?"

Unable to speak, I pointed. He looked, not comprehending, then his knees buckled and I thought he'd fall, but he started walking. Going to the cemetery.

I must close this journal, grab the Kerr .45, and follow.

Same day, late evening

Just enough pages left in this journal to finish my story.

Heart racing, I left the house with the big revolver in my right hand, and took the trail to the graveyard, stopping beside the old captain's former grave, sweating like I'd never sweated before, staring at that ragged figure standing over Pa's grave.

A few months after Pa's death—a lifetime ago—*Señor* Vee had placed a marble cross over Pa's grave. Nothing fancy, just a cross, not even a name chiseled into the stone, but the only marker of any kind in this cemetery.

My hand wouldn't stop shaking, and that .45 never felt so heavy. Ahead of me, Julian sobbed a bit, and slowly turned to face me, to die.

The wind blew harder, kicking up whirlwinds of dust.

The Kerr fell into the dirt.

That wasn't my brother I saw standing there. The beard. The one arm. So frail, so foreign. I saw my father, and then saw nothing but tears.

"How?" Julian managed to choke out the question. "When?"

Blocking the tears, the pain, I straightened. "Was a year ago February." I shook my head. "He just give out. Wore out."

If he noticed the Kerr, Julian never spoke of it, merely turned back to Pa's grave, and then he was on his knees, bawling like a newborn babe, wailing in such miserable torment, choking out things like: "It's my fault . . . I'm so sorry. . . ." And a broken word that chilled me:

"Forgive. . . ."

I don't remember walking up to him, don't remember putting my hands on his shoulders, but there I stood, hearing words from some strange voice, far away. My voice!

"He never held any grudge against you."

Julian looked up, his face so gaunt, red-rimmed eyes so . . . I don't know a word that can describe them. "I failed him, Smith."

The numbing, humbling truth of what I was about to say shook me, but I had to be strong. "No. I failed him. You did what you thought was right."

His trembling head shook, and he looked back at that cross.

"No. I was wrong."

"We were both wrong," I said, thinking Pa had been wrong, too, only he knew it. "Let's go back to the house. Get out of the wind. A monsoon's blowing up."

The rain fell in torrents as I filled his cup with chicory and sat across from him.

"What kept you here?" he asked.

I started to answer, but couldn't, realizing I had left that revolver outside at the grave, chilled at how hate had driven me for four years. I wondered about that last word Pa wrote, wondered if he had been asking for forgiveness, had forgiven Julian, or was begging me to forgive. Forgive who? Julian? Pa? Myself?

I saw no need in telling my brother how Breed had came close to killing us both, or that Pa had spent his last few years as a walking whiskey vat. It didn't seem to matter. Nothing mattered.

Julian changed the subject. "How's Mr. Velásquez and his family?"

"Haven't heard from them in a spell. Alyvia got married, though."

He nodded as if he knew. We drank coffee. The rain fell. The roof leaked. The wind wailed.

"What?" My throat felt dry, and the wind brought a chill into the cabin. I pointed to the pinned up sleeve. "Happened?"

"Franklin," he said. "Big battle in Tennessee. Battle!" He spit out a mirthless laugh. "Wasn't anything short of murder, and I don't blame the Yanks who took my arm. It was our fool general, Hood." The head bowed, slowly shook again. "He got his whole army slaughtered." He was looking at me now as he spoke. "I learned something, Smith. The Confederate officers . . . some of them, at least . . . were no better than the Union martinets I fought with out West."

"You didn't join Wade Hampton?"

"No." He brushed away a tear. "Pa saw to that. Wrote Hampton a letter. When I got to South Carolina, requested the honor of joining Hampton's Legion, Hampton said he had heard of my atrocities . . . that's his word . . . my betrayal of family and honor. Hampton wouldn't have me. Almost challenged me to a duel. Said I wasn't fit to serve under any Southern command. No, Smith, you'll find no record of a Julian Munro anywhere in the Confederate Army. I enlisted under another name. Fought with the 1st Texas."

"What . . . ?" My head dropped, but I had to know. "And the money you took?"

He blurted out his answer, then stopped to regain his composure. "Pa was right about that, too!" The storm had stopped when he continued. "After we left here, after Breed rejoined us, Cassady sent Howell on to Burchville. My mule had thrown a shoe, so Howell and I switched mounts, figured he could nurse Sweet Ainsley to the mining camps. Later, he sent Breed back to watch our back trail. I didn't understand until later that Cassady had paid off those two. The rest of us rode to Santa Rita, then took a trail through the mountains to the river. I don't know what became of Breed or Howell."

I didn't tell him.

"And the others?"

"We also split up. Cassady took most of the money, rode up the river toward Santa Fé. Pinto and I started across the Jornado. I guess by then I had my suspicions, but . . . well, I'd crossed the Rubicon. Pinto knew the country. I don't know how. I was such an idiot. We hit the Pecos, turned south for Texas, rode to Fort Davis. The Yanks had abandoned her by then. That's when I knew for certain that I'd been played for a fool. Pinto kept riding for Mexico, and I . . . well . . . I lit out for Carolina. Maybe I should have turned myself in, but. . . ."

"And Cassady? Pinto?"

Julian shrugged. "For all I know Pinto's still in Mexico, rich. You remember Richardson Day, that lieutenant?"

I nodded, but didn't inform him of his friend's fate, either.

"I met his brother, campaigning in Georgia. He was a captain with the Second Kentucky Mounted Infantry. Kenny told me a story he'd heard about some rich Southerner who showed up in Denver City in the spring of '61 and opened a gambling hall before being run out of town by Unionists. He was killed, they say, by Cheyenne Indians on his way to Kansas in '63. That could have been Cassady. I'd like to think it was. Can't be sure, though."

There was another question I had to ask, for my brother, and for me.

"What's next?"

He finished his coffee, and rose. "I'll drift." He stood in the doorway, staring outside. The ground, the air smelled new. "Tucson, maybe. California. Oregon. Maybe. . . ." Turning to me, he said: "You've grown. Taller than me now." His eyes hardened, but just as quickly softened. "I thought you'd kill me." He stood a little straighter. "Nobody would blame you. Not even me."

"Pa would," I said, and we both knew it was true. "And I don't want to kill you, Jules." Not any more, I thought.

Oh, it wasn't that we could ever go back to how things had been, me the doting kid brother, him the strong one I'd admired and envied. He had been wrong, but I'd been wronger, letting hate drive me so. Maybe if I hadn't been so consumed, so blind, I could have pulled Pa back on his feet, stopped the drinking, made him raise mules, or I could have hauled him far away from these cursed ruins. I'm not sure I really forgave my brother, certainly couldn't bring myself to shake his hand. That would take time.

After a long while, still staring outside, he asked: "What are your plans?"

What about me? Suddenly I longed to see Tori, to beg her forgiveness, and then I got another notion. Crazy, maybe. Forlorn. But. . . .

Take up where Pa left off. Become a jackstock man. Maybe, maybe I could go to work for *Señor* Vee. He couldn't get around well, could use some help, and a smart man could learn a lot from Alejondro Velásquez. Besides, I could teach him about mules, teach him some of what Pa taught me. I'd leave Soldier's Farewell to the desert, to its ghosts. I'd left all the hate I had, left it with that unfired pistol up at the cemetery.

I never answered my brother, but I knew then what I'd do. I'd shave, clean myself up, get things in order. Maybe *Señor* Vee will banish me. Maybe Tori will send me packing. I wouldn't blame either of them. *Vamos a ver.* We shall see.

"Good bye." Julian walked outside.

"Take the mule!" I called out suddenly, unexpectedly, and he stopped, but never looked back. "She's yours anyway," I said. "It's Sweet Ainsley."

After another long pause, he shook his head, his voice breaking again. "You'll need her."

"No." I pictured myself at the Velásquez place, pitching my proposal to *Señor* Vee, and maybe, God willing, in a few years making another proposal. "I'll walk. I don't have far to go."

ACKNOWLEDGMENTS

Special thanks to the New Mexico State Archives, the Santa Fe and Vista Grande public libraries, and Butterfield-Overland historian, Melody Groves, of Albuquerque, New Mexico, for research help with this novel.

And to my son, Jack, who kept an eye out for rattlesnakes while I scouted out the southern New Mexico locales in this novel around Soldier's Farewell, Besse Rhodes (Bessie Rhoads on today's maps), and elsewhere between Gage and White Signal in Luna and Grant counties.

Recommended reading about the John Butterfield's Overland Mail Company includes *That Old Overland Stagecoaching* by Eva Jolene Boyd (Republic of Texas Press, 1993); *The Butterfield Overland Mail*, three volumes, by Roscoe and Margaret Conkling (Arthur H. Clark, 1947); *The Butterfield Trail in New Mexico* by George Hackler (Yucca Enterprises, 2005); *The Butterfield Overland Mail* by Waterman L. Ormsby, edited by Lyle H. Wright and Josephine M. Bynum (The Huntington Library, 1942); and *A Compendium of The Overland Mail Company On the South Route, 1858-1861 and the Period Surrounding It* by G.C. Tompkins (Talna Corp, 1985).

ABOUT THE AUTHOR

Johnny D. Boggs has worked cattle, shot rapids in a canoe, hiked across mountains and deserts, traipsed around ghost towns, and spent hours poring over microfilm in library archives—all in the name of finding a good story. He's also one of the few Western writers to have won two Spur Awards from Western Writers of America (for his novel, *Camp Ford,* in 2006, and his short story, "A Piano at Dead Man's Crossing", in 2002) and the Western Heritage Wrangler Award from the National Cowboy and Western Heritage Museum (for his novel, *Spark on the Prairie: The Trial of the Kiowa Chiefs,* in 2004). A native of South Carolina, Boggs spent almost fifteen years in Texas as a journalist at the *Dallas Times Herald* and *Fort Worth Star-Telegram* before moving to New Mexico in 1998 to concentrate full time on his novels. Author of dozens of published short stories, he has also written for more than fifty newspapers and magazines, and is a frequent contributor to *Boys' Life, New Mexico Magazine, Persimmon Hill,* and *True West.* His Western novels cover a wide range. *The Lonesome Chisholm Trail* (Five Star Westerns, 2000) is an authentic cattle-drive story, while *Lonely Trumpet* (Five Star Westerns, 2002) is an historical novel about the first black graduate of West Point. *The Despoilers* (Five Star Westerns, 2002) and *Ghost Legion* (Five Star Westerns, 2005) are set in the Carolina backcountry during the Revolutionary War. *The Big Fifty* (Five Star Westerns, 2003) chronicles the slaughter of buffalo on the southern plains in the 1870s, while *East of the Border* (Five Star Westerns, 2004) is a comedy about the theatrical offerings of Buffalo Bill Cody, Wild Bill Hickok, and Texas Jack Omohundro, and *Camp Ford* (Five Star Westerns, 2005) tells about a Civil War baseball game between Union prisoners of war and Confederate guards. "Boggs's narrative voice captures the old-fashioned style of the past," *Publishers Weekly* said, and *Booklist* called him "among the best Western writers at work today." Boggs lives with his wife Lisa and son Jack in Santa Fé. His website is www.johnnydboggs.com. His next Five Star Western will be *Río Chama*.